CLASSICAL ECONOMIC MAN

ADVANCES IN ECONOMIC METHODOLOGY

General Editor: Warren J. Samuels
Michigan State University, US

This major new series presents original and innovative work in economic methodology, including all aspects of the philosophy, sociology and rhetoric of economics as well as the relationship of economics to other disciplines.

The series reflects the renewed interest in all aspects of economic methodology as well as the deepening sense both of conceptual and technical crisis plaguing the economics profession and that the crisis involves deep methodological considerations. It is hoped that the series will contribute to the better understanding and solution of the economic problems of both mature and developing countries.

The series is open to all points of view and approaches.

Truth versus Precision in Economics
Thomas Mayer

John Maynard Keynes: Language and Method
Edited by Alessandra Marzola and Francesco Silva

Classical Economic Man
Human Agency and Methodology in the Political Economy
of Adam Smith and J.S. Mill
Allen Oakley

The Nature of Economic Thought
Essays in Economic Methodology
Johannes J. Klant

Classical Economic Man

Human Agency and Methodology
in the Political Economy
of Adam Smith and J.S. Mill

Allen Oakley

Department of Economics
University of Newcastle
Australia

Edward Elgar

Published by
Edward Elgar Publishing Limited
The Lypiatts
15 Lansdown Road
Cheltenham
Glos GL50 2JA
UK

Edward Elgar Publishing, Inc.
William Pratt House
9 Dewey Court
Northampton
Massachusetts 01060
USA

This book has been printed on demand to keep the title in print.

A catalogue record for this book
is available from the British Library

Library of Congress Cataloguing in Publication Data
Oakley, Allen
    Classical economic man: human agency and methodology in the
political economy of Adam Smith and J.S. Mill/Allen Oakley.
        p. cm. — (Advances in economic methodology)
    Includes bibliographical references and index.
    1. Classical school of economics. 2. Economic man. 3. Smith,
Adam, 1723–1790. 4. Mill, John Stuart, 1806–1873. I. Title.
II. Series.
HB94.023 1994
330.15'3—dc20   93–29339
                                                                                                CIP

ISBN 978 1 85278 708 0

Printed and bound in Great Britain by
Marston Book Services Limited, Didcot

For Renate

Contents

Preface   ix
Abbreviations for cited primary works   xiv

1. Introduction: methodology and economics as a human science   1

PART I   ADAM SMITH

2. Intellectual foundations   7
    2.1   The philosophical heritage   7
    2.2   Human nature and philosophical inquiry   19

3. Modelling morally situated human agents   31
    3.1   Introduction   31
    3.2   The sentimental human agent   39
    3.3   Balancing the moral virtues of human agents   45

4. The human agent in economy and society   62
    4.1   Introduction   62
    4.2   Justice and political economy   65
    4.3   Human agency and the organization of production   71

5. Human agency in a 'commercial' economy   84
    5.1   Introduction   84
    5.2   The 'ideal' operation of a 'commercial' economy   86
    5.3   Human agency in the operations of a mercantilist economy   98
    5.4   Containing human agency by reforms   107

6. Human agency and Smith's methodology   113

PART II   JOHN STUART MILL

7. 'Economic man' and the formation of classical methodology   123
    7.1   Introduction   123
    7.2   The transition to classical methodology   124
    7.3   David Ricardo   129
    7.4   Reactions to Ricardo   134

8.   J.S. Mill and classical methodology   142
     8.1   Introduction   142
     8.2   Reflections on the methodological inheritance   148
     8.3   Comte's positivism and the human sciences   158

9.   Mill's extended methodological inquiry   169
     9.1   Introduction   169
     9.2   The essentials of situated human agency   171
     9.3   Methodology and the representation of human agency   179
     9.4   Metaphysical intrusions   194

10. Human agency and socioeconomic reform   205
     10.1 The intentions and design of the PPE   205
     10.2 Essentials of production and distribution   211
     10.3 Reflections on the free market   218
     10.4 Human agency and socioeconomic progress   222
     10.5 Interventions and reform: pros and cons   234
     10.6 Human agents in political economy: some final
           observations   239

Bibliography   244
Index   253

Preface

The themes and theses argued in this book, I think more fully and completely than has been achieved in the classical economics literature to date, may be presented in outline as follows. It is well known that, from its beginnings as a separate discipline in the eighteenth century, political economy was taken for granted as being an integral part of the total human science of the period known as moral philosophy. Adam Smith had no occasion to question the idea that, if one sought to understand the working of an economic system, one would have to begin with as complete an analysis of human nature as possible. He treated it as self-evident that any explanation of economic phenomena should give primary emphasis to the fact that they are the consequence of human action. It followed, therefore, that political economy should be founded on a proper comprehension of what drives the choices, decisions and actions of the agents when they engage in economic activities. So it was that Smith's total project on moral philosophy began with a long inquiry into human nature in general, with the economic dimensions of human existence treated within the framework of analysis so established. In Smith's theory of the moral sentiments of human nature, in which contact with the realities of character and conduct was never lost, the motive of self-interest was ever dominant, but its effects were always either tempered by counteracting sentiments, where intersubjective relations had a dominant emotional content, or directed by situational conditions into collective consequences which could, in principle, be optimized, where the relations were functional in their objectives. In the case of economic conduct and relations, the optimal collective results comprised the maximization of the periodic flow of real per capita wealth and of its rate of growth.

My inquiries begin with this reading of Smith's project in an endeavour to demonstrate that it was as a consequence of his acceptance of human agency as the root of economic understanding that the methodological strategy which, with the benefit of hindsight, we find implicit in his work, was one with no conscious preconception or dominant direction. Smith was well aware of the wonders of Newtonian physics and of Hume's advocacy of the application of Newton's principles to human science. But, in the *Wealth of Nations*, the degree of conscious penetration by the methodology of the burgeoning physical sciences was confined to the principles of empirical observation and the representation of phenomena as systemically organized. Smith applied a mix of inductive and deductive technique in his analyses, with the shifting emphasis being in accordance with the singular demand that his explanations and exposition should be clear and cogent. Sometimes this meant adopting an approach comprising the simplification of observations and subsequent deductive argument, at other times the requirement was for empirico-historical description and consequent inductive generalization. The significant point here is that, for Smith, it was always accepted that the way to approach explication and understanding was to let the ontology of the object, that is, the nature of its generation and the character of its existence, determine the logical form to be taken by the argument.

Some of Smith's most important successors in political economy did not continue to see this as an appropriate approach. Soon after the turn of the nineteenth century, the science was beset by a methodological self-consciousness that was driven by the epistemological ambition to emulate the physical sciences. Physical scientists could demonstrate an empirical accuracy and logical security in their arguments and it was these achievements that James Mill and David Ricardo set out to claim for political economy. The effect was to turn the methodological imperative driving economic analysis on its head. Although Smith had given priority to the maintenance of empirical accuracy, he had not been concerned about the precise logical form in which his arguments were presented. James Mill's demand for logically exact argument, and Ricardo's genius for delivering it, shifted the immediate imperative in the design of political economy from providing for empirical accuracy to ensuring consistency with the principles of axiomatic–deductive methodology. It was now methodological predilections and ambitions that were driving economic analyses and the representation of the object phenomena was moulded to fit the demands thereof by whatever degree of abstraction from reality was required.

For better or for worse, economic phenomena turned out to be peculiarly suited to the application of this methodological inversion. For one thing, their manifestations were immediately in quantitative terms, terms which were able readily to be expressed in deductive logical sequences and thus to give an impression of precision as great as that expected in mechanics or astronomy. Moreover, and just as importantly, the status of self-interest as the most essential and dominant motivating force of human agents in their economic actions, which already had the imprimatur of Smith, was readily converted to the unqualified axiom of 'economic man'. Use of this concept represented human agents in a way that rendered their conduct as single-minded, reliable and predictable. Contingent dimensions of conduct were relegated to a second tier of inquiry that could legitimately be left aside in establishing the essential principles of political economy. This legitimation was grounded on the widely held belief that, in their concerns with matters economic, human agents really did operate exclusively so as to maximize individual material wealth and to minimize pecuniary and non-pecuniary costs. This whole strategy of designing economic analyses on the foundation of the axiom of 'economic man' and through the application of deductive logic gave them an air of unqualified veracity. In the public pronouncements of economic arguments, the 'disturbing causes' of contingent human actions were readily ignored in the interests of maintaining scientific pretensions.

It was into this intellectual environment that John Stuart Mill was inculcated under the exclusive tutelage of his father James. He started out as a defender of the 'Ricardian' faith in all its dimensions, but his subsequent intellectual career led him increasingly to deviate from these principles. Nowhere did this occur earlier and become more evident than in the matters of the application of the abstract–deductive methodology as exclusively appropriate to the moral sciences and the consequent adoption of 'economic man' as the sole representation of the human agent in economic argument. Having critically assessed the methodology of what had become the orthodox political economy of his age, Mill embarked on an ambitious endeavour to assess its bona fides by means of a comprehensive investigation of the extant logic of science. It became apparent to him in the process that the key methodological issue with which all moral sciences had to contend was that their phenomena were of human origin. They were thus distinct from the physical sciences in at least this respect and the challenge was to assess the implications this had for their 'correct' methodology. This led him back to the approach adopted by Adam Smith, in which selection of a valid methodology was decided by the criterion that it be the most consistent with the meaningful representation of its object phenomena. Mill was convinced that human sciences in general, and political economy in particular, could adhere to the principles of scientific logic, albeit in a form suitably adapted to the demands of its objects of inquiry.

An immediate outcome of his investigation of scientific logic was a recognition that there existed an essential incompatibility between logical precision and empirical accuracy in all human science analyses. Especially was this so in political economy, whatever its claims to the contrary, with the most significant manifestation of the difficulty being the failure of 'economic man' adequately to represent the true nature of human agents. The retention of a logic with scientific validity called for a compromise and Mill found it by rendering political economy an 'inexact science': its deductive methodology had to work from empirically sound axioms derived from observation and introspection, and its conclusions, together with the understanding and facility for prediction that they delivered, could only approximate their object reality. Such a position left economic theory and calculations as merely very complex examples of those worked out in the physical sciences. He drew the analogy of tidology as the epistemological target for economic analysis to aim at. It, too, experienced intractable degrees of difficulty in getting its explanations and predictions right, in particular because the interactions of lunar gravity and the oceans were subject to the 'disturbing causes' of a diverse and ever-changing complex of local conditions. There remained, though, a sufficient core of reliable analysis to allow a useful degree of understanding and predictions of the tides. Political economy was in a similar position, Mill reasoned. However he also allowed for inquiries to adopt an inductive methodology and devise empirical generalizations where the observed phenomena were too complex for the above methodology to be applied directly. Such empirical arguments as resulted carried the proviso that they were always to be regarded with scepticism until they could be shown to be consistent with some deductive explanation.

Mill's economic magnum opus, the *Principles of Political Economy*, perhaps not unexpectedly in the light of the foregoing observations, reflected a mix of methodological characteristics. The treatise went well beyond its 'Ricardian' roots both methodologically and substantively. In particular, in its whole argument, there was nothing to parallel the abstract and decisive logic of Ricardo's published analyses. And there was no dependence on a strictly circumscribed 'classical economic man' in its representations of human agents. Quite consciously and unashamedly, Mill set out to emulate and update the achievements of Smith in the *Wealth of Nations* by blending theory with historical inquiry and with its application to the formulation of policy. The methodological strategy of the work was pluralistic in ad hoc response to the demands of properly representing his various analytical objects. The conduct of human agents was portrayed as determined by the situational conditions in and through which they operated, although, in the end, the full import of this insight was never realized because it was left without its intended theoretical support from the science of Ethology. Ultimately he left his successors in much the same position as Smith had done. He wrote the dominant economic text of his age, but his readers were presented with no definitive conclusion about the 'correct' methodology to be applied in the further development of its analyses.

Quite contrary to the future direction that Mill's own thinking on the issues of human agency and methodology in the human sciences was to take, economic theory in the hands of his most influential successors returned to the principles of deductive stringency with a vengeance. As for Mill himself, the later years of his intellectual career were marked by an ever more decisive retreat from the defence of deductive methodology, even in its most fully qualified forms. His uneasiness became more acute when he took on the metaphysicians around him in an attempt to consolidate his argument that the character and conduct of human agents should be accounted for by biography and situational environment rather than by innate psychological determinants. In his critique, he was forced to confront and came to accept the fact that the empirical observation of human conduct, including introspection and the extrapolation of its revelations to others, always left a transcendental remainder of psychological effect. Explaining this effect was beyond the reach of the instruments of intellectual inquiry and representation, for it was directed largely by the forces of origination and creativity that are constituents of the human imagination. These forces could be expected to have a contingent effect on individual responses to situations that could not, therefore, be represented analytically or understood within human science at the time. Mill's final resignation to the existence of what we would now refer to as a phenomenological dimension of the determination of human conduct was indicated when he referred to it as the 'final inexplicability ... [of] ultimate facts' about which 'by far the wisest thing we can do, is to accept the inexplicable fact, without any theory of how it takes place'. In the end, then, Mill implicitly accepted that the phenomena of the human sciences were of a different ontological nature from those of the physical world. He made nothing of it explicitly and, anyway, by this time, his capacity to influence the development of methodology in political economy had waned and his further philosophical writings had no impact in that direction.

The ten chapters that comprise my exposition of this historical inquiry are based to a very large extent on direct exegesis from primary sources. I have not sought to confront extant contributions to the issues of interpretation with which I deal, except where they provide direct support for my own argument and thereby assist in its development and improve its cogency. My intention has not been to challenge the existing readings of the classical methodological legacy, about which there is now a fair measure of consensus, but rather only to draw attention to a relatively neglected facet of it. The aspects that I have pursued had their most profound effect through the impact of Smith and Mill on the foundations of human science in Germanic Europe. But that really is another story.

Allen Oakley
Medowie, Australia,

Abbreviations for cited primary works

(The publication details of each work are provided in the Bibliography at the end of the book.)

Adam Smith

EPS *Essays on Philosophical Subjects*, Smith (1980)
LJ   *Lectures on Jurisprudence*, Smith (1978)
TMS *The Theory of Moral Sentiments*, Smith (1976)
WN   *An Inquiry into the Nature and Causes of the Wealth of Nations*, Smith (1961)

John Stuart Mill

CW   *Collected Works of John Stuart Mill*
DPE 'On the definition of political economy; and on the method of investigation proper to it', Mill (1967)
SOL *A System of Logic*, Mill (1973)
PPE *Principles of Political Economy*, Mill (1965)
EHP *An Examination of Sir William Hamilton's Philosophy*, Mill (1979)
ACP *Auguste Comte and Positivism*, Mill (1969)
AUT *Autobiography*, Mill (1981)

1 Introduction: methodology and economics as a human science

The British classical period of political economy, covering the approximately 100 years from Adam Smith to W.S. Jevons, saw the formation of the methodological and epistemological standards to which orthodox economic theory still largely adheres today. What has not been adequately analysed in expositions of this development process is how it was related to the burgeoning philosophy and psychology of human nature of the period. My intention is to argue that this comprises a vital, but relatively neglected, connection which, when elaborated in detail, enables us to account more completely for the dominant acceptance and adoption of the concept of 'economic man' as the only representation of the human agent required to legitimate economic analyses.

It will become evident that the classical period was characterized by the fact that most political economists distanced their analyses from the complicating methodological implications of contemporary understandings of human nature. The impetus for this retreat came from the widespread conviction that economics should aspire to be a science with characteristics and standards of analysis that emulated those of Newtonian methodology as it applied to the physical sciences. Two things ultimately facilitated the ostensible realization of this aspiration. One was the development of the concept of 'economic man' itself, which enabled analysts to isolate and to operate with only those definitive and reliable facets of human nature and motivation that could be represented by formal logic. The other was the progressive recognition that, amongst the moral sciences of the time, political economy was unique in that its object phenomena immediately presented themselves *in exact physical cum quantitative terms*. They could thereby be manipulated in analyses in the same way as the natural objects of the physical sciences. Economics was able, therefore, to focus only on the manifested *results* of the complex processes of human agency. What went on underneath the quantitative surface was irrelevant and quite quickly lost from sight. In particular, this meant that theories could apparently be formulated with only minimal consideration of the problem of representing human agents who, in reality, comprised an infinite number of unique psychological entities, all with their own genetic make-ups, cumulative biographies of experiences and current situations. The overwhelming acceptance of theories known to be grounded

on such a meagre representation of the most complex of all natural beings is
something which warrants inquiry and explanation.

My study of this historical theme proceeds from a belief that, if economics
is to be thought of as a science, then it should explicitly be as a *human*
science. Especially does this require a recognition that its 'human' appellation derives from the ontological nature and constitution of its object of
study, for, whatever else economic phenomena may be, the one irreducible
characteristic that they all have in common is that they originate in the
choices, decision making and actions of human agents. An immediate question posed by this recognition is the extent to which this ontology should
influence the methodological and epistemological aspirations of the human
sciences. My presumption in what follows will be that the influence should
be a dominant one. Most particularly, methodological choices should be
made that can be shown to be consistent with the proper representation of
object ontology. To work the other way around, with methodology driving
and delimiting the representation of object phenomena, is to have the cart
before the horse, as it were. It will soon become apparent that, very early on,
political economists effectively denied the chronically human status of their
science and adopted this perverse approach. From being a 'soft' moral
science, political economy was rapidly transformed into a quantitative,
pseudo-physical science. One of the critical consequences of this denial and
transformation was the rise to prominence of 'economic man' as the only
axiom which allowed the objectively expressed, physical–scientific arguments to proceed.

Human agents, in the economic dimension of their existence, are concerned, directly or indirectly, with the wresting of material provisioning
needs from the natural environment. The essence of this process is the physical transformation of selected contents of the environment in a way that must
go beyond the mere spatial rearrangement of resources. This is due to the fact
that the substantive constituents of raw nature rarely meet directly the biologically and socio-historically determined needs of the human agents, a fact
that is complicated further by any problems of scarcity relative to demand
that emerge. Because of the need to undertake this transformation, it is
appropriate to refer to human involvement in it as an *agency* process, for that
involvement is one of physical mediation. Additionally, the process includes
psychological dimensions that are intimately part of the individual and social
composition of the agency concept. For this reason, the phenomena relating
to the material provisioning process were originally studied as a part of moral
philosophy and later as comprising one of the separable moral sciences. And,
as human economic organization became more sophisticated over historical
time, the cerebral aspects of the provisioning process increased in importance. This can be attributed to the human ramifications of increasing spe-

cialization and division of labour in production, together with the increasing complexity of the income distribution and exchange – circulation institutions and processes required to mediate between production and consumption. Paradoxically we will find that it was as this increasingly complicated involvement of human agents in economic processes developed that the representation of the human dimension in political economy was being consolidated as the highly abstract and simplified concept of 'economic man'.

It is an obvious fact of life, but one that is worth emphasizing in the present context, that, for the vast majority of people, it has always been the case that involvement in the material provisioning process dominates the character of their existence more than any other factor. Not only does it pre-empt a large proportion of their daily time and intellectual and physical effort, but also the mode of their participation in it provides and determines the means they will have available to undertake all other aspects of their lives; that is, to meet all their other desires and aspirations. Thus it is that the economic dimension of human life invokes imperatives that give it a logical and a very real priority over all other aspects. One way or another, the need to be involved in the provisioning process is mandatory for all human agents. Economics is *the* human science par excellence in this respect.

It is reasonable to expect, therefore, that the form of presentation of economics as a science, in both its methodology and its substance, would give a clear primacy to the need to represent formally the nature of the existence and being of human agents as they are manifested in the processes that generate its object phenomena: that is, to give expression to the ontological nature of these phenomena. The inherent difficulty of this expectation can be emphasized by setting out some of the crucial characteristics of real-world human agents with which any human science should endeavour to deal analytically.

First, human agents are, in an absolute and ultimate sense, existentially free beings who may choose and act in any way that they may wish. In any exercise of this right they draw upon their constituent innate and learned emotions, sentiments, capacities to reason and accumulated states of knowledge. Their conduct has, as a consequence, an ever-present element of contingency. Secondly, in virtually all respects, though, human agents exist, make decisions and do their choosing and acting with some cumulative biography behind them and in *some individually particular situation*. These individual human exigencies are, for many short-term imperatives, given as inherited from period to period. Their situations comprise a complex totality of human and non-human, natural and artificial, environmental conditions made up of social, institutional, physical and spatial dimensions. The importance of human situations is that their selectively relevant aspects always serve to contain and/or facilitate the agents' otherwise free decisions, choices and actions. A third consideration is that, as human agents are self-conscious and autonomous, they subjectively reason about, interpret and formulate meanings for their situations. It is in response to these considerations that they choose, decide and act in pursuit of their equally subjective preferences and goals. Here we reach a point where the analytical complications of representing human agency really begin to set in, for, in addition to these considerations, it must be recognized that the capacity to reason includes the ability to be *creative and to originate* in forming the substantial bases upon which choices, decisions and actions are undertaken. The result is that these agency processes are highly contingent and potentially open-ended phenomena that necessarily involve the metaphysical cum transcendental dimensions of human existence. These are beyond the capacities of the human senses to 'observe' in any way other than through personal introspection, with all its individualistic overtones. Fourthly, in spite of these subjectivist complexities, within their respective situations, historical observation suggests that agents' individual and decentralized choices, decisions and actions in the social and economic facets of their life-world, pursued more or less freely and guided by their personal self-interest and objectives, generate, reproduce and change a collective *cosmos*. This ordered outcome, while it is characterized by varying degrees of coherence and stability over time, is somehow preserved from chaotic degeneration by some quality of the reason that the agents bring to their situations and operations. What may be anticipated is that, while the agents have little immediate control over their periodically inherited situations, the reality is that, when they confront the immanent rules, directions, facilities and constraints that are the institutional manifestations of these situations, they are most frequently inclined to reason that it is in their best interests to cooperate with them: that is, to so orient their conformist conduct as to get the best out of the system for them. Renegades will always exist, but the presence of a core of social and economic order suggests that they are usually in the minority.

The above considerations become pertinent when we press the classicals for an answer to the question: what mode of generalized and abstracted representation of the situated agents and their agency can be defended as feasible and legitimate in the formal analysis of economic phenomena? A further question that follows is: given the particular nature of its object, what sort of science can economics legitimately claim to be within the totality of the sciences? And, as a matter of potential comparison and contrast, it is appropriate to pose the cognate question: what sort of science does economics claim to have become? The interplay between the search for an answer to the former two questions and the evolving answer to the third during the classical period constitute the central theme of my inquiries.

PART I

ADAM SMITH

2 Intellectual foundations

2.1 The philosophical heritage

The eighteenth-century intellectual context, of which Adam Smith was so much a part, was characterized by a high degree of physical scientific optimism. One anticipated outcome of this optimism as far as moral philosophy, or human science, was concerned was that it could expect to emulate the intellectual achievements of physical science. In particular, it was the discovery of Newton's principle of gravitation 'which made it possible to found on a single law a complete science of nature' which led to the 'conception of the hope of discovering an analogous principle capable of serving for the establishment of a synthetic science of the phenomena of moral and social life' (Halévy, 1972, p. 3). A further dimension of optimism involving human science was the expectation that the free exercise of human nature in society and economy would deliver up the maximum potential psychic and material well-being for all people. The human sciences 'were thought to be finding in the world of men and all their voluntary doings, full indications of the possibility, and the reforms needed for realization, of a ... harmonious, human–social cosmos' (Taylor, 1960, p. 2). This cosmos would comprise 'a world of free individuals, rationally pursuing satisfactions of all their "natural" desires, *and in so doing,* always acting in the ways that would fit in as appropriate parts of an orderly system of "natural" social processes' (ibid., original emphasis). Such containment and direction of the pursuit of self-interest as was required, it was thought, could be achieved so that the resulting order emerged as 'on the whole conducive to the highest attainable welfare of all mankind' (ibid.). In the chapters which follow, I will show how Smith was able to advance both of these aspects of the optimism of his era.

The general methodological and epistemological sources upon which the creators of this image of the human cosmos drew were the achievements of John Locke (1632–1704) in philosophy and ethics and of Isaac Newton (1642–1727) in astronomy and physics. Newton showed how the empiricism of Locke could be applied to an understanding of the physical universe and this set the standard which the human sciences were challenged to emulate. The Newtonian perception of science was one which defined it 'as being no longer contemplative and theoretical, but active and practical, as aiming at securing our domination over external nature through the knowledge of natural laws' (Halévy, 1972, p. 6). Martin Hollis neatly sums up the era as one dominated by 'a Newtonian picture of nature as a mechanical, law-governed, humanly empty system, whose workings were hidden from the naked eye, rather as the springs and wheels of a fob watch are invisible to those who see only its face'. The reaction of natural scientists to this empirical presentation of nature was to learn how to 'prise the back off the watch' in order to reveal 'the forces acting on the cogs' and to learn 'the secrets of the innermost particles of matter'. The challenge that this posed for moral philosophers was thus: 'Could the same not be done for human nature and society?' (Hollis, 1987b, p. 2) That is, they sought to defend the ambitious claim that in the formation of a science of mind and a science of society,

> it is possible to conduct one's study of man as an individual and as a social being in the same way as the physicist studies other matters, and here again to apply the Newtonian method with a view to determining the smallest possible number of general simple laws which, once discovered, will enable the detail of phenomena to be explained by a synthetic and deductive method. (Halévy, 1972, p. 6)

It will be my purpose in the first section of this chapter to present an outline of the way in which Adam Smith's immediate antecedents were involved in this endeavour to expose and comprehend the natural workings of human nature and society.

Adam Smith's own unified project in moral philosophy began with an investigation of some specifically methodological aspects of Newtonian science as they related to the dominant psychological principles of the period. He focused most particularly on the nature and role of the human mind and its complex of sentiments in the processes of constructing natural science and, although his endeavour was set in the context of the history and philosophy of science, his objective is more aptly interpreted to have been an inquiry into the mental characteristics of human agents that were revealed by their scientific activities. At this stage of his project, human agents were looked at as natural philosophers, that is, as observer-analysts of their physical environment. This was soon to change to a more general perspective in which Smith's study of human nature was directed at humans in their life-world situations and thus as active subjective agents within, not only a physical environment, but also a humanly created social and institutional environment which their own participation was instrumental in helping to construct and reflexively to change. Just how his psychological and methodological inquiries in relation to science prepared him for this transfer of focus is the subject of the second section of this chapter.

Adam Smith's treatment of human nature was developed from a conscious mix of rejection and extension of his antecedents' work. The dominant intellectual figure of the era in moral philosophy was Thomas Hobbes (1588–1679) who portrayed the essence of human nature as an egoism which manifested itself as the unrestrained and destructive pursuit of self-interest. This portrayal generated such outrage in so many disparate quarters that he may be considered to have initiated much of the philosophical inquiry that followed. The result was that the intellectual history of the century between the publication of his *Leviathan* (in Latin in 1642 and in English in 1651) and Adam Smith's early philosophical works, as far as it involved moral issues, was dominated by reactions to Hobbes. The literature of the period was characterized by a myriad of efforts by philosophers and men of letters generally, as well as by churchmen and politicians, to negate, or at least to contain the influence of, in one way or another, the claimed abhorrent and pernicious human, social and political implications of the doctrine. For the purposes of the present study, it is appropriate to regard Adam Smith's work on human nature as representing the confluence and culmination of antecedent Hobbesian influence and anti-Hobbesian struggles (see Taylor, 1960, chapters 1 and 2; Myers, 1983, *passim*, especially chapters 8 and 9).

The warlike social state of human nature was attributed by Hobbes to the overwhelming and all-consuming obsession of human agents with the pursuit of their selfish interests. It was this egoistic motive that remained when Hobbes abstractly conceptualized the most essential and natural state of human nature itself, in isolation from any situational containments such as customs and institutions. Milton Myers reads this as a mathematical-like process of abstraction because Hobbes 'is subtracting elements from what makes up the totality of man's condition and nature, the remainder being the denominator common to all individuals'. That is, argues Myers, Hobbes 'intends to get down to the irreducible in man' (Myers, 1983, p. 30). Moreover, he tells us, even as a pre-Newtonian, Hobbes was inclined to apply mechanistic analogies to the study of human nature (ibid., p. 37), a claim that is supported by Halévy's assertion that Hobbes had applied the gravity principle to the problem of accounting for moral determinism (Halévy, 1972, p. 6n).

For Hobbes, unlike for many of his antagonist successors, there existed no natural containment for the destructive force of self-interest in society and economy. The continuous actions of all human agents were motivated by an insatiable acquisitiveness, combined with the natural condition that 'every man has a Right to every thing', the 'right of all to all'. And, in the consequent struggle 'of every man against every man', the result was a state in which 'nothing can be Unjust' and the 'notions of Right and Wrong, Justice and Injustice have there no place'. Man in this extreme and raw state was condemned to a life in which only the perpetual race for survival mattered and thus to a life that was 'solitary, poore, nasty, brutish, and short' (quoted by Myers, 1983, p. 32). In such a state, human agents lacked security in the betterment of any aspect of their existence and, therefore, had no incentive to lift themselves beyond their brutish and animal-like pursuits. A crucial legacy of Hobbes which remained as a consequence of this image of humankind was one in which the individual pursuit of self-interest was given priority as the driving force behind the character and conduct of human agency in all life-world matters. But he envisaged it as functioning only in a form moderated by the constraining and facilitating institutions of the political state constructed and operated by human reason. There was no evidence in Hobbes's conclusions that human agents were ever to be credited with anything but an underlying abhorrent and naturally selfish character or that any authority other than the omnipotent civil and secular state could bring harmony to human relations.

It was Hobbes's portrayal of human nature as overwhelmed by egoistic concerns, and as lacking any of the innate moral virtues that should be associated with the capacity to reason and/or the sentiments that were said to constitute the human psyche, that brought him such widespread condemnation. Many considered this to be a scandalous defamation and deformation of the God-given goodness of humankind and reacted accordingly in the moral–philosophical literature. However, increasingly during the eighteenth century, it came to be accepted that self-interest represented a vital force in the existence and *prosperity* of human beings (Halévy, 1972, pp. 14f). The focus of the debates in moral philosophy was, as a consequence, on the containment and direction of individual human self-interest such as to generate acceptable moral and social outcomes. For Hobbes, it was necessary to impose upon individuals an extensive structure of sociopolitical controls, and the sanctions that go with them, in order to bring moral cohesion to society. Against this need for an 'artificial identification of interests' were arraigned two alternative perceptions: one was the 'fusion of interests' and the other was the 'natural identification of interests' (Halévy, 1972, pp. 13ff). In the former case, egoism was claimed to be adequately contained by the immanent countervailing effect of other-directed sentiments such as benevolence. Individuals were thus perceived as spontaneously morally self-sufficient prior to their entry into society. Where a 'natural identification of interests' was assumed, the balance of sentiments was to be struck by means of some automatic process of social interaction. What was really required for this to occur was the evolution of an appropriate systemic situation of human activities, just as was required in the 'artificial' identification case. The difference was that the 'natural' thesis claimed that perfectly free agents pursuing their individual self-interest in a society comprising only institutions which had developed largely without conscious human interventions, including aspects of the law and the market exchange mechanism, could be relied upon to deliver an optimal social and moral outcome. It will become apparent later that Smith borrowed from all three of these alternatives in creating his moral and economic analyses.

One prominent writer who took issue with Hobbes on human nature was Anthony Ashley Cooper, third Earl of Shaftesbury (1671–1713). The tenor of Shaftesbury's diametric opposition has been perceived as 'asserting the native "natural goodness" of mankind, and [in] attributing this more to "good, natural" emotional dispositions than to "reason", and [in] regarding mankind as all too easily corrupted by the misuse of the latter on the higher levels of its cultivation and achievements' (Taylor, 1960, p. 30). Importantly Shaftesbury worked on a quite broad canvas, in that he drew attention to more diverse aspects of the innate psychology of human nature that could be elicited to account spontaneously for the reconciliation of the individual pursuit of self-interest with social harmony. Human agents, he thought, were morally self-contained and self-sufficient by virtue of their design. They could, in principle, as a consequence of their inbuilt 'moral sense', operate socially in a morally acceptable way independently of their situation, an argument which placed Shaftesbury squarely in the 'fusion of interests' camp. That is, active human agents were an integral part of the great and proper design of the harmonious universe that autonomously functioned in the best interests of all. So, although self-interest remained a central, inborn and legitimate senti-ment, it was one that had its effects balanced by a range of other passions, including benevolence. Such balance was analogous to the balanced func-tioning of the organs of the body. The public good was thus taken care of by 'a due balance and counterpoise in the affections', referred to by Shaftesbury also as an 'economy of the passions' and as a 'tuning of the passions' (quoted by Myers, 1983, pp. 54, 55). There remained a qualification to this optimism, though, in that any malevolent sentiments and actions that human agents may exhibit were considered by Shaftesbury to be the unnatural result of environ-mental influences stemming from bad social conditions. This, of course, begs the question of just what would comprise the appropriate environment to avoid distortions of human nature, and the 'natural' thesis enters by the back door, as it were. Shaftesbury's espousal of social reforms aimed at ensuring the dominance of the innate goodness of humankind reinforced the notion that the social and moral state of humankind cannot be determined prior to the definition of its situational conditions.

Shaftesbury was typical of his era in espousing a dominant thesis in the reaction against Hobbes that claimed the existence of an harmoniously de-signed natural universe of which the character and conduct of human agents, both individually and collectively, was an integral part. The same sort of order of nature endowed by the Creator in the physical universe was there to be discovered in the 'natural identification of interests' as the basis for the order of society as well. All such thinking could only have been reinforced by Newton's theory that the harmony of the physical universe could be explic-itly accounted for by the operation of the binding force of gravity. The apparent empirical confirmation of this finding turned speculation about a natural order into a scientific fact. As things turned out, the influence of Newton on all subsequent scientific thinking, including that in the moral–human sciences, was profound and durable. The concepts of 'system' and 'mechanism' pervaded much of the discussion of human relations and activity and it was largely taken for granted that human science should set out to discover the natural laws of society. It was similarly to be expected that the harmony of society would be attributed to some sort of 'moral gravity', by means of which the socially centrifugal forces of self-interest were able to be depicted as balanced by the centripetal forces of more benign sentiments. This broad notion of the relevance of a gravitationally ordered material universe to the understanding of the order of the human universe was taken up especially by one of the key figures in the intellectual life of Adam Smith, his much admired teacher, Francis Hutcheson. However, before Hutcheson, in his turn, rose to defend humankind against the libels of Hobbes, a new antagonist with decidedly Hobbesian views appeared on the popular literary scene in the person of Bernard de Mandeville (1670–1733). Hutcheson and his followers thus had to aim their critical reactions at a compounded and reinvigorated version of Hobbes's doctrine.

Bernard Mandeville's attack on the moral sentimentalism of Shaftesbury and his ilk stirred the coals of Hobbesianism again during the first quarter of the eighteenth century. In his widely read and notoriously influential publication, *The Fable of the Bees: or, Private vices, Publick Benefits; with ... a Search into the Nature of Society*, that appeared in several ever-expanding editions during the period, Mandeville graphically reiterated the thesis that the conduct of human agents is primarily and predominantly motivated by selfishness. Contrary to what some of the sentimental moralists had been arguing, Mandeville denied that any natural or acquired virtues that human agents may possess, such as benevolence, or any innate 'moral sense', could impede or counterbalance the power of the self-interest drive. Most importantly, he compounded this claim by arguing that it was, in fact, fortunate indeed for humankind that this is so, for it was the determined individualistic pursuit of a maximum of all things material, necessities and luxuries alike, together with the associated psychic returns of pride and vanity, that ensured the most active operation of human industry in all its forms and the consequent collective prosperity of the society and economy. What Mandeville defended in particular was the image of human nature overwhelmingly dominated by the pursuit of *situated* self-interest. Such pursuit was situated in the sense that it was always to be contained and constrained by institutional structures of some kind. Different readings of his work have emphasized that these were created by constructed state intervention (cf. Taylor, 1960, pp. 37ff) and/or that they resulted from spontaneous evolution without conscious human design (cf. Hayek, 1978, *passim*). In the former case, Mandeville was argued to espouse an 'artificial' thesis and in the latter case a 'natural' thesis as concerns the confluence of egoisms. The important point remained, independently of this reading, that the pursuit of self-interest was argued cogently to be a crucial driving force in the realization of an harmonious and prosperous social and economic order. Both representations of situated self-interest became an integral part of the intellectual heritage from which Adam Smith worked (cf. Cannan, 1904, pp. xliiff).

One crucial influence on Adam Smith's intellectual life was his teacher, Francis Hutcheson (1694–1746). Hutcheson was a disciple of Shaftesbury and continued the attack on the egoistic doctrines of human nature espoused by Hobbes and Mandeville. He, too, gave priority to the notion of an innate, natural 'moral sense' in the determination of the character and conduct of human beings and considered it to operate through the sentiments, including the all-important aesthetic sense, rather than through reason. Most significantly, he maintained the notion of humankind's inbuilt moral self-sufficiency and effectively defended the 'fusion of interests' thesis. Hutcheson found the key to moral virtue in the sentiment of benevolence and proceeded to give it pride of place in his ethical theory. Indeed it was with respect to the central role of benevolence that the strongly Newtonian influence on him surfaced most clearly when he quite baldly drew an analogy between gravity and benevolence: 'This universal Benevolence toward all Men, we may compare to that Principle of Gravitation, [which] like the love of Benevolence, increases as the distance is diminish'd, and is strongest when Bodys come to touch each other' (quoted by Myers, 1983, p. 69). The significance of this passage goes beyond its immediate implication that it is benevolence that is the intersubjective force that holds human society together as a system. It is important to notice, too, the reference to the inverse relation between the 'distance' between human subjects and the strength of the benevolent 'gravity' which they experience in their contacts with each other. This is an important idea, for it allowed for some social relations needing more than the innate balance of sentiments to ensure moral harmony and cohesion. Once again, a role for a 'natural' or even an 'artificial' identification of interests was implicit, but not addressed.

This limitation of Hutcheson's argument was even more prominent when he considered the sentiment of self-interest in the specific context of the nature of moral cohesion in commercial relations: 'It is well known, that general Benevolence alone, is not a motive strong enough to industry' so that 'Self-love is really as necessary to the Good of the whole, as Benevolence.' He went on to recognize self-love 'as that Attraction which causes the Cohesion of the Parts, [and that it] is as necessary to the regular State of the Whole, as Gravitation' (quoted by Myers, 1983, p. 69). However it seems that, for him, benevolence would remain of sufficient innate strength to counter any socially adverse consequences of the rising effect of self-interest. Hutcheson thus maintained an image of human nature in which a sufficient concern for its own well-being was juxtaposed to and 'fused' with a similar degree of concern for others so that an harmonious and materially adequate socioeconomic order would prevail.

Following D.D. Raphael and A.L. Macfie in their 'Introduction' to the definitive Glasgow Edition of Smith's *Theory of Moral Sentiments*, it is evident that the intellectual influence of David Hume (1711–76) on Adam Smith, his friend and contemporary, was even greater than that of Hutcheson. It is not to be thought from this, though, that Smith was simply a follower of Hume. As we shall see below, there is good reason to agree with Raphael and Macfie that 'Smith rejects or transforms Hume's ideas far more often than he follows them, but his own views would have been markedly different if he had not been stimulated to disagreement with Hume' (1976, p. 10). For, while Smith may well have been critical of some of Hume's ideas on certain basic philosophical themes, he followed him closely in much of what was pertinent to the development of his political economy. As with all his antecedents, though, Smith himself only gave the sketchiest of indications of Hume's influence on him. Scholars of eighteenth-century thought have combed their respective texts and revealed a number of particular points of agreement and disagreement. For example, D.D. Raphael suggests that 'Adam Smith was one of the few people of his time who took the measure of Hume's positive achievements in philosophy; Smith's emphasis on the constructive role of the imagination in his theory of scientific method, and the function which he assigned to nature in his ethical theory, must both have come from an appreciation of Hume' (1975, p. 84; cf. Thomson, 1984, p. 331; Raphael and Skinner, 1980, pp. 15ff). Andrew Skinner is even more specific in referring to 'three characteristic positions' that Smith adopted from Hume. These were, first, that any study of human activity, including scientific activity, must be preceded by a proper study of human nature; secondly, that all scientific study, including that of human nature itself, must proceed by means of the observation and experience emphasized in Newton's methodology; and thirdly, that certain principles of human nature are uniform and constant across space and time (1979, pp. 14f). As we shall find in subsequent chapters, these were indeed key premises from which Smith worked in his analyses of human agency and its place in political economy.

In his theory of human nature, Hume's key critical focus was on ethical and scientific rationalism which attributed the character and conduct of human agents to their innate capacity to reason. He put his position on reason quite emphatically in his *A Treatise of Human Nature* when he asserted that, in the 'combat of passion and reason' as directives of human conduct, the passions will take precedence in the sense 'that reason alone can never be a motive to any action of the will' and 'that it can never oppose passion in the direction of the will' (1962, II, pp. 154, 155). Passages such as these led D.G. Macnabb to conclude that the 'consequences of Hume's philosophy are no less than the death of all rationalistic metaphysics and ethics' (1962, p. 11). Hume's emphasis was on the activating role of the entire complex of passions or sentiments in the constitution of human nature and this immediately broadened his outlook on the subject beyond the confines of Hutcheson's 'moral sense' (cf. Raphael and Macfie, 1976, p. 14). Any claim to find a 'fusion' of interests between agents on the basis of an innate balancing of sentiments would be rather more complicated to defend than previously suggested. Indeed it is difficult to classify Hume's views within the above threefold taxonomy except to suggest that he drew upon each ad hoc.

As part of this wider perspective on the determination of human character and conduct, Hume sustained the utilitarian view of morality that 'all virtue is connected with beneficial effects'. Thus, while he accepted that benevolence 'is a motive natural to man and that it naturally evokes approval ..., he did not agree that [it] is the sole motive of virtuous action or that moral approval is an innate basic feeling' (Raphael and Macfie, 1976, pp. 12, 13). Justice was an important virtue, too, but it was perceived to need an 'artificial' identification of interests rather than being able to depend on a 'fused' or 'natural' one. The common factor in all such virtue was that acts which can be designated as virtuous were those that draw sympathetic approbation from an indifferent and uninvolved spectator because of their perceived human benefits. So, instead of being innate, moral standards were manifested through the sympathetic pleasure of a situated human judge in the form of a representative but detached spectator. The 'natural' virtue of benevolence elicits sympathetic pleasure directly, whereas the 'artificial' virtue of justice can elicit it only via the utility that its rules bring in the form of a happy and harmonious society (cf. Raphael and Macfie, 1976, pp. 12f).

To the extent that he broadened his concerns explicitly to include the structures and operations of the human mind, Hume worked with a psychology of the association of ideas. This approach to mental inquiry proved to be extremely popular and durable, and we will find it still dominant in the work of J.S. Mill about a century later. It is reasonable to suspect that a part of this popularity and longevity of the doctrine can be attributed to the apparently scientific status of its argument. The association of ideas drew on an analogy with the natural attraction between objects of the universe that was an integral part of Newtonian physical science. Mental phenomena were envisaged as comprising ideas that were attracted by the 'force' of their substantive and contiguous association. As Hume himself put the point, this associative 'force' comprised 'a kind of *attraction*, which in the mental world will be found to have as extraordinary effects as in the natural [physical world]', with 'the actions of the mind ..., in this respect, the same with those of matter' (quoted by Myers, 1983, p. 67, Hume's emphasis). Moreover, for Hume, the Lockian empiricist, the ideas of which the mind is constituted were able, directly or indirectly via the memory, to be traced back to sensory impressions (Hume, 1962, I, pp. 45ff). Some ideas, he argued, are simple in the sense that they are singularly able to be linked to a sense impression that was their exclusive source without leaving a remainder. Complex ideas, by contrast, comprise arrangements of simple ideas drawn from immediate simple singular or complex multiple sense impressions that may or may not be combined with elements of memory. It was through his notion of complex ideas that Hume introduced the potential for human imagination. The importance of this was that it meant granting that some dimensions of the human mind had no direct source in any sense impression, but rather could only be attributed to a *creative and original* rearrangement of accumulated past impressions. Such application of memory involves a process of *reflection* that is quite distinct from the acquisition of immediate sensations. Complexes of ideas may still exist that can be traced to their sensory origins to some greater or lesser degree. These provide the substance of memory that can be accounted for by sensory associations. Those pure or perfect ideas that do not have such associations in their present format constitute the human imagination.

From a methodological perspective, Hume had been enthusiastic about the achievements of Newton in astronomy and classical physics and they had an important influence on the way that he addressed his inquiries into the human mind and human nature generally. It was his ambition, expressed in his *Treatise of Human Nature*, to emulate these scientific advances in the formalization of the methodological bases of moral philosophy. The immediate manifestation of this is to be found in the sub-title of the *Treatise:* 'Being an attempt to introduce the experimental method of reasoning into moral subjects'. The rationale for his intention was expressed by noting that 'all the sciences have a relation, greater or less, to human nature; and that, however wide any of them may seem to run from it, they still return back by one passage or another'. So sciences such as mathematics, natural philosophy and natural religion 'are in some measure dependent on the science of MAN; since they lie under the cognisance of men, and are judged of by their powers and faculties'. Then he came to the sceptical thrust of these assertions: 'It is impossible to tell what changes and improvements we might make in these sciences were we thoroughly acquainted with the extent and force of human understanding, and could explain the nature of the ideas we employ, and of the operations we perform in our reasonings.' In this he stressed that bane of the life of serious human scientists still today: 'we ourselves are not only the beings that reason, *but also one of the objects concerning which we reason'* (1962, I, pp. 40–41, emphasis added).

Despite these misgivings about human science in particular, Hume envisaged that all sciences would become part of 'a complete system of the sciences' in which they would all depend upon a methodology of 'experience and observation'. As he expressed this objective in 'An Enquiry Concerning Human Understanding' (Hume, 1975), it would be history which would enable philosophers 'to discover the constant and universal principles of human nature, by showing men in all varieties of circumstances and situations and furnishing material from which we may form our observations and become acquainted with the regular springs of human action and behaviour' (quoted by Halévy, 1972, p. 9). That is to say, he anticipated that it should be possible legitimately to apply at least the observational component of Newton's 'experimental philosophy to moral subjects' (Hume, 1962, I, pp. 41, 42). However, as we have begun to notice, he was sensitive at the same time to the potential problems and limitations of such an application where the complexities of human nature were the object of study, for, although he remained adamant that no science 'can go beyond experience, or establish any principles which are not founded on that authority', the force of that authority was ultimately weak. He was sceptical of all claims to knowledge which depend upon observation and the reasoned association of ideas and he resisted any assertion that induction in its demonstrative cum causative sense could be sustained as a means to establishing the nature of real events. Clearly this sort of scepticism hits the moral sciences with a vengeance. Hume candidly admitted to the 'impossibility of explaining ultimate principles' in the science of human being (1962, I, p. 43). He expressed his awareness that such science had the 'peculiar disadvantage, which is not found in natural [physical sciences], that in collecting its experiments, it cannot make them purposely, with premeditation, and after such a manner as to satisfy itself concerning every particular difficulty which may arise' (1962, I, pp. 43–4). His resolve, though, was to press on with the empirical methodology, as far as he judged that it could be meaningfully and securely taken in human affairs.

The simple but crucial fact of intellectual life that Hume had recognized here is that there is an irreducible difference between the nature of the objects confronted by the physical, and even the biological sciences, and of those confronted by the human sciences. With an outstanding astuteness and subtlety for his time, he realized, if he were to set up and participate in a formal intersubjective experimental situation akin to that which could be used for two physical bodies, 'it is evident ... [that my] reflection and premeditation would so disturb the operation of my natural principles, as must render it impossible to form any just conclusion from the phenomenon [observed]'.

The only solution would be to avoid experiment per se and to proceed to 'a cautious observation of human life' and to take the observations 'as they appear in the common course of the world, by men's behaviour in company, in affairs, and in their pleasures'. He boldly concluded that, where such behaviourist pseudo-experiments as these 'are judiciously collected and compared, we may hope to establish on them a science which will not be inferior in certainty, and will be much superior in utility, to any other human comprehension' (1962, I, p. 44).

It is apparent, then, as Macnabb observes, that, whatever developments had gone before in formulating a theory of human nature, Hume saw himself as more explicitly founding such a theory upon sound, empirically dependent principles (1962, pp. 12–13). But, aware of the problems posed by the peculiar nature of the object of study confronted by moral philosophers, he recognized that the empirical research required would demand extensive observations of human activities in everyday life. As Macnabb also perceptively notes, though, concerning the two locations in Britain and France where Hume prepared for and wrote his *Treatise* between 1726 and 1737, that 'one wonders whether Ninewells and La Fléche were really favourably situated man-watching stations' (1962, p. 12). The suspicion must begin to dawn on us that the 'observations' that dominated Hume's 'data' collections were largely those of personal experience together with, in his case, the introspection and plain common sense of a highly intelligent and thoughtful social philosopher. Presumably, too, he was not alone in this empiricist delusion, for all who claimed access to the internal dimensions of the human psyche by means of observational cum behavioural approaches in this era, and for some time to come, would have had to accept the same limitations. We can assume, in particular, that the 'man-watching stations' available to Adam Smith and J.S. Mill were no better than Hume's. Taylor (1960) makes this clear as a general concern about the methodological claims of the period: those moral philosophers 'who sincerely professed their adherence to the Lockeian "empiricism" and the natural-science method of observing facts and testing theories for agreement with them', as we may well expect, 'generally fell very far short of actually performing, or even realizing or conceiving, all that was needed in the way of thorough, careful, systematic, empirical research, and critical testing of their plausible, "rational" theories for agreement with "experience"'. As things really were, they could, for the most part, only '"reason" from or upon simple, plausible, general assumptions arising from or suggested by their limited amounts of informal, casual, "everyday" experience and observation and their "common sense"'. And, finally, Taylor adds the insightful caveat that this sort of methodological approach 'really differed less than they often supposed from the avowed method of the all out "rationalists", who regarded their "common sense" beliefs not as summaries of everyday experience, but rather as "self-evident" intuitions of pure reason' (ibid., pp. 4–5).

In my treatment of Adam Smith's work and beyond into the ideas argued especially by J.S. Mill, this and the other caveats suggested by Taylor will often reappear. All philosophers of the period had ultimately to confront the insoluble dilemma that the mental phenomena of other human agents are not accessible by any process that can legitimately be called observation. They were then, and remain today, transcendental and beyond access to experience. Any science that has as its objects of study empirical phenomena that originate in the mental processes of human agents should explicitly contend with this dilemma when formulating its methodological principles and strategies and when making claims about the epistemological status of its analyses. Such a science is economics, and the endeavours by writers of the classical period of its evolution to grapple with this dilemma comprise the subject of the chapters to follow.

2.2 Human nature and philosophical inquiry

Earlier on above, I drew attention to the fact that, in his initial endeavours to understand the interface between moral philosophy and physical science, Adam Smith's focus was on human agents as observer-analysts of their environment. We recall immediately the words of Hume, worth reiteration at this point, to the effect that 'all sciences have a relation ... to human nature ... [and] are in some measure dependent on the science of MAN; since they lie under the cognisance of men, and are judged of by their powers and faculties' (1962, p. 40). Here, as we shall see, we have in summary form the guiding threads of Smith's philosophical inquiry into the nature and progress of science. The vision of human nature that he immediately adopted for the purposes of his inquiry was that of the sentimentalist tradition that he had inherited, with added insights provided by Hume's associationist psychology. It will soon become apparent that, as a consequence of this vision, Smith's approach to science was strongly psychological and he emphasized the subjectivist aspects of its procedures, together with the conventionalist aspects of its achievements. His focus was on the dynamics of knowledge acquisition from the perspective of the psychological states experienced by the observer-analyst and the effect that these could have on the activity of scientific inquiry. It was, Smith argued, the disturbance of the mental harmony of the scientist that comes from some observation that is inconsistent with or unexplained by existing knowledge that elicits the desire to inquire. That is, some observation that does not fit readily into the range of established patterns of association of ideas in the mind of the observer stimulates the imagination to search for a revised pattern, more or less radical, that restores intellectual order. And it was only order, including its aesthetic form, that could induce tranquillity in the human mind. Once it was disturbed, the agent would experience pressure to relieve the resulting mental anxiety.

Quite apparently, then, for Smith, the essence of understanding progress in scientific knowledge and the form that knowledge takes could only be rooted in the sentiments and imagination of the scientists. The former accounted for the stimulus further to pursue knowledge, while the latter provided the means to establish its ideational format and bona fides. Either way, conceiving of the mind as a passive receptor of empirically explicable sensory inputs was ruled out by Smith's approach. Indeed we will find him straying towards the borders of transcendental cum metaphysical inquiry as a matter of necessity, or, perhaps, in spite of himself, as it were. In the end, though, he had to be satisfied with *asserting* an unspecified, but mandatory, active function for human reason in understanding the dynamics of scientific inquiry: 'In short, the task of *establishing* a system of thought must be conducted in terms of the combination of reason *and* experience' (Raphael and Skinner, 1980, p. 1, original emphasis).

Very early in his academic career, probably during the late 1740s and early 1750s, Adam Smith wrote a series of short papers dealing with a range of contemporary philosophical issues. Fortunately for future scholars, these *Essays on Philosophical Subjects* (EPS) were exempted from the general order to destroy his manuscripts that Smith issued on his death-bed. (EPS, p. 32). Three of these papers were gathered under the rubric 'The Principles which lead and direct Philosophical Enquiries', and their importance today has much more to do with their methodological theme than with their ostensibly historical substance. In our reading of them, we need to give due recognition to Smith's rider that the historical dimensions of the pieces were designed only to 'illustrate' the former, more general theme (EPS, pp. 31, 106, 118). By far the most well known and significant of the essays was that which sought the above 'Principles' in the history of astronomy (EPS, pp. 31ff). And, apropos the point just made about the contents of the pieces, the original editors, the executors of Smith's literary remains, were moved to add a note to its final page that reads in part: '[The essay above] ... must be viewed, not as a History or Account of Sir Isaac Newton's Astronomy, but chiefly as an additional illustration of those Principles of the Human Mind which Mr. Smith has pointed out to be the universal motives of Philosophical Researches' (EPS, p. 105). What, then, were these motives and principles that Smith found to 'lead and direct' philosophical inquiry and research? It is my objective in this section to give an answer to this question.

Following in the tradition of Locke and Hume, for Smith the ultimate source of knowledge and of changes therein was sensory stimulus from the observed environment. The immediate form of the human response to such potentially knowledge-engendering stimuli he identified as the 'allied' but 'distinct' sentiments of wonder, surprise and admiration (EPS, p. 33). Of these wonder was the most directly relevant, for it was the reponse induced by what is 'new and singular', by what are 'extraordinary and uncommon objects', and by 'all the rarer phaenomena of nature' – that is, 'everything, in short, with which we have before been either little or not at all acquainted'. This response remains so even if we are 'forewarned of what we are to see' (EPS, p. 33). From an associationist perspective, wonder is the response to ideas, as reflections and representations of observed objects, that do not readily fit into the agent's established mental patterns. Wonder may be accompanied by the further response of surprise, where the sensory encounter is unexpected or out of its normal context. Much of what is to be wondered at will elicit surprise, too, but many surprising stimuli will not stimulate wonder to any extent beyond the superficial curiosity about the object's appearance at an unfamiliar time and/or place. The sentiment of admiration comprised yet another response that may be experienced by agents, and it, too, may occur in isolation or in combination with one or both of the other two nominated by Smith. He cited the 'great and the beautiful' as the key characteristics of objects that stand out from their surroundings and elicit this sentiment (EPS, p. 33). In philosophical inquiry, it was the aesthetic appeal of the coherence and beauty of a piece of analysis that may contribute to its scientific acceptance.

Of the former two sentiments which will be in focus here, surprise was investigated first by Smith because of the frequency with which it provides the initial response that triggers the onset of wonder (EPS, pp. 34ff). To begin with, an expected object of experience that is familiar in all respects will stimulate only a passive emotional response from agents. Human sanity in everyday life must depend upon this more or less unemotional sort of response to the majority of environmental stimuli that agents must confront and contend with, for, by contrast, when an object is unexpected, much more is demanded by way of mental activity. Here Smith emphasized the point by noting that these latter occurrences have the potential to generate 'violent and convulsive emotions', to 'disjoint the whole frame of the imagination', to cause agents to exhibit 'frenzy or habitual lunacy', or at least 'almost always ... [to experience] a momentary loss of reason, or of that attention to other things which our situation or duty requires' (EPS, pp. 34–5). Smith was, in this argument, already positing a highly active role for the human mind in its endeavours to cope with things and events that do not 'glide gradually and easily into the heart'. The sentiment of wonder was depicted as an active form of the disturbance of the potentially passive state of the mind which ensues when an unfamiliar object or event is encountered and its stimuli cannot be readily accommodated within the agent's existing associations of ideas. According to Smith, this sort of disruption to the 'career' of the mind engenders a state of mental discomfort, a 'tumult of the imagination', that calls for active resolution (EPS, p. 46). It objects to ideas that do not form ready associations with existing patterns of ideas and which stem from a 'chaos of jarring and discordant appearances' (EPS, pp. 45–6). On the basis of such an understanding of the human mind, Smith was led to conclude that it is the 'repose and tranquillity of the imagination [that] is the ultimate end of philosophy' (EPS, p. 61).

In this search by the mind for a state of 'repose' through the establishment and maintenance of stable associations of ideas, we can identify the origins of the appeal of the notion of *system* that Smith was to make the methodological foundation piece of his theories of human nature and associated dimensions of human agency. The mind was envisaged to have an innate sense of the aesthetic which calls for all sources of wonder to be absorbed into associations of ideas by a process of pattern adjustment: the mind thus 'endeavours to arrange and methodise all its ideas, and to reduce them into proper classes and assortments' (EPS, p. 38). That is, the imagination comprises a taxonomy of typified and associated ideas, with appropriate sequential and situational linkages, that originate in cumulative past experiences that have been successfully absorbed as knowledge. Some components of the imagination will then form regularized associations which may be referred to as a *system of ideas*, comprising ideas that 'have acquired a tendency to go on of their own accord', independently of any particular empirical 'chain of events presented to the senses' (EPS, p. 41). I will return to a consideration of the methodological import of this theme below.

The source of wonder is novelty of experience in some absolute or relative sense. It is overcome when what 'obstructed the movement of the imagination is ... removed' by means of 'the clear discovery of a connecting chain of intermediate events' which enables the mind to situate the novel object or event meaningfully in some association of ideas. So the back is removed from the Enlightenment watch (section 2.1) and the disparate movement of its hands is linked into a coherent chain of mechanical events with which the mind can cope. In the terms of Smith's similar analogy, 'who wonders at the machinery of the opera-house who has once been admitted behind the scenes?' (EPS, p. 42). Thus it was that he conceived it to be 'the end of Philosophy, to allay ... wonder' (EPS, p. 75).

Perhaps most importantly in the longer-term view of Smith's burgeoning methodological ideas, we have found that he applied subjectivist criteria to his reading of all understandings of the universe of nature. Most generally stated: 'Philosophy ... may be regarded as one of those arts which address themselves to the imagination ....' And, he continued, the veracity of bodies of formal argument could be assessed by 'how far each of them was fitted to soothe the imagination and to render the theatre of nature a more coherent, and therefore a more magnificent spectacle, than it would have appeared to be' (EPS, p. 46). These observations were directed at even the contemporary theories of classical physics and astronomy that had been posited by Newton and, at the end of his essay on the history of astronomy, Smith included a brief but penetrating summary of Newton's work and its origins in the calculations of classical mechanics (EPS, pp. 97ff). Significantly he ascribed the widespread acceptance of the theory that he outlined to the sentimental responses associated with the *familiarity* of the notion of gravitation around which it centred. But here it was also its capacity to account for a wide range of empirical observations and to make sound predictions that Smith cited as amongst the theory's key attributes.

Smith gave most weight to the subjective dimensions of Newton's theory in that he continued to emphasize the crucial and all powerful role of the mind in system and theory creation. In this regard, he also emphasized his general Humean scepticism concerning the real-world verisimilitude of claims to knowledge. In what is probably the most important piece of the whole essay on astronomy for our purposes, he concluded by pointing out that the work had been an effort *'to represent all philosophical systems as mere inventions of the imagination'* which serve 'to connect together the otherwise disjointed and discordant phenomena of nature' (EPS, p. 105, emphasis added). To this point, he immediately added, with a striking degree of boldness for the period, that, with respect to his summary of Newton's theory in particular, 'even we ... have insensibly been drawn in, to make use of language expressing the connecting principles of this ... [system], *as if they were the real chains which Nature makes use of to bind together her several operations'* (EPS, p. 105, emphasis added). Small wonder, he finally concluded, that the theory had been accepted as 'the discovery of an immense chain of the most important and sublime truths, all closely connected together, by one capital fact, of the reality of which we have daily experience' rather than as what it actually was, simply another, more sophisticated and comprehensive *'attempt to connect in the imagination* the phenomena of the Heavens' (EPS, p. 105, emphasis added).

The minimum message that flows from the above considerations is that, for Smith, all philosophical inquiry had a strongly subjectivist dimension and that this was attributable to the active and independent intervention of the human mind in the *creation* of knowledge. The stimulus and the raw material for the process of generating increments to knowledge remained the sensory inputs consequent upon current experience of the object and it was only in this limited sense that Smith's primary methodology was inductive–empirical. And, apropos this point, it is worth noting in passing that, perhaps unconsciously, Smith had not been prepared to take Newton's methodological assertions at their face value. It is now apparent that there were sound reasons for this, for Newton's claims to have derived his celestial theory from observations have been subjected to a severe critique by Karl Popper and found to be false on several counts (Popper, 1972, pp. 184ff). Smith had been astute enough to realize the import of Hume's thesis that this empirical experience, in and of itself, could not add directly to knowledge. His associationist psychological premisses, also adopted from Hume, were always invoked in order to allow for the mediation of the mind in the formation of claims to knowledge. But, beyond the assertion of the existence of chains and systems of ideas that this entailed, he was not prepared to delve into the operations of the mind. Such inquiry would, as he saw things, lead him along the treacherous path to metaphysical speculation. Raphael's insight is correct when he observes that, *in this particular respect*, 'Adam Smith's bent was scientific rather than philosophical' so that 'despite his philosophic interests, shown in a tendency to make connections and to raise general questions, ... [he] was *in one way* markedly unphilosophical: paradoxical metaphysics left him cold' (1975, p. 84, emphasis added). In these latter arguments, too, Smith was apparently well in tune with Newton himself. Newton also avoided attempting to give any trans-empirical account of the nature of gravity, even though he stated categorically his belief that it 'existed' in some real sense, and he accepted that scientific knowledge could only ever be contingent pending further pertinent evidence (Losee, 1972, pp. 91, 93–4).

What had been made clear by Smith in the above treatment of Newtonian science was his belief that all intellectual systems of explanation, including those concerned with even the most firmly established empirical observations, are found to be but conjectured 'inventions of the imagination' of the analyst, once their epistemological foundations are actually exposed. Now if this belief could arise in the context of a system of physical science as highly regarded as Newton's, then it applied with a vengeance to systems of moral sentiments, including Smith's own yet to come, that purported to provide an understanding of human nature as the basis for a theory of human agency and for the associated theory of economy and society. Thus Smith's subjective and sceptical view of empirically derived knowledge of the real world was made even more apparent when the object to be investigated was human nature itself. When he turned his attention from the human agent as observer–analyst to a focus on active, subjective human agents per se as the object of science, Smith revealed a consciousness that he was now dealing with a scientific inquiry that had certain particular and distinguishing logical and substantive characteristics compared to the physical sciences. The key to these distinctions was to be found in the special ontological nature of its object-in-itself. One crucial difference was that, as an object of scientific inquiry, human nature had the unique status of being immanently familiar to the analyst *qua* human agent in a way that could never be so with objects of the non-human world. More on this most significant point for Smith in a moment.

Another pertinent distinction here was the Humean one that the 'observation' of and experimentation with the operational dimensions of human *nature* posed profound intellectual and practical problems (cf. section 2.1 above). This is for the ever-present and insurmountable reason that whatever is observed concerning human agents is the *product* of the activities shaped by that nature and not the nature-in-itself. On both of these counts, the analyst of human agency must deal with an object-in-itself that is at once, quite paradoxically, more accessible and totally inaccessible to observation. The former is made possible through the personal introspection of the analyst, but the pertinence of this sort of self-inquiry to establishing the nature of other agents will always be subject to an irreducible margin of doubt and must remain, strictly speaking, inaccessible to any modes of external sensory observation. Yet a third ontological distinction may be argued as follows: on one level, moral philosophy could, subject to the above riders, purport to be a 'positive' discipline to the extent that it described what *is* in the case of human nature, at least as it was exhibited in observed behavioural form. This would be consistent with the objective of all philosophical inquiry. But, on another level, moral philosophy could include in its arguments elements of a *normative* kind (cf. Bitterman, 1940, p. 506). Such elements were not always easy to keep separate from the 'positive' aspects of human science. Most significantly, they have no counterpart in the world of natural sciences. It simply makes no sense to set up a normative inquiry into a phenomenon of the physical or biological world with a view to espousing change to what *is*.

From these three distinctions, Smith himself was to pursue the first, the self-consciousness and self-awareness of analysts of their own humanness, in most explicit detail. He realized that any purported understanding of human nature, individually or socially, must confront the immediate phenomenological 'test' of being consistent with *what we all know of ourselves*. This 'test' has no meaning in the world of natural sciences. Smith's awareness of the matter can be most clearly demonstrated by referring ahead to that part of his *Theory of Moral Sentiments* (TMS) where he considered the lessons of Mandeville's *Fable of the Bees*. Smith raised the idea that Mandeville's doctrine had gained some acceptance and caused widespread social alarm because of the elements of generally recognizable apparent truth about human nature that it contained. There are, he wrote, 'some appearances in human nature, which, when viewed in a certain manner, seem at first sight to favour' Mandeville's portrayal. And 'how destructive soever this system [of Mandeville's] may appear, it could never have imposed upon so great a number of persons, nor have occasioned so general an alarm ..., had it not in some respects bordered on the truth' (TMS, pp. 308, 313). That is, he felt that if the lay public can somehow identify a degree of veracity in and the import of a scientific argument, then they will accept its thesis. In order to convey his point, Smith noted that it is possible for a 'system of *natural* philosophy ... [to] appear very plausible, and be for a long time very generally received in the world, and yet have no foundation in nature, nor any sort of resemblance to the truth' (TMS, p. 313, emphasis added). He chose to use the example of Descartes's intellectually ill-fated vortices of ether argument to illustrate what he meant. This argument had purported to give 'substance' to the notion of gravitational force, but it had been refuted by Newton as involving an unnecessary hypothetical dimension in the explanation of the phenomenon (Losee, 1972, p. 91; cf. Smith's exposition in EPS, pp. 93ff). By contrast to such potentials, 'it is otherwise with systems of moral philosophy', for anyone who claims 'to account for the origin of our moral sentiments, cannot deceive us so grossly, nor depart so very far from all resemblance to the truth' (TMS, pp. 313–14).

Smith resorted to an analogy in order to make his argument clearer. He referred to a traveller who is retailing the wonders of a journey to his/her readers. Such a traveller, returning from a distant and unknown land, could tell stories more or less as he/she wished and the readers would be receptive. By contrast, one who tells of a local journey has less flexibility in the contents of the stories told because of the readers' potential familiarity with the territory concerned. Thus 'an author who treats of natural philosophy, and pretends to assign the causes of the great phaenomena of the universe, pretends to give an account of the affairs of a very distant country, concerning which he may tell us what he pleases ... as long as his narration keeps within the bounds of seeming possibility'. He contrasted this situation with that of the philosopher who sets out to explain human sentiments, the very stuff of our own daily lives. The latter 'pretends to give an account, not only of the affairs of the very parish that we live in, but of our own domestic concerns'. Any attempt in this case to appeal to any but the most familiar principles would 'appear absurd and ridiculous to the most injudicious and unexperienced reader' (TMS, p. 314).

To sum up the above argument, we can see that, for Smith, the task of accounting for human nature in terms of moral sentiments carried with it the need to be sensitive to the ontological particulars of the object of study. What he chose to stress in his earliest treatment of the matter was that human agents have an unchallengeable access to their own natures as evidence of the general characteristics of the phenomenon. For human agents as philosophers, this is indeed fortunate, because it is the only evidence that they have to draw upon about which they can claim some degree of epistemological security. But, at the same time, they can only extrapolate from this introspective insight to other agents, perhaps with the supporting evidence of familiar behavioural manifestations. As I will develop more fully in subsequent chap-

ters, the result for Smith was a sensitivity to the idea that claims to knowledge in moral philosophy are of a different epistemological status from those
of the physical sciences.

Finally in my investigation of Smith's perception of the nature of philosophical inquiry, I turn to a more operational aspect of the methodology that
he worked out. As indicated above, his interpretation of the products of such
inquiry were always mind-dependent as much as object-dependent. The one
dimension of the mental input per se that he was prepared to develop more
fully, and to which I have made passing references above, was the capacity of
the mind to create *systems of ideas* by means of their qualities of association.
These transcendental systems were expected to represent the functionalist
and machine-like operations of what can be discovered in the real world as
systems of objects and/or events, even though the latter may appear to be in
total disorder in their raw observed state.

As was argued earlier, the impetus for philosophical inquiry according to
Smith was the sentiment of wonder. Now, on a more practical level, as
concerns 'the Wonders of nature, ... it rarely happens that we can discover so
clearly ... [a] connecting chain' of associated ideas that will fully bridge the
intellectual gaps left by novel observations. This was the constant challenge
for philosophers, for Smith saw 'philosophy ... [as] the science of the connecting principles of nature', as 'that science which pretends to lay open the
concealed connections that unite the various appearances of nature' (EPS, pp.
45, 51). It confronts a natural state which observation most frequently reveals
'to abound with [objects or] events which appear solitary and incoherent with
all that go before them, which therefore disturb the easy movement of the
imagination'. Here, the function of philosophy was, 'by representing the
invisible chains which bind together all these [apparently] disjointed objects
[and events], ... to introduce order into this chaos of jarring and discordant
appearances, to allay the tumult of the imagination'. And, from another
perspective, it was 'the more practised thought of the philosopher, who has
spent his whole life in the study of the connecting principles of nature, [that]
will often feel an interval betwixt two objects [or events], which, to more
careless observers, seem very strictly conjoined' (EPS, pp. 45–6). So, when
the back is taken off of the Enlightenment watch, or when we go behind the
scenes at the theatre, it is the philosopher who accompanies us in order to
provide an explanation for the phenomena that, as lay people, we normally
observe only from the front and accept at face value. At most, we may
wonder at the appearances, but never resolve them.

Most generally, Smith stated that what philosophers observe as systems 'in
many respects *resemble* machines', and he went on to define a machine as 'a
little system, created to perform, as well as to connect together, *in reality,*
those different movements and effects which the artist has occasion for'

(EPS, p. 66, emphasis added). At first sight, there is a certain air of circularity and ambiguity in this passage. However what Smith was trying to convey may be readily clarified. Systems of the real world that comprise observed phenomena that we wish to understand may or may not have been created by humankind – in the case of the physical universe, obviously not; in the case of society, obviously so, albeit largely unconsciously on the part of individuals and making due allowance for the possibility of divine guidance. But, independently of this, the human agent (as 'the artist') can and does create 'little systems' *in reality* called machines in order to accomplish certain designated tasks and objectives. By analogy, then, what the human mind creates to replicate the functioning real-world systems in the imagination is a 'little system' of ideas that has machine-like capabilities. The imagined associationist system produces knowledge from the sensory inputs stimulated by empirical observation and realizes the objective of understanding. Thus '*a system [of ideas] is an imaginary machine invented to connect together in the fancy those different movements and effects which are already in reality performed*' (EPS, p. 66, emphasis added). The analogy was later argued along similar lines (TMS, pp. 19, 289), but there as a prelude to aligning human society with machine-like functionalist characteristics. At least, then, 'when we contemplate it in a certain abstract and philosophical light, [society] *appears like* a great, an immense machine, whose regular and harmonious movements produce a thousand agreeable effects' (TMS, p. 316, emphasis added; cf. p. 326).

What we will find Smith carrying forward into his subsequent writings is a Newtonian concept of the system as a mode of organizing formal abstract argument. Joseph Spengler reminds us of the extent to which the system mode of conceptualizing the terms of inquiry pervaded Smith's work: 'Conceptualization played an important role in Smith's mode of analytical inquiry into the nature of science and its development ... [in the EPS], into the organization of society and the nature of man and his response to the socio-economic environment encasing him ... [in the TMS and the *Lectures on Jurisprudence* (LJ)], and into the structure of economies and the response of individuals to differences in economic structure ... [in the *Wealth of Nations* (WN)]' (1975, p. 394). Robert Heilbroner notices the same dominance of the system concept in Smith's works when he refers to 'that love of "system" (theoretical explanation) that first appears in the *Astronomy* [EPS], surfaces again in *TMS*, and finally emerges for the last time in *WN*, itself a vast exercise in system building' (1982, p. 435). In particular, the system concept applied by Smith involved the identification of some singular, or at least minimal, and familiar means by which the system could be shown to establish and maintain its coherent and stable order. In Newton's own case, it was the principle of gravitation that provided the means in question. Smith wrote of this discovery in glowing terms: 'The superior genius and sagacity of ... Newton ... made the most happy, and, we may now say, the greatest and most admirable improvement that was ever made in philosophy, when he discovered, that he could join together the movements of the Planets by so familiar a principle of connection, which completely removed all the difficulties the imagination had hitherto felt in attending them' (EPS, p. 98). On the subject of economy in the use of explanatory principles, Smith wrote in the TMS of that 'propensity, which is natural to all men, but which philosophers in particular are apt to cultivate with a peculiar fondness, as the great means of displaying their ingenuity, the propensity to account for all appearances from as few principles as possible' (TMS, p. 299). The idea was reiterated in the WN when he referred to the 'beauty of a systematical arrangement of different observations connected by a few common principles' as it first appeared in natural philosophy and was later 'attempted in morals'. In the latter context, the 'maxims of common life were arranged in some methodical order, and connected together by a few common principles, in the same manner as ... [the philosophers] had attempted to arrange and connect the phenomena of nature' (WN, pp. 768–9).

More specifically, the Newtonian idea that Smith adopted, as Hutcheson had done before him (see above, section 2.1), was concerned with the way in which the phenomenon of gravity manifested itself as the centripetal force that counteracts the centrifugal force of motion that would otherwise pull the solar system asunder. What I will show, in the next two chapters, is how Smith applied this principle of a balance between opposite forces to human relations and to the make-up of a coherent social order. The principle centrifugal 'force' in this context will be the pursuit of self-interest by individual human agents. Those sentiments that stem from the sympathetic links between human agents will provide the basic counteracting centripetal 'force' structure that keeps a society together as a system. But I will also argue that Smith carried forward the Newtonian idea that the force of gravity diminishes with the increasing distance between the bodies concerned. He did so in recognizing that, as the intersubjective 'distance' between agents increases, manifested as an increase in the degree of anonymity and functionality of their relationship, the strength and reliability of the centripetal 'force' that can be derived from sentiments of sympathy, especially benevolence, decreases. This means that some other construction must be introduced if the human order is not immanently to destroy itself. In Smith's analysis, this was especially the case where commercial relations were concerned and the harmony of the economic base of the social order generally could be put at risk as a consequence of the unbridled pursuit of self-interest within an inappropriate situational context. These aspects of human agency will thus be found to have influenced profoundly the form taken by Smith's normative analysis of the institutional reforms needed to correct the economic and social distortions that had evolved with mercantile capitalism.

3 Modelling morally situated human agents

3.1 Introduction

At this point it is appropriate to say something about the particulars of the bibliographical and substantive structure of Smith's moral philosophy. The premiss from which I intend to work in this respect is that his often apparently disparate writings and the reports of his lectures are of a piece, in the sense that they all constitute components of an unfinished holistic project. Of course, to modern readers, he was involved in a number of now quite separate academic fields of inquiry, but, in Smith's day, the norm was to treat psychology, philosophy, theology, sociology, history, jurisprudence and political economy as branches of the broader rubric of moral philosophy. As Robert Heilbroner has been moved to observe, concerning this character of Smith's work, 'there is a reinforcing interaction of philosophy, psychology, history, and social analysis in Smith that has no equal in political economy, save for Marx.' And, indeed, 'in many ways it is this trans-disciplinary coherence that gives to Smith's work its depth and lasting interest' (1982, pp. 435–6). One result of the present study will be further to reinforce this reading of Smith.

Now it has not always been accepted that Smith worked consistently on such a unified project. One reason for this doubt is that, at times, there does appear to be, across the stages of his thought, some evidence of a shift of position on vital matters concerning human agency. These especially involve the operational status of self-interest, in relation to more other-directed sentiments, as this was treated in Smith's two magna opera, the TMS (1759 and beyond) and the WN (1776 and beyond). On this theme, Jacob Viner rather cryptically observed in 1927 that it was the Germans 'who, it seems, in their methodical manner commonly read both the TMS and the WN, ... [and] coined a pretty term, *Das Adam Smith Problem*, to denote the failure to understand either which results from the attempt to use the one in the interpretation of the other' (1984b, p. 145, original emphasis). Viner's main implication here was that reading either work in isolation, and applying its immediately apparent representation of human nature to the reading of the other, can result in a failure to comprehend the shifts of emphasis in this representation which Smith correctly undertook in the transition from the TMS to the WN. It will be an integral part of my argument that accounting for the pattern of shifts remains an essential part of any complete exposition of Smith's treatment of human agency. *In this sense,* the so-called 'Adam

Smith problem', with its history of extensive intellectual controversy, especially in Germanic Europe during the nineteenth century (cf. Raphael and
Macfie, 1976, pp. 20ff), is still of significance. This is so even though most
modern Smith scholars now agree that there never was really a 'problem' in
the way that it was originally understood.

Many Smith scholars have commented upon the importance of reading his
work as a coherently organized project. James Bonar appreciated this very
early on, in 1893: 'Adam Smith undoubtedly started with the purpose of
giving to the world a complete social philosophy' (quoted by Lindgren, 1973,
p. x). Similarly Ronald Meek refers to Smith's 'general sociological system'
(1967, p. 35). The editors of the Glasgow Edition of the WN have more
recently observed that Smith's 'contribution to what would now be defined as
the "social sciences" is contained in his work on ethics, jurisprudence, and
economics, which correspond in turn to the order in which he lectured on
these subjects while Professor of Moral Philosophy at Glasgow'. Most especially, though, they go on to point out that his work is 'marked by a degree of
systematic thought of such a kind as to reveal a great capacity for model-
building ... [and] an attempt to delineate the boundaries of a single system of
thought, of which these separate subjects were the component parts' (R.H.
Campbell and Skinner, 1976, pp. 3–4).

It has been the apparent separation between the substance of Smith's
various writings that has often led to the neglect of his total system, especially by some economist readers. Meek makes the point that, while 'the
elements of ... [Smith's] sociological system can, indeed, be easily enough
detected in the *Wealth of Nations* ... for a more complete outline of it we
have to go back to [his] *Glasgow Lectures* and to his *Theory of Moral
Sentiments*'. And Meek draws our attention to the fact that these *Lectures on
Jurisprudence* (LJ) are the only remaining guide that we have to 'the elements of that great sociological treatise on the development of law and
government which Smith always intended to write but never managed to
finish' and which would have constituted the bridge from TMS to WN (1967,
p. 35). The three works were to form what may be thought of as a philosophical triptych, but the middle panel on which the TMS, on the left, and the WN,
on the right, are hinged is only present as a sketch provided by two of his
students from their records of his lectures in Glasgow (see LJ). The status of
the missing work may be gleaned from an 'Advertisement' that Smith added
to the sixth edition of the TMS in 1790. He referred there to 'what remains
[of my project], the theory of jurisprudence, which I have long projected ...'
as being unlikely to be completed 'to my own satisfaction ... because of my
advanced age' (TMS, p. 3). Whatever he may have done towards the completion of 'this great work' we must assume was destroyed on his death in
accordance with his instructions regarding the bulk of his manuscripts.

Be this as it may, we do have enough of a record of the total project to enable R.H. Campbell and Skinner, for example, to elicit some common threads that bind its pieces together. First, 'in each case Smith sought to explain complex problems in terms of a small number of basic principles'. Secondly, all three parts 'make use of the typical hypothesis that the principles of human nature can be taken as [uniform and] constant, and all employ the doctrine of "unintended social outcomes" – the thesis that man, in following the prompting of his nature, unconsciously gives substantial expression to some parts of the (Devine?) plan'. Thirdly, he revealed 'a keen sense of the fact that manners and institutions may change through time and that they may show striking variations in different communities at the same point in time'. These common threads reinforce their claim to have identified a unity in Smith's work so that his 'economic analysis as such may be seen to be connected with the other areas of ... [his] thought in the sense that it begins from a specific stage of historical development [of law and government] and at the same time makes use of the psychological assumptions established by the TMS' (R.H. Campbell and Skinner, 1976, p. 4). And, apropos the latter connection, Campbell and Skinner write of how one aspect of Smith's 'achievement was ... to see all these different subjects [ethics, jurisprudence and economics] as parts of a single whole, while at the same time differentiating economics from them'. From this perspective, Smith is seen to have adopted 'a high degree of abstraction' such that 'in his economic work, ... [he] was concerned only with some aspects of the psychology of man and in fact confined his attention to the self-regarding propensities [in] a situation where the minimum condition of justice obtains' (ibid., pp. 18–19). Later on, below, we shall be called upon to qualify the use of the term 'abstraction' in contexts such as these where the transition from the TMS to the WN analyses is concerned. What we shall find is that what changed between the two works was rather the dimensions of human nature which Smith chose, for good reasons, to emphasize. But the general thrust of the Campbell and Skinner summary will be sustained and elaborated in what is to come.

The observations that have just been outlined may be compared to those made by Dugald Stewart some 200 years earlier, soon after Smith's death. In his 'Account of the Life and Writings of Adam Smith, LL.D.', read before the Royal Society of Edinburgh early in 1793, Stewart spoke of themes similar to those considered above. He noted how, in 'Mr Smith's writings, whatever be the nature of his subject, he seldom misses an opportunity of indulging his curiosity, in tracing from the principles of human nature, or from the circumstances of society, the origin of the opinions and the institutions which he describes'. Stewart went on explicitly to reinforce this emphasis on the essential role of *situated human nature* in Smith's thought by arguing that, with reference to the WN in particular, 'the great and leading object of his speculations is, to illustrate the provision made by nature in *the principles of the human mind, and in the circumstances of man's external situation,* for a gradual and progressive augmentation in the means of national wealth' (1980, pp. 295, 315, emphasis added). Furthermore Smith's endeavour was designed to demonstrate that the most appropriate means for realizing this national outcome was 'to maintain that order of things which nature has pointed out ... by allowing every man, as long as he observes the rules of justice, to pursue his own interest in his own way, and to bring both his industry and his capital into the freest competition with those of his fellow citizens' (ibid., p. 315). Stewart underestimated the complexity of Smith's message about human nature and competition, but, as with the ideas of R.H. Campbell and Skinner above, the main substance of his observations, which keep human nature to the fore in reading Smith, is consistent with the theses to be pursued further below.

What I intend to emphasize about Adam Smith's work, in this chapter and the next, is his pursuit of a theory of human agency in economics which gives due weight and prominence to autonomous individual self-interest as the essential driving force behind the phenomena of the material provisioning process. In developing such a theory, it is crucial, though, that the agents be represented as *situated* in a particular environment that facilitates, as well as contains and constrains, their actions in such a way as to generate and sustain an observed coherent social and economic order. An integral part of this confrontation between agents and their situation is the reflexive effect that the latter has on their character and conduct through moral socialization. The result is that the containment and constraints which they experience include an internalized component which ensures some degree of volitional conformity to the social–moral standards of the society in which they live. The actions of agents also reflexively affect their situation, so that there is altogether a dynamic *interaction* between individual agents and their environment as they both evolve over time. All of these arguments are to be found adumbrated and more or less developed in Smith's theory of moral sentiments.

From within Smith's detailed treatment of human nature, as it was very largely presented in the TMS, it is possible to distil a core sequence of ideas that provides the essential substance of the interpretative argument to be developed below. The sequence begins with the existential individual human agent considered in isolation in order to build up a profile of the sentiments that Smith regarded as the main constituents common to all human nature. As Robert Heilbroner argues, these constituents are founded upon some 'primal human nature' about the details of which Smith was never very specific (1982, p. 429). This was a point that G.R. Morrow had noticed some years earlier in his 1923 work: '[Smith] does not clearly state what these primitive instincts are, sometimes regarding them as pleasure and pain, sometimes as gratitude and resentment' (1969, p. 40). Heilbroner's reading is that human nature at this level has two components: one includes the 'sensory and cognitive properties of man', of which the capacity to reason is that which will be of most concern to us later on; the other is 'the array of instincts, drives, emotions, affects, and propensities to which Smith, following in the tradition of his age, gives the label "passions"' (1982, p. 430). Concerning these latter, Morrow cites Smith as 'describing the growth of the moral sentiments from originally pre-moral elements', a process in which 'certain "original passions" ... gradually grow into morality under the influence of the social principle' (1969, p. 40). Moreover, as T.D. Campbell observes, 'Smith's belief in "necessary" sympathetic emotions ... presuppose[s] a basic uniformity in human nature'. In this respect, Smith may be regarded as 'an empirical natural law theorist, for he takes for granted that there exist certain "natural sentiments of all mankind" ... which properly directed observation can discern behind the complex variety of human behaviour' (1975, p. 78).

These essentials of all human nature provide the foundations for the socialization process that agents must traverse as a consequence of growing up in a world of intersubjective relations with others. The insight that I will look for in Smith is not so much the ambiguous 'primal' vision of human nature as such, but a *typified* vision that includes the established socialized elements, which he proceeds to situate in an existing environment with a given, but unspecified, history. It is not suggested here that the resulting profile has any existential status. Rather the model of human nature that is depicted can only be an analytical convenience for the very reasons that are the substance of the next steps in building up Smith's conception of the human agent. For, while it may be possible to imagine an isolated human agent and to outline his/her innate and learned, typified and uniform senti-mental make-up, in reality, all human agents have a natural and social biogra-phy which has shaped their present sentimental profile. Then, given this profile, they must live in some current complex situation with multiple di-mensions through which these accumulated sentiments are made operational as character and conduct. It is this biography to which Heilbroner refers in the following passage: 'the passions are the raw material on which the socialization process will work its effects, shaping or blunting their impact to change human behavior from that which it might be, were man solely the product of his unfettered drives, into that which expresses his character after he has been tempered to live in the company of his fellows' (1982, p. 431). Thus the agents' sentiments are affected by and affect the environment in which they find themselves placed.

Implicit in these considerations are the two subsequent steps that the developing interpretation should include. First, the individuals must be situated relative to other agents around them and with whom they have varying degrees and kinds of involvement. This aspect of their situation involves both the effect that agents' actions have on others and the effect that the latters' reactions, potential and actual, have on the sentiments of the agents as the performers of those actions. The mutuality of the intersubjective sentiments that are an integral part of the structured set of relations into which agents enter with others was important to Smith, as we shall see in the sections to follow. Secondly, as well as existing in some prestructured social context, individuals confront an inherited physical and institutional situation which is largely beyond their immediate choice, influence or control. It is this conglomeration of situational characteristics that presents to agents the medium in and through which they must decide, choose and act in the various facets of their daily lives. It acts as both a facilitating and a constraining mediation which the agents must understand in order to optimize their conduct and the material and other benefits that flow to them as a consequence. Smith's primary objective was to show how the principles of human nature could generate such relations between, and actions of, free, self-interested individual human agents that the collective outcomes constitute a coherent and well-ordered social and economic cosmos. There was quite evidently such an observable inherent dynamic order in the aggregated results of independent actions by interdependent agents. With all agents pursuing their own self-interest, the requirement was to provide an understanding of the means by which this collectively undirected activity was, in fact, channelled so as effectively to coordinate it. The pattern of material and social consequences of this coordination may not turn out to be consistent with what are perceived as the best interests of all the agents concerned, as Smith was to find in the case of his own era. The challenge then was normatively to argue out the reforms to the system that would provide a more socially desirable outcome.

At the most basic level, Smith accepted the Hobbesian image of human nature as dominated by egoistic motives. He saw this, though, both as a virtue, to the extent that it led agents to act in pursuit of their own prudent self-interest, and as a vice, to the extent that the consequences of such actions impinged negatively upon the psychic and material well-being of other agents. What he set out to show, *contra* Hobbes, was that the latter aspect of this most fundamental of the sentiments could be counterbalanced without the need for the all-pervasive constructivist interventions by government that dominated the Hobbesian position. That is, as a matter of first principles, appropriately situated human agents are morally self-contained and self-sufficient to a dominant extent. At first, Smith confined his attention to potential for such counterbalance within the natures of isolated human agents. That is, was there to be found amongst the typical sentiments of human nature one that would induce agents, when confronted with other agents with whom they form relationships, to temper and/or redirect their pursuit of self-interest when its effects on the others proved to be adverse? A positive answer to this question would suggest an innately ensured 'fusion' of interests amongst human agents as distinct from the identification of interests that may flow from an appropriate 'natural' or 'artificial' social environment (see above, section 2.1). Smith identified such a sentiment as the general one of fellow-feeling that was referred to more formally as *sympathy*. It is important to mention that the term that would be used today to convey much of what he intended is *empathy,* in that it is defined as the supposed capacity to understand by imaginatively entering into another person's feelings. What Smith saw as the sentiment of sympathy involved, in part, an ostensible act of intersubjective identification in the forms of taking notice of, of taking in and of coping with the feelings of others. In all, as we shall see, Smith considered sympathy to be a sentiment of some considerable power in the human psyche. He relied upon it to a significant extent, in conjunction with the sentiment of self-interest, to explain the conduct of human agents and the core of harmony that existed between such self-centred agents once they were thrown together as interdependent beings. In short, what we will find Smith struggling with eventually is the preservation of sympathetic sentiments as the autonomous 'cement' of society; or, more dynamically expressed, as its centripetal force of cohesion. He struggled with these cohesive potentials in the face of the need to recognize self-interest as simultaneously the 'engine', or the dominant mobilizing force of industry and material welfare, and the crucial centrifugal force affecting society.

For Smith, the Stoical ideal of self-command by individuals that he associated with the exercise of sympathy always remained important in understanding the basics of social harmony in terms of a 'fusion' of interests amongst agents. He envisaged that their consciences, which he represented as the internalized form of an ideal–typical impartial spectator and moral judge of actions and their effects on others, would lead them to exercise the necessary restraints on self-interest to behave ethically towards others in the interests of harmony. There was no innate 'moral sense' to draw on as some of the Sentimentalists had suggested, but there was the socialized and learned capacity of agents to provide a balance between the sentiments that would have the same effect. The makings of collective harmony were present within the internal, moral–sentimental constitutions of socially situated human agents and Smith had quite some degree of faith in this possibility. He also made us aware, though, that the balance of sentiments required would not always be present in all facets of human society. The main source of its unreliability was the uneven intersubjective distribution of the reach and strength of the sympathy-based sentiments. What has to be recognized is that the binding force of these sentiments could begin to fade with any shift of focus onto inter-agent relationships with a different nature. As the 'distance' and the anonymity of the relation increases, an imbalance in favour of egoism may well emerge unless a 'natural identity of interests' has resulted as an integral consequence of the immanent evolution of the social system in which agents are situated. Smith's additional concern in this respect was that injustice between agents may result. At the same time, he felt that the sentiment of justice is an absolutely essential precondition for social harmony. For these reasons, he made full allowance for the constructed intervention of a system of jurisprudence that would provide explicit sanctions for transgressing the commonly agreed and/or legislated tenets of justice. In this respect, the identification of interests could only be 'artificial'.

To summarize, then, the moral–sentimental foundations of Smith's theory of economy and society are those of self-interest and sympathy. As a matter of principle, the maintenance of a correct balance between these two basic sentiments could account for the character and conduct of human agents and for the order and harmony in the intersubjective relations established between them. In the view of two prominent Smith scholars, 'the TMS may be seen to offer an explanation as to the way in which so self-regarding a creature as man succeeds (by natural as distinct from artificial means) in erecting barriers against his own passions' (R.H. Campbell and Skinner, 1976, p. 4). Smith explored this potential extensively before he went on to identify the characteristics of agents, and the aspects of their situations and actions, that would engender its breakdown and necessitate the intervention of some institutionally constituted corrective measures. Thus the above two scholars continue that Smith's argument in this respect 'culminates in the proposition that some system of magistracy is generally an essential condition of social stability' (ibid., p. 4). As we shall see in the next chapter, it was this matter of justice, the 'system of magistracy' just referred to, that became most significant for Smith in the economic sphere once he recognized that the mercantile capitalist order was built upon some principles and institutions that were in conflict with it. The point is put by Viner (1984b) that the TMS 'is an unqualified doctrine of a harmonious order of nature, under divine guidance, which promotes the welfare of man through the operation of his individual propensities'. However, as he immediately goes on, 'of these, self-interest is the most important one, in so far as economic life is concerned, *though it is subject to the regulations of natural justice, to which it must conform*', where such justice 'is likely to be more effective if it is administered by a magistrate' (ibid., pp. 148–9, emphasis added). These notions of justice will be followed up more fully in section 3.3 below. Our immediate concern in the interim will be with Smith's endeavours to sort out the moral–sentimental make-up of human nature. This will serve to highlight the potential that he found to exist for social harmony to emerge from a 'fusion' or a 'natural identification' of interests amongst agents; that is, from the innate, internalized and socialized structure and functioning of the moral sentiments per se. He was also directly concerned about the potential for such harmony to break down because of the bias towards the dominance of egoism that can arise in certain facets of the total pattern of inter-agent relations.

3.2 The sentimental human agent

In the TMS, Smith sought to provide a psychological theory of human nature that could account for the character and conduct displayed by human agents who are active in their life-world. He recognized that the actions of human agents are designed most immediately to serve the self-interested objectives of their choice and that the expected outcomes comprised a mix of material and psychic returns. In addition to this, Smith was always conscious that the actions of individuals take place in a particular situation which they inherit from the past and over which they have little immediate control; it is, for the purposes of immediately ensuing decisions and actions, effectively given. Such situations impinge upon the character and conduct of agents in a number of ways that Smith pursued in great detail in the TMS.

At the most general level, the situations that agents confront in their decisions and actions have two interrelated dimensions. One consists of the natural and constructed physical environment that surrounds them and which provides the medium for their actions. As Smith was later to argue, it both facilitates and impedes action, with his concerns in this respect focusing especially on economic actions in pursuit of material provisioning. In the context of the TMS, though, this aspect of the agents' situations was largely left implicit. The present focus is to be on the other of the dimensions of their situation, namely the complex of human relations in which they find themselves placed. This social aspect of agents' situations, consequent upon the existence of a range of interdependencies, combined with the sympathy-based sentiments, similarly mediates in their actions and both facilitates and impedes what they set out to do. In the process of mediating in agents' actions, their situations affect the returns that they actually realize through such actions. The situations also have a reflexive effect on the agents which stems from their reactions to the material and sentimental outcomes that they experience. Of particular concern to Smith in the TMS were the sentimental consequences of actions that flow from the intersubjective relations between agents. These he found to have two immediately interdependent dimensions: one is the sentimental effect that the agents' actions have on the various other agents that comprise the complex relations in which they are involved; the second is the sentimental reaction that the agents themselves experience as a consequence of their perceived effects on others.

It was Smith's thesis that it is of the essence of human nature that agents care about the material and the reflexive sentimental consequences of their actions, both as they affect themselves and as they affect other agents. In this sense, human agents are always social beings who assess their own actions in these dual terms: 'We may say that [for Smith,] the moral judgement of the individual is the expression of the social consciousness' (Morrow, 1969, p. 32). Smith devoted a massive effort in the TMS to a formalized explication of the multiple facets of this intersubjective caring that characterize the moral–sentimental make-up of human agents. Most simply stated, he sought to explain how human agency is directed and affected by the extent to which agents pursue various social–moral virtues as an integral part of the psychic returns that they expect to flow from their actions. Attention to these virtues, he argued, is the manifestation of the agents' concern for the well-being of others, together with the agents' own affective need to be viewed with approbation by others. Morality for Smith, then, was never an individual matter, but always one in which the agent had to confront moral standards that are largely externally established by what others expect of him or her.

In the opening lines of the TMS, Smith referred directly to the two sentiments that were to form the foundations of his theory of human nature, with its focus on the nature and origins of moral virtue in the character and conduct of agents. As individuals, all human agents were characterized by a feeling for themselves and by a juxtaposed feeling for others, both of which could affect their decisions and actions in their life-world. For Smith, 'how selfish soever man may be supposed, there are evidently some principles in his nature, which interest him in the fortune of others, and render their happiness necessary to him, though he derives nothing from it except the pleasure of seeing it'. This is the interest in the well-being of others that was referred to by the broad concept of *sympathy* and Smith found it to be one of the 'original passions of human nature [which] is by no means confined to the virtuous and humane', for even the 'greatest ruffian, the most hardened violator of the laws of society, is not altogether without it' (TMS, p. 9). Because of its central importance in his theory of human nature, we should pause to consider this concept in more detail.

It has long been recognized by Smith scholars that the basis for the sympathy notion is what in more recent terms is referred to as *empathy*. The key psychological operation involved here is the identification by one agent with the circumstances and feelings of another by means of introspection and the imagination. That is, there is a claimed human capacity to understand others by 'entering into' another agent's psyche, a capacity that can only be based on the extrapolation to the other of the agent's own psychological make-up and experiences. As Morrow observes, 'this participation in the feelings of others is sympathy' (1969, p. 29). More pointedly, in Taylor's words, '"sympathy" is an acquisition into one's self – one's own feelings – of a kind of echo or reflection of the other, observed, active person's apparent feelings, which results from a successful, imaginative "identification" of the self with that other person [and] which a more modern psychological theory calls *empathy*' (1960, pp. 58–9, original emphasis; cf. Heilbroner, 1982, p. 428). In the TMS, Smith himself referred to the 'imaginary change of situation upon which ... sympathy is founded' and proceeded to build his theory of moral judgements around it (p. 21, cf. p. 19). For him, it was this assumed ability that was to form the basis of interpersonal comparisons and judgements of moral standards. To quote Morrow again, 'the fundamental principle in Adam Smith's ethical theory is that all moral judgements are based upon an imaginary change of situation, whereby the individual judging places himself in the situation of the individual judged, and feels to some extent as his own the sentiments and passions of the latter' (1969, p. 29).

But two related qualifications to the above argument should be noted immediately. One is that Smith recognized the potential limitations of the empathy phenomenon as the basis for his moral theory. In the opening lines of the TMS he included an implicit, but in hindsight clear, admission that the inquiry concerning human nature would have to confront the transcendental character of all claims to knowledge about other agents. Both as active subjective agents and as observer analysts, 'we have no immediate experience of what other men feel, we can form no idea of the manner in which they are affected, but by conceiving what we ourselves should feel in the like situation'. That is, our senses can never 'carry us beyond our own person, and it is by the imagination only that we can form any conception of what are his sensations'. The imagination facilitates this 'by representing to us what would be our own [sentiments], if we were in his case'. So, 'by the imagination we place ourselves in his situation, ... we enter as it were into his body, and become in some measure the same person with him' (TMS, p. 9). The outcome is that the agents can extrapolate to others what they would feel in the same circumstances, but Smith was aware that, epistemologically, this is an insecure and speculative claim to knowledge. The methodological ramifications of this insight have a significance that he did not go on explicitly to recognize. However what it means in terms of the ontological nature of the objects of moral science will be kept to the fore in my subsequent interpretation. Smith granted, in particular, that what the observing agent feels in the imagination will 'always be, in some respects, different from what ... [the other] feels ... because the secret consciousness that the change of situations, from which the sympathetic sentiment arises, is but imaginary, [and] not only lowers it in degree, but, in some measure, varies it in kind, and gives it a quite different modification'. The strict consequences of this difficulty were not pursued by Smith, though, because he was prepared to accept that the 'correspondence with one another' of the shared sentiments will be 'sufficient for the harmony of society'. Thus, while the sentiments 'will never be unisons, they may be concords, and this is all that is wanted or required' (TMS, p. 22; cf. p. 21).

The other related qualification relevant here is that, while sympathy is a pervasive characteristic across human agents, its strength in the sense of the degree of correspondence between the shared sentiments varies widely as a consequence of the different natures of the inter-agent relationships in which it may be involved. This recognition is significant because of the tempering effect that the various sympathy-based sentiments were said by Smith to have on the pursuit of pure self-interest. Already what was emerging here was a consciousness that sympathy will not always be able to curb the excesses of self-interest where the agents concerned exist in a more distant, and thus more anonymous, relationship. So it is that, in our dealings with other agents, 'we expect less sympathy from a common acquaintance than from a friend ... [and] we expect still less sympathy from an assembly of strangers' (TMS, p. 23). What Smith adumbrated in this piece was the idea of a pattern of counterbalances to the pursuit of self-interest, the existence of which revealed variations in the degree to which sympathy could be relied upon to maintain a balance between these two core components of human nature. This very important idea will resurface from time to time at strategic points in the argument to follow.

Most essentially Smith argued that it was the agents' concern for others that made society viable: 'Nature, when she formed man for society, endowed him with an original desire to please, and an original aversion to offend his brethren ... [and] she taught him to feel pleasure in their favourable, and pain in their unfavourable regard' (TMS, p. 116). It was this latter pleasure–pain interaction that Smith applied in the development of his understanding of the moral rules that basically governed the conduct of and relations between agents. In order to give some substance to this moral theory, Smith invoked the idea of an impartial observer of inter-agent actions and responses who assesses the two critical qualities of those processes, namely propriety and merit. Propriety and impropriety are judged in accordance with the spectator's approbation or otherwise of the conditions and motivations confronted by the agent that initiated the action concerned. The judgement of the merit or demerit of an action shifts the focus of the spectator from the origin of the action to its impact on the agents affected by it. Actions that bring benefits are approved of by the spectator and are judged to have merit, while those that cause hurt are disapproved of and elicit judgements of demerit (TMS, pp. 18, 21–2, 27ff, 67ff). Smith summarized his argument by noting that 'the propriety of conduct arises from what I shall call a direct sympathy with the affections and motives of the person who acts, ... [while]

our sense of its merit arises from what I shall call an indirect sympathy with the gratitude of the person who is ... acted upon' (TMS, p. 74).

What is involved in this spectator idea can be set out to begin with by considering the individual agent as the uninvolved and unaffected, and hence impartial, observer of the action of another agent and of the responses of the beneficiary of that action. Smith's analysis was based upon the hypothetical observer agent's exercise of the assumed capacity for empathy outlined above. In observing the acting agent, the impartial observer will identify to some degree with the circumstances that surround and motivate the actor and judge the propriety of the action on the basis of how he/she would have acted if put in the same position. The degree of correspondence that this comparison elicits determines the assessed degree of propriety of the action. The observer also takes in the reactions of the party at whom the action is directed and identifies to some degree with the responses observed. In this case, the outcome is an assessment of the merit of the action on the basis of how the observer would have reacted to the same effects. The action is one of high merit where it brings vicarious pleasure to the observer and so on down a continuum towards the experience of vicarious pain in the case of actions judged to warrant demerit to a large degree. As Smith put it most generally, the above analysis is based on the thesis that 'to approve of the passions of another ... as suitable to their objects, is the same thing as to observe that we entirely sympathize with them; and not to approve of them as such, is the same thing as to observe that we do not entirely sympathize with them' (TMS, p. 16).

Smith's next interim step in setting up the spectator device as a practical mode of moral judgements was effectively to generalize from the specific case of an agent observer to that of an impartial and typical spectator to whom Viner refers as 'the "real spectator" or the outside observer manifesting in some way, perhaps in the guise of a visible "public opinion", approval or disapproval of one's own behavior'. (1972, p. 78). In Morrow's similar reading of Smith, 'the impartial spectator is the personification of that which is permanent, universal, rational, natural, in the phenomena of sympathy'. The point here is that, while 'all sympathies partake in a greater or lesser degree of ... [an inherent] quality of contingency ...[, when] taken together in their mass, there is a stability about the phenomena ... which is not found in the inspection of individual instances; and it is these permanent stable elements of sympathy which we regard as embodied in the personality of the impartial spectator' (1969, p. 37). This view is also taken by T.D. Campbell: 'in talking of the judgements of the impartial spectator as "natural", Smith implies both that these judgements express the average reactions of normal human beings who are in the position of observing the behaviour of others, and that they are, for this reason, morally correct'. Campbell goes on to conclude that 'the impartial spectator represents the common denominator which unites men in their attitudes towards conduct and to which men approximate in their pursuit of the "pleasures of mutual sympathy"'. (1975, pp. 68, 71).

In the argument so far, the agent as observer and the typified impartial spectator have taken only a passive role in the exposition. This was sufficient to establish the principles of the approach to moral theory that Smith adopted. However it was the subjective agent in action with whose individual moral judgements and standards he was ultimately concerned. Part III of the TMS carried the title, 'Of the Foundation of our Judgements concerning our own Sentiments and Conduct ...'. Its opening lines then inform us that 'in the two foregoing parts of this discourse, I have chiefly considered the origin and foundation of our judgements concerning the sentiments and conduct of others' and that 'I come now to consider more particularly the origin of those concerning our own' (p. 109). In order to realize this shift of focus, he recentred the analysis on the acting agent's own perspective and ascribed to him/her a concern for the impartial spectator's imagined reaction to any action and its effects on the beneficiary: 'we suppose ourselves [to be] the spectators of our own behaviour, and endeavour to imagine what effect it would ... produce upon us' (p. 112).

What emerged from this step in Smith's theory was the effective internalization of the spectator concept and its reappearance as the agent's conscience, or the impartial spectator 'within one's breast' (cf. Viner, 1972, p. 78). As a second step, Smith posited the existence of 'a much higher tribunal' before which the agents' actions and their consequences must appear, namely 'the tribunal of their own consciences, ... that of the supposed impartial and well-informed spectator, ... that of the man within the breast, the great judge and arbiter of their conduct'. And he stressed that 'the influence and authority of this principle is, *upon all occasions*, very great' (TMS, pp. 128, 130, 134, emphasis added; cf.137). Raphael summarizes this notion of conscience as 'a social product, a mirror of social feeling' (1975, p. 89). He goes on, though, to point out that, while this assertion can be inferred from Smith's arguments, it poses a problem for moral theory in that it calls for a wholly socially dependent conscience. This ignores the role of the agent's mind with its capacity for independent imagination that Smith had long ago accepted, even in relation to the formation of theories based on empirical observations of the physical universe (see section 2.2 above). The simple fact of the matter is that the agent's own conscience must judge differently from what any external spectator could, however impartial, because only the agent has full information about his/her actual experiences and true situation. Thus, continues Raphael: 'The voice of conscience reflects what I imagine that I, *with all my knowledge of the situation,* would feel if I were a spectator instead of an agent' (1975, p. 90, emphasis added). As a consequence, 'the judgement of conscience is superior to that of actual spectators simply because the agent can know better than bystanders what he has done or not done, and what was his motive for acting as he did' (ibid., p. 95).

In this respect, as Smith himself ultimately recognized, the mirror of the mind could reveal an image of the agent's action that did not slavishly follow social attitudes. So, as Raphael also notes, by 'the second edition [of the TMS,] he trusted the imagination more and society less' (1975, p. 92). In so doing, Smith inclined himself towards the transcendental role of reason which makes the constitution of the mind more than the sum of its associated cumulative experiences and ideas. The result was that he had to resort to some ultimate, trans-social authority over the free reign of reason if moral standards were ever to have a solid foundation. To this end, he invoked the notion of the Deity as the former of consciences. We receive a hint of this early in the TMS: 'When by natural principles we are led to advance those ends, which refined and enlightened reason would recommend to us, we are very apt to impute to that reason, as to their efficient cause, the sentiments and actions by which we advance those ends, and to imagine that to be the wisdom of man, *which in reality is the wisdom of God*' (TMS, p. 87, emphasis added). Morrow's comment on this is that 'in this one sentence Adam Smith has given expression to and shown the fallacy in the fundamental assumption of the social rationalism of the eighteenth century', in particular of the notion that reasoned constructions and contracts are the stuff of social morality and order (1969, p. 41). In the next section, we will have occasion to look more deeply into Smith's references to the role of reason in the establishment of moral codes for society.

3.3 Balancing the moral virtues of human agents

What Smith sought in his theory of moral sentiments was to identify the maximum possible potential for human agents collectively to generate social order and stability as an immediate consequence of their immanent moral virtues. The origin of these virtues was both innate and learned through the socialization process, and they were always effectuated through the medium of the agents' situations, comprising the institutions and moral rules of various sorts that had evolved over time. My concern now is with Smith's understanding of the relationship between moral sentiments and the origin and nature of these situational aspects of the social existence of human agents. The issue that this will lead us to confront is how he struck a balance in his analysis of their character and conduct between the subjectivity of individual moral attitudes and the containment of such attitudes within the objectivity of the agent's situation.

In order to understand Smith's treatment of this subjective–objective nexus we should examine his analysis of the links between the moral sentiments of agents and the formation of moral rules and institutions through which they collectively operate. The principle of morality that Smith's arguments enabled him to formulate was, as we have seen, that all agents look to an imaginary spectator within their own psyche, a conscience based on reason guided by God, for revelations as to the degree of propriety and merit that their actions involve. Moral virtue could then be claimed for those actions that on both counts receive the *justified* approbation of the internal spectator. The emphasis upon the justified nature of approbation was carefully set down by Smith in order to distinguish the genuine side of virtue from that which is based only on vanity. For this reason, then, the 'most sincere praise can give little pleasure when it cannot be considered as some sort of proof of praiseworthiness' (TMS, p. 114; cf. pp. 115, 117).

The challenge for Smith at this point was to situate agents with this established desire for the realization of individual virtue in an operational model of society. That is, he felt obligated to show how the virtuous character and conduct of agents could be turned into an active principle that brings and sustains social cohesion. Smith's dominant focus in this analysis, as far as it went in the TMS, was on the origin and nature of the *moral rules* to which agents could be expected, more or less, to conform in their conduct. These amounted to objective and practical guides to the realization of virtue in action. If agents are seen to conform to them, he soon came to recognize that this called for some subjective rationale on their part for so doing. The effect was that such a rationale made the moral sentimental constitution of human nature the active basis for human agency, but Smith still wanted to steer clear of any taint of resorting to rationalism per se in making this connection.

For Smith, reason remained only secondary in the setting up of morality, with the primary role being ascribed to the sentiments. As T.D. Campbell notes, 'reasoning comes into the process [of moral judgement] in so far as men form, by induction, general rules which serve as everyday moral guides as to the sorts of conduct which are generally approved and disapproved of, but, in the end, *all moral judgements are based on that species of "immediate sense and feeling" ... which is the product of the imaginative consideration of specific actions'* (1975, p. 70, emphasis added). So, Smith himself argued, although 'reason is undoubtedly the source of the general rules of morality, and of all the moral judgements which we form by means of them; it is altogether absurd and unintelligible to suppose that the first perceptions of right and wrong can be derived from reason' (TMS, p. 320). In this regard, Viner's perception is that 'the important thing for the interpreter of Smith to note is how low down ... [on a scale of significance] reason enters into the picture as a factor influencing social behavior. The sentiments are innate in man; that is man is endowed with them by providence. Under normal circumstances, the sentiments make no mistakes. It is reason which is fallible' (1972, p. 78). Joseph Cropsey, concurring with Viner, describes as a 'theme of the utmost importance' Smith's emphasis on 'the inadequacy of reason to the furtherance of the principal objects of [human] existence' Rather, he continues, 'Nature causes men to seek their good by making their good attractive to their passions' and that the 'attribution of natural pre-eminence to the passions as causes ... signifies the intransigence of the passions to merely rational governance' (1977, pp. 5, 8). In contrast to these readings, it is not readily apparent how Macfie argues to the contrary that 'while sympathy is the essential social sentiment for Smith ..., [it] is always *united with reason*, with the operation of the impartial spectator; and that, on a broad estimate, it seems true to say that Smith specially stressed the rational rather than the emotional side' of human agency (1959, p. 216, original emphasis). However, he makes a valid point in asserting that the 'rational element in ... [Smith's] argument needs special stress, because without it we [will] fail to see the link between our social feelings and the actual growth of judicial and economic systems' (ibid., p. 217). As we shall see in the next chapter, the 'rational element' really does enter once agents are confronted with social relations in which moral imperatives are not the dominant influence on conduct.

Smith was ever conscious of the innate limitations that nature had left built into the essential make-up of human agents and we will find this surfacing from time to time throughout what follows. He saw it as his challenge to show how social harmony could emerge and be sustained in spite of human nature, rather than because of it. This theme is apparent in the notion that moral rules are set up because the fundamental weakness of human agents is their incapacity to be fully objective in assessing the virtue of their own actions, given that these are most immediately driven by the pressures of self-love. It is reason, though, that implicitly mediates so that 'our continual observations upon the conduct of others, *insensibly lead us* to form to ourselves certain general rules concerning what is fit and proper either to be done or to be avoided' (TMS, p. 159, emphasis added).

In order to reveal the nature of human virtue, Smith first asked the direct question, 'wherein does virtue consist?' (TMS, p. 265). On the most general level, he identified two general categories of virtue involved in the process of assessing the morality of an action. On the spectator's efforts 'to enter into the sentiments of the person principally concerned' as the beneficiary of the action, are founded the 'soft, the gentle, the amiable virtues, the virtues of candid condescension and indulgent humanity'. Then, to the extent that the agent perpetrating the action tempers the degree and form of his/her passions in order to gain the sympathy of the internalized spectator, there exists the need for 'the great, the awful and respectable, the virtues of self-denial, of self-government, of that command of our passions which subjects all the movements of our nature to what our own dignity and honour, and the propriety of our own conduct require' (TMS, p. 23). It was the proper exercise of the latter set of virtues, that is, 'to feel much for others and little for ourselves, ... [and] to restrain our selfish, and to indulge our benevolent affections', which constituted 'the perfection of human nature' that 'can alone produce among mankind that harmony of sentiments and passions in which consists their whole grace and propriety'. In accordance with this duality, Smith portrayed the 'man of the most perfect virtue [as] he who joins, to the most perfect command of his own original and selfish feelings, the most exquisite sensibility both to the original and sympathetic feelings of others' (TMS, p. 152).

According to Smith's judgement, though, both of these sets of virtues were lacking to various degrees amongst the ordinary run of human agents that he called 'the rude vulgar of mankind'. Most agents could manage to ensure only the 'mere propriety' of their actions, because it 'requires no more than that common and ordinary degree of sensibility or self-command which the most worthless of mankind are possest of'. But, more optimistically, although the 'coarse clay of which the bulk of mankind are formed, cannot be wrought up to ... perfection ...[, there] is scarce any man ... who by discipline, education, and example, may not be so impressed with a regard to general [moral] rules, as to act upon almost every occasion with tolerable decency, and through the whole of his life to avoid any considerable degree of blame' (TMS, pp. 25, 162–3). What a satisfactory delivery of intersubjective harmony between agents would ultimately require, then, in Smith's view, was that the realization of the innate and learned moral virtues here referred to should be close enough to perfection for only a minimum of constructivist support systems to be needed. Later on, we will see that the most essential of such systems was that which ensures justice.

It has been mentioned earlier that one of Smith's intentions was to argue, in contrast to Hobbes, that, at least from one perspective, the pursuit of self-interest by agents should be treated as an immediate virtue to be promoted rather than as a vice to be curbed. Thus 'The crux of the question [that he sought to answer] is *the place of self-interest in human excellence*' (Morrow, 1969, pp. 7–8, emphasis added). In this vein, Smith wrote at one point that 'regard to our own private happiness and interest ... appear [*sic*] upon many occasions very laudable principles of action ... [with the] habits of oeconomy, industry, discretion, attention, and application of thought ... generally supposed to be cultivated from self-interested motives, and at the same time ... apprehended to be very praise-worthy qualities, which deserve the esteem and approbation of every body' (TMS, p. 304). That is, the agent's concern for the well-being of the self should be represented as a legitimate one alongside the concern for the well-being of others. Smith was prepared to grant, though, that, given the moral foibles of real human agents, it was potentially a *socially* problematical virtue if left unchecked. However, as a matter of first principle, he expressed a confidence that the human powers of self-command and the tempering powers of the sympathy-based sentiments of benevolence and justice would ensure that the necessary checks to maintain social harmony and equity were effective in much of the life-activity of human agents. He was soon to discover the vital flaws in this first principle, and they will constitute the theme of the next chapter. For the present, our inquiry must focus upon the foundations that this belief in an internalized and autonomous moral balance provided for his treatment of human agency.

Smith captured the particular notion of self-interest that he wanted to convey as pertinent to the actual actions of agents by using the concept of *prudence* in association with it. This virtue comprised that 'wise and judicious conduct' directed towards the 'care of the health, of the fortune, of the rank and reputation of the individual, the objects upon which his comfort and happiness in this life are supposed principally to depend' (TMS, pp. 216, 213). In their pursuit of self-interest, prudent human agents were portrayed by Smith as having several objectives in mind. The most obvious need to accrue material returns, the economic facet of their objectives, was but a part of a more complex set of desires, but it remained of fundamental importance in his exposition because of its immediacy in the inducement for agents to make decisions that result in action. Indeed, in the definition of the character of the prudent man implied above, Macfie notes, 'Smith quite explicitly underlines his economic side' even in the TMS (1959, p. 221, cf. p. 223). Macfie's consequent suggestion that this adumbrates a concept of 'economic man' to be used in the WN will receive critical scrutiny in my later discussion (Chapters 4 and 5 below). The other general expectation of return from self-interested actions, given the material outcomes already referred to, was less substantive and comprised a profile of sentimental outcomes. These included the approbation and admiration of the actions by the self and by others, the realization and maintenance of status in terms of the distinction of ranks and the order of society, a possible touch of vanity, and an ultimate state of mental tranquillity.

What Smith did was to refer to all these objectives as related to the primary notion that 'every man ... is first and principally recommended to his own care; and every man is certainly, in every respect, fitter and abler to take care of himself than of any other person ... [because] [e]very man feels his own pleasures and his own pains more sensibly than those of other people'. But he also found in this 'desire of becoming the proper objects of this respect ... perhaps, the strongest of all our desires', at least in the sense that it tempers the pursuit of the primary desires of sustenance and procreation that must precede it (TMS, pp. 219, 213). This emphasizes the idea that the material and the psychic cum sentimental dimensions of the rewards that agents expect to flow from the pursuit of self-interest are quite interdependent and to be kept in the appropriate balance. It provides us with an image of the human agent who is cautious in economic decision making and actions and content to accumulate an external fortune at a rather leisurely and secure pace. What should be noted for future reference is that this image appeared in the part of the TMS added in 1790, and, therefore, it was one that Smith still found to be relevant in some positive and/or normative sense even after his deliberations on the nature and operations of the burgeoning capitalist economy. Thus 'The prudent man of TMS ... is the frugal man of WN' (Raphael and Macfie, 1976, p. 18).

All in all, what Smith argued here was that any action in pursuit of material self-interest must be motivated by more than the merely self-centred, utilitarian rewards that are expected. Agents were represented as self-conscious beings who care about the effects that they have on others and their consequent image in the eyes of those around them. They temper and direct their pursuits accordingly. The *virtue* of self-interest then flowed from the combination of a concern for the self and for the reaction of the affected other, together with the capacity of self-command that would enable the concerns to be effected. In this respect, the first counterbalances to the potentially disturbing forces of self-interest were to be found built in, as it were, as an integral part of that virtue itself. For Smith, the pursuit of prudent self-interest by individual agents was the most fundamental of all the virtues because it provided the substantive means by which the collective material well-being of the society could be satisfied. In the process, of course, it also satisfies the material objectives of the individual, but some caution is called for in interpreting Smith on this aspect of his theme. At the individual level, material ends were, he argued, intimately tied up with the non-pecuniary rewards of vanity and interpersonal esteem and prestige. Indeed his downgrading of the material impetus to the pursuit of self-interest led him also to invoke the need for some degree of delusion on the part of agents in order to explain the extent of the industry that they were prepared to apply to the accumulation of external fortunes. The amount of these fortunes, the somewhat ascetic Smith felt, went far beyond the agents' capacity ever to make effective use of all the material objects actually and potentially made available to them. However it remained the case that little respect would be due to an agent 'who did not exert himself to gain an estate, or even a considerable office, when he could acquire them without either meanness or injustice'. What is evident, then, is that this 'spirit and keenness constitutes the difference between the man of enterprise and the man of dull regularity', a distinction that has clear implications for their respective capacities to contribute to the wealth of nations (TMS, p. 173).

Now be this spirit of industry as it may, Smith's message was that, in the end, an agent could derive little that really gave satisfaction from an ever-increasing access to wealth if utility per se was to be the measure of things. He asked rhetorically, 'for to what purpose is all the toil and bustle of this world? what is the end of avarice and ambition, of the pursuit of wealth, of power, and preheminence?' It could not be 'to supply the necessities of nature ... [for the] wages of the meanest labourer can supply them'. The implication is rather that 'if we examined ... [an agent's] oeconomy with rigour, we should find that he spends a great part of ... [his rewards] upon conveniencies, which may be regarded as superfluities' (TMS, p. 50). What Smith saw as the ultimate end of the pursuit of riches was not the individual items of pleasure, but rather the systematic access to them that wealth could facilitate. Thus 'We are then charmed with the beauty of that accommodation which reigns in the palaces and oeconomy of the great; and admire how every thing is adapted to promote their ease, to prevent their wants, to gratify their wishes, and to amuse and entertain their most frivolous desires'. It is the prospect of this arrangement that leads the 'pleasures of wealth and oeconomy ... [to] strike the imagination as something grand and beautiful and noble, of which the attainment is well worth all the toil and anxiety which we are so apt to bestow upon it'. The conclusion that Smith drew from this perspective on the pursuit of wealth was that 'it is well that nature imposes upon us in this manner ... [, for it] *is this deception which rouses and keeps in continual motion the industry of mankind'* (TMS, p. 183, emphasis added). In this way he linked the agents' pursuit of self-interest with the industry capable of ensuring their own individual material welfare and that of the society which they constitute.

That individuals are prepared to pursue material fortunes was also an important *social* phenomenon, for one of the results was that it situated the agent in a particular position in the structure of order and ranks that were so evident in the society of Smith's era. The principle of human nature that Smith elicited in this argument was that, for agents, 'to deserve, to acquire, and to enjoy the respect and admiration of mankind, are the great objects of ambition and emulation'. Once again, the utility of material things was pushed into the background by more sentimental concerns: 'From whence ... arises that emulation which runs through all the different ranks of men, and what are the advantages which we propose by *that great purpose of human life which we call bettering our condition?'* (TMS, p. 50, emphasis added). The response here, even given the emphasized reference to what would become the most fundamental driving force of economic behaviour in the WN, was that the agent sought to be 'observed, to be attended to, to be taken notice of with sympathy, complacency, and approbation, ... [as] all the advantages which we can propose to derive from it' (ibid.).

This outcome was reinforced by an asymmetry in human sentiments that leads agents 'to sympathize more entirely with our joy than with our sorrow, [so that] we make parade of our riches, and conceal our poverty'. As a result, the order and ranks of a society are built upon agents' 'disposition to admire, and almost to worship, the rich and the powerful, and to despise, or, at least, to neglect persons of poor and mean condition'; and, moreover, it is frequently the case that 'the vices and follies of the powerful [are] much less despised than the poverty and weakness of the innocent' (TMS, pp. 50, 61, 62). Later in the TMS, this thesis was reiterated: 'The peace and order of society, is of more importance than even the relief of the miserable. Our respect for the great, accordingly, is most apt to offend by its excess; our fellow-feeling for the miserable, by its defect' (p. 226). This inclination to accept the existence of poverty as integral to the ranks and order of society was compounded by an indifference to the evident maldistribution of wealth and income that is responsible for it. At one stage, though, Smith did attempt to induce his readers to overlook the obvious. He suggested that, while it was the 'natural selfishness and rapacity' of the rich which drove them to maximize employment and production, the end result was the sanguine one that 'they divide with the poor the produce of all their improvements'. More specifically he claimed that 'they consume little more than the poor ... [and] are led *by an invisible hand* to make nearly the same distribution of the necessaries of life, which would have been made, had the earth been divided into equal portions among all its inhabitants, and thus without intending it, without knowing it, advance the interest of society' (TMS, pp. 184–5, emphasis added). Whatever the message intended in this passage, he would ultimately recognize in the WN that the realities of capitalist competition in pursuit of material ambitions would give rise to the appearance of both winners and losers in the observed material outcomes of economy and society. The 'invisible hand' would not always be as benevolent as suggested here, and this aspect of the actual mercantile system of his day was to become one of the issues confronted in considering the design of reforms to the system. But, as we will find in the next chapter, even when positing his 'ideal' alternative, he continued to defend the economics of the distinction of ranks and the order of society on the basis of the moral asymmetry suggested above (cf. Heilbroner, 1982, pp. 438–9).

The next stage in the argument of the TMS was devoted to raising the possibility that any negative effects of the imprudent exercise of self-interest on the collective harmony and well-being of the order of society could be autonomously offset. What Smith sought was to show that there existed a potential for at least some degree of counterbalance by the sympathy-based sentiments that appear as the virtues of benevolence and justice, in combination with the general virtue of self-command driven by the conscience's demand for propriety in actions. What his investigation actually turned up was that benevolence had a very limited potential in this respect and that the desire for justice would only be able to be met with the support of an extensive constructivist system of formalized rules and associated sanctions. While the exposition of the latter lacked detail in the TMS, enough was said to indicate that social and economic harmony and stability depended heavily upon that virtue being realized. The counterweight of benevolence and the exercise of self-command just would not be sufficient to balance the empirically pervasive and socially detrimental consequences of the pursuit of *economic* self-interest in particular.

Consider first the nature and role of benevolence in the TMS exposition. Smith specified this virtue as an active one in the sense that it involved action on the part of an agent that is expressly designed to benefit others. Its origin is able to be traced to the qualities of humanity and generosity, with the former being a necessary but not sufficient condition for it. Smith was anxious to keep these two qualities distinct, because the 'most humane actions require no self-denial, no self-command, no great exertion of the sense of propriety'. It is quite otherwise with generosity and he made the all-important observation that the self-sacrifice involved means that 'we never are generous except when in some respect we prefer some other person to ourselves, and sacrifice some great and important interest of our own to an equal interest of a friend or of a superior' (TMS, p. 191). We find that, here, Smith conceived of the idea that benevolence is connected to the strength of the intersubjective relationship between the acting and benefiting agents. I will return to argue the importance of this point below. Two of the other important characteristics of this virtue were expressed in the following passages: 'Beneficence is always free, it cannot be extorted by force, the mere want of it exposes to no punishment; because the mere want of beneficence tends to do no real positive evil'; and, to reiterate the latter point, 'the mere want of the beneficent virtues, though it may disappoint us of the good which may reasonably be expected, neither does, nor attempts to do, any mischief from which we can have occasion to defend ourselves'. Thus benevolence was depicted by Smith as a voluntary virtue, the absence of which does no explicit harm to others. The immediate implication that he drew from this was that, as a social force, it is a desirable virtue for agents to exhibit, but it remains an optional one with respect to the viability of the social order (TMS, pp. 78, 79, 86).

With respect to sympathy-based sentiments generally, and to benevolence in particular, Smith's position was that these have an influence on the human agent that has a very limited reach into inter-agent relations. That is, their impact on agents' decisions, choices and actions is rapidly weakened by the 'distance' that separates them from others. He set the stage for this important insight by making the following point: 'That we should be but little interested ... in the fortune of those whom we can neither serve nor hurt, and who are in every respect so very remote from us, seems wisely ordered by Nature ....' The sense of his viewpoint may be gleaned further from his subsequent observation that 'the administration of the great system of the universe, ... the care of the universal happiness of all rational and sensible beings, is the business of God and not of man. To man is allotted a much humbler depart-ment, but one much more suitable to the weakness of his powers, and to the narrowness of his comprehension; the care of his own happiness, of that of his family, his friends, his country' (TMS, pp. 140, 237). Again we read here of Smith's consciousness of the moral and intellectual limitations of real human agents, but now as contributing to their ordered approach to the scope and range of sentimental influences on their motives and actions. According to Smith's assessment of human nature, there is instilled into each agent an *'Order in which Individuals are recommended by Nature to our care and attention'* (TMS, p. 219, original emphasis). This order is manifested as the 'order which nature seems to have traced out for the distribution of our good offices, or *for the direction and employment of our very limited powers of beneficence'*. To these insights Smith added that the order of nature's recom-mendations is, as always, *'stronger or weaker in proportion as our benefi-cence is more or less necessary, or can be more or less useful'* (TMS, p. 218, emphasis added).

Smith argued this point out further by working more specifically through the various categories of relationships that agents will normally be involved in and assessing the degree of care and concern that they are likely to assign to others in each case. He did so by beginning with the potential for sympa-thetic feelings and benevolent actions that could be expected from an agent towards the members of his/her own family. In this context, the agent finds the people who are 'naturally and usually the persons upon whose happiness or misery his conduct must have the greatest influence'. Also he is 'more habituated to sympathize with them ..., and his sympathy with them is more precise and determinate, than it can be with the greater part of other people'. The significance of the idea of intersubjective distance in affecting the strength of sympathy directed at others begins to become clear once the immediate family situation is compared to that involving more remote relations. In the latter case, the 'mutual sympathy is less necessary, so it is less habitual, and therefore proportionably weaker ...; and the affection gradually diminishes as the relation grows more and more remote' (TMS, pp. 219, 220). The need to accommodate to others in relationships does extend beyond the family, though, and again this highlights the potential for sympathetic concern for others to be present so long as it has some rationale. This happens, for example, where 'the necessity or conveniency of mutual accommodation, very frequently produces a friendship not unlike that which takes place among those who are born to live in the same family'. And, what is more, 'Colleagues in office, partners in trade, call one another brothers; and frequently feel towards one another as if they really were so' (TMS, pp. 223–4).

From an even more extensive perspective, agents exist in society at large, within which they will form identifications with groups of other agents on the basis of functional needs rather than on the grounds of sympathetic or benevolent feelings as such, even though the latter may be present *as a result*. These relationships are a reflection of the fact that, in order to operate effectively within an economy or a society, individual agents have no real alternative but to form dependencies upon others. Where the resulting interdependencies have an established and continuing nature, the inclination is present for the formation of more or less formalized mutual interest groups: 'Every independent state is divided into many different orders and societies, each of which has its own particular powers, privileges, and immunities. Every individual is naturally more attached to his own particular order or society, than to any other'. The nature and strength of the intersubjective bonds that these groups elicit will vary, but at one point Smith envisaged them to be such as to make even benevolence possible: 'The wise and virtuous man is at all times willing that his own private interest should be sacrificed to the public interest of his own particular order or society' (TMS, pp. 230, 235). Given the location of the references to these mutual interest group relations in Part VI of the TMS, added in 1790, it is reasonable to suggest that their inclusion was prompted by what emerged to be an important component of economic and social organization in the WN.

From the above argument it is apparent that Smith envisaged agents as situated within a structure of intersubjective relations with others, one in which the strength of the sympathetic feelings and attachments involved decreases as the distance, or degree of anonymity, increases. Viner reminds us that this idea was not original to Smith, referring to Hume's discussion in his *Treatise of Human Nature* and to earlier writers (1984a, p. 115). Moreover Viner notes elsewhere the additional and compounding factor that the 'concrete nature of the contacts of man with man can also affect the extent to which they involve "distance" in the psychological sense' (1972, p. 81). Or, as he puts it in the former work quoted above, the 'moral sentiments operate at different levels of intensity according to the nature and the strength of the external stimuli impinging upon men' (1984a, p. 115). The implication of most concern here is that this increasing remoteness of the relationships between agents makes it increasingly improbable that they will consider benevolence to be a relevant virtue in the process of deriving satisfaction from the relationship. Anspach supports this reading: 'Between oneself and one's family at one extreme and generalized humanity at the other, there exists ... a continuum of individuals and groups organized in concentric circles around the individual ... [so that in] each case, ... people very practically tend to allocate their benevolent feelings and actions in such a way as to optimize the effectiveness of their efforts' (1972, p. 195). Ultimately, too, the *nature* of the relationships reached will be of such anonymity that the *scope and need* for any sympathy basis, and hence for any inclinations to benevolence, will fade away completely. In these cases, some of which will be vital to the well-being of individuals, a different rationale for the operation and preservation of the relationships must be found. In the WN, Smith cited economic and commercial relations as of such a kind, a fact that Viner expresses quite explicitly:

> To understand the relationship of 'sympathy', of the 'sentiments', to Adam Smith's economic views as expounded in *The Wealth of Nations* it is essential to appreciate the role Smith assigns, in the operations of 'sympathy', to what I ... call here ... 'distance', in the spirit of the term 'social distance' sometimes used by modern social psychologists with reference to the relations to each other of members of different social classes. (1972, p. 80)

For these more distant relations between agents, the rationale for and the nature of which are dominated by the functions which they serve, no sympathy feelings strong enough to elicit benevolence are likely to be present. More specifically, to quote Viner again, Smith 'took for granted that the participants in a large number of the transactions which occur in the market [are] (in the metaphorical sense) at an extreme distance from each other; they are, in relation to each other, anonymous, or strangers, so that there is limited occasion for any moral sentiments other than justice to come into operation' (1984a, p. 115 – the point about justice will be addressed below). Indeed the presence of such extraneous concerns between agents could disrupt the realization and impede the efficiency of the functional purposes for which the relation was established in the first place.

The crucial point that Smith was driving at in the above argument was that benevolence is a virtue that demands of the agent such a self-conscious act of sacrifice that its main impact will necessarily be directed towards those other agents who are closest to him/her in an intersubjective sense. As the distance in this sense increases between agents, that is, in particular, as the degree of anonymity in their relationship increases, the scope and need for, and the expectation of, the appearance of the sympathy based sentiments, from which benevolent actions are bound to flow, falls away. Readers familiar with the WN will recall that this virtue makes but a brief appearance in that work, only to be dismissed as a relevant force in economic relations between agents. It is my argument that the rationale for this desultory treatment is to be found in the TMS and provides one of the most important of the links between the two books.

Most importantly, though, for the present stage of the exposition, the continuum of decreasingly effective sympathy feelings in inter-agent relations implies that their tempering effect upon the pursuit of self-interest decreases along with them. That is, the chance of an autonomous harmony emerging in the social order must be reduced accordingly because of the need for agents to enter into functionally important relations with others that, for the vast majority of them, are not founded upon any mutual expectation of beneficence. The result is, according to Smith, an increasing probability of infringements of the virtue of justice due to a rising prominence of self-interest. He recognized in this possibility much more serious implications for economy and society than could be drawn from the existence of relations that function without benevolence alone. The distinction that he posited between the two other-directed virtues of benevolence and justice was a crucial one because he was of the opinion that without the general and substantial presence of the latter, no society could be viable. The essential basis for this more fundamental concern with the exigencies of justice was presented by Smith as the need for agents explicitly to avoid doing harm to others. So, whereas a failure of benevolence did no direct harm to anyone, 'the violation of justice is injury: it does real and positive hurt to some particular persons, from motives which are naturally disapproved of ... [and it is] the proper object of resentment and of punishment'. A further contrast between these two virtues to which Smith drew attention was that, while the presence of benevolence in an action could be the stimulus for reward, 'the observance of the rules of ... [justice] seems scarce to deserve any reward ... [because] as it does no real positive good, it is entitled to very little gratitude'. So it is, then, that the 'man who barely abstains from violating either the person, or the estate, or the reputation of his neighbours, has surely very little positive merit' (TMS, pp. 79, 82).

Quite apparently, Smith was conscious at this point that he was dealing with a virtue of significantly greater imperative for human well-being than benevolence. The exercise of justice is so vital to social harmony because it means the avoidance of the hurt and consequent resentment that can flow from the uncontrolled pursuit of self-interest by any particular agent. He went so far as to assert that a society

> cannot subsist among those who are at all times ready to hurt and injure one another ... [, for the] moment that injury begins, the moment that mutual resentment and animosity take place, all the bands of it are broken asunder, and the different members of which it consisted are, as it were, dissipated and scattered abroad by the violence and opposition of their discordant affections. (TMS, p. 86)

But, in spite of this profound status, its exercise brings little intersubjective reward of a positive nature for individual agents and they, therefore, have no immediate or immanent incentive of any significance to do so.

Smith did argue that there exists some negative internalized incentive to act with justice in the form of the agents' avoidance of the retribution of the impartial spectator, of the conscience. The effect on the agents is to cause them to temper their self-interested actions so as to retain the approbation of the spectator, although it remains the case that prudent self-interest is a virtue to be espoused. He sketched the nature of the situation in the following passage:

> In the race for wealth, and honours, and preferments, ... [the agent] may run as hard as he can, and strain every nerve and every muscle, in order to outstrip all his competitors. But if he should justle, or throw down any of them, the indulgence of the spectators is entirely at an end. It is a violation of fair play, which they cannot admit of. (TMS, p. 83)

Once again, though, Smith ultimately expressed a very limited confidence in the power of *autonomously generated*, other-directed virtue to offset the excesses of the driving force of self-interest. His rationale was here, too, the breakdown of the immanent concern of one agent for another due to the existence of the significant intersubjective distances that many important relationships between them involve. The most fundamental point was that '*all the members of human society stand in need of each others assistance, and are likewise exposed to mutual injuries*' (TMS, p. 85, emphasis added). From this perspective, a society can function quite well autonomously where 'the necessary assistance is reciprocally afforded from love, from gratitude, from friendship, and esteem' and the potential for 'mutual injuries' is reduced as a consequence. But, as was indicated in relation to benevolence, such affections have a limited scope and range, so that their powers of social bonding and the protection from injury that they offer are insufficient to ensure the viability of society at large. The limitations of humankind in this respect were all too apparent to Smith: 'Men, though naturally sympathetic, feel so little for another, *with whom they have no particular connexion*, in comparison of what they feel for themselves; the misery of one, *who is merely their fellow-creature*, is of so little importance to them in comparison even of a small conveniency of their own'. (TMS, p. 86, emphasis added).

A further potential element of autonomous social cohesion that Smith cited can stem from the economic and utilitarian facets of human interdependence: 'Society may subsist among different men, as among different merchants, from a sense of its utility, without any mutual love or affection; and though no man in it should owe any obligation, or be bound by gratitude to any other, it may still be upheld by a mercenary exchange of good offices according to an agreed valuation' (TMS, p. 86). Here we have a remarkable piece of insight in which was foreshadowed a crucial problem of political economy that Smith confronted in the WN. What emerged in this argument is that the social ties that incline agents to treat one another with justice can be generated by mutual economic and utilitarian concerns. But their scope, too, is constrained by the requirement that the agents can benefit each other through such an alliance. The effect, as Smith observed it empirically, is to facilitate the formation of intra-societal agent groups with common economic interests that may not reflect, or at least may not serve optimally, the needs of the members of the society generally. They are thus, in themselves, a potential source of the collective material injustice which became characteristic of economic organization in the mercantile states of Smith's era.

Smith went on to espouse the need for a formalized, constructivist system of laws which he envisaged would reliably facilitate the ends of justice in all aspects of the life-world of all agents. What he wanted to convey, most especially, was that injustice is of such a highly destructive nature because justice 'is the main pillar that upholds the whole [social] edifice ... [and if] it is removed, the great, the immense fabric of human society, ... must in a moment crumble into atoms'. This imperative made it appropriate for societies to defend against such destructive influences by constructivist means. Such means would require the creation of explicit laws which include sanctions against transgressors that reach beyond their own inner self-disapprobation: 'A society cannot subsist unless the laws of justice are tolerably observed, as no social intercourse can take place among men who do not generally abstain from injuring one another; the consideration of this necessity, it has been thought, was the ground upon which we approved of the enforcement of the laws of justice by the punishment of those who violated them' (TMS, pp. 86, 87; cf. p. 88).

Two further aspects of justice were at least outlined in the TMS and served to emphasize further the unique status and overwhelming social importance of this virtue. One of these concerned the particular nature of its rules. In his consideration of the moral rules to which human agents may be expected to conform out of a sense of their social duty, Smith noted that those which relate to the realization of justice are able to be specified with a definitude that is not possible with the other virtues. To clarify his meaning in this case, he resorted to the following analogy: 'The rules of justice may be compared to the rules of grammar; ... precise, accurate, and indispensable', while those of the other virtues are 'loose, vague, and indeterminate, and present us rather with a general idea of the perfection we ought to aim at, than afford us any certain and infallible directions for acquiring it'. More directly stated, the 'rules of justice are accurate in the highest degree, and admit of no exceptions or modifications, but such as may be ascertained as accurately as the rules themselves, and which generally, indeed, flow from the very same principles with them' (TMS, pp. 175–6, cf. p. 327). As we shall see, this characteristic rendered possible their systematic and formalized expression and their universal applicability across the society.

The other principle of the nature of justice that was addressed by Smith in the TMS focused upon the way its rules are made operationally effective. The basic requirement that he stressed in this respect was that the most effective system of laws will be that to which individual agents are prepared to conform voluntarily. This requires that they understand the laws and can perceive that it is in their interests, and in the interests of all members of the society, to comply with them. As Lindgren emphasizes, in Smith's vision, 'except in the case of [legal] coercion, all actions of men in society are determined by criteria which they regard as their own'. For this purpose, an agent 'may regard such criteria as his own either because they are his own by nature, i.e., his original passions, or because they are the norms of conduct which obtain within a group or society with which he identifies' (1973, p. 56). A system of laws, then, that will elicit such social qualities must be allowed to evolve consistently with the dominant needs and concerns of the agents who comprise the society. In this way, the rules of natural justice are derived from the moral–sentimental experiences of agents themselves (cf. Skinner, 1979, pp. 64, 65). Inevitably, though, as Smith was all too well aware, what emerges in any social system is a body of positive laws enacted by governments in an endeavour to capture the ideal of these natural rules. Thus 'Every system of positive law may be regarded as a more or less imperfect attempt towards a system of natural jurisprudence, or towards an enumeration of the particular rules of justice'. However it is the case that 'in no country do the decisions of positive law coincide exactly, in every case, with the rules which the natural sense of justice would dictate' (TMS, pp. 340, 341). Smith had further explained his position in this matter earlier in the TMS by considering the case of a possible all-wise 'man of system' who is bent upon imposing an ideal set of positive laws in order to reform a society (pp. 232ff) Such a man

> ... is apt to be very wise in his own conceit; and is often so enamoured with the supposed beauty of his own ideal plan of government, that he cannot suffer the smallest deviation from any part of it. ... He seems to imagine that he can arrange the different members of a great society with as much ease as the hand arranges the different pieces upon a chess-board. He does not consider that the pieces upon the chess-board have no other principle of motion besides that which the hand impresses upon them; but that, in the great chess-board of human society, every single piece has a principle of motion of its own, altogether different from that which the legislature might chuse to impress upon it. (TMS, p. 234)

The image of the wise law-maker that Smith presented, *contra* the 'man of system', was he who 'will accommodate, as well as he can, his public arrangements to the confirmed habits and prejudices of the people; and will remedy as well as he can, the inconveniencies which may flow from the want of those regulations which the people are adverse to submit to'. And, if 'he cannot establish the right, he will not disdain to ameliorate the wrong; ... [and] when he cannot establish the best system of laws, he will endeavour to establish the best that the people can bear' (TMS, p. 233).

The message is emphatically that only where the legislation imposed by a government moves *self-conscious and autonomous agents* to choices and actions closely consistent with their own predispositions and preferences can an harmonious social and economic order be expected to emerge without the need for a system of positive laws and sanctions of Draconian severity. For Smith, this finding was a vital one in arguing out the balance involved in the maintenance of individual freedom within the facilities and confines of a system that was integral to the reforms defended in the WN. How he saw human agency involved in the need for and in the nature of these reforms is the subject of the next two chapters.

4 The human agent in economy and society

4.1 Introduction

Human agents and their life-world situations have so far been depicted in quite general terms and we have emphasized their intersubjective relations as mediated only by the broad moral rules and obligations of society that have evolved to preserve the balance between self-interest and sympathy based sentiments. It is now time to inquire more specifically into the economically relevant aspects of these situations and to provide an interpretation of Smith's treatment of their composition. One challenge here is to understand the extent to which Smith actually dealt with the theory of economic agency by making these extensions to the situations of agents explicit and thus making due allowance for the more particular influences on character and conduct that resulted. The general principle that is potentially applicable in this context is that human agents are born into and thus inherit a particular situational structure and environment of functions and operations. By virtue of this inheritance, combined with their experiential biographies, they make decisions and choices and initiate actions that are both facilitated and constrained. A second challenge in the present chapter is to provide an assessment of Smith's representation of human agents and agency within these economically pertinent situations as the foundation of his analysis in political economy.

In order to understand fully the message of Smith's WN, it is well established that an appreciation of his work on human nature in the TMS is crucial. In his treatment of this basic aspect of Smith's writings, Heilbroner sets out to show how it is possible 'to ground the economic drives and social constraints of the ... [WN] in the considerations on human nature featured in the ... [TMS]' so that, in effect, 'the end point of the first book [TMS] becomes the starting point of the second [WN]' (1982, pp. 434, 435). More specifically, 'the economic man who is the active agent of the ... [WN] is the prudent man who is the product of the ... [TMS]', for 'whereas TMS covers the socio-psychological process of the socialization of the individual, WN explores the socio-economic consequences brought about by socialized man through the institutions appropriate to ... [the commercial] stage of development' (ibid., pp. 427, 434). This unity of Smith's project referred to by Heilbroner will be sustained in my argument, with one of the most crucial points to be expanded upon here being its precise nature. In this respect, it is misleading to infer that a distinct 'economic man' concept emerged in the WN, as this has connotations that will be shown to have been avoided by

Smith as irrelevant to the nature and direction of his inquiry. It was rather the case, as Heilbroner begins to notice, that Smith developed a single general conception of the human agent, based upon the Humean image of the essential uniformity of human nature, as the unifying core of his inquiries. The typified particulars of the character and conduct of agents in focus were then an elicited product of their situations, including the variety of role specifications within which they choose or are socially coerced to operate in serving the functional dimensions of their relations with others. What follows is that the apparently different sort of human agents who populate the world of political economy in the WN, with their innate inclinations to pursue self-interested objectives to the fore, are, in fact, the same ones who have all the potentials for sympathetically motivated virtuous conduct discovered in the TMS.

A failure to recognize this particular feature of Smith's treatment of human agents has led in the past to the so-called 'Adam Smith Problem' which was referred to in section 3.1 above. Although this problem was proved to be spurious and no longer has any currency as such, it remains the case that, in particular, the TMS revealed agents to be capable of a complex of virtuous behaviours to offset the existence of raw self-interest, whereas the image of agents in the WN gave the impression that such virtues were overwhelmed by the exigencies of self-interest. So, even though it is now accepted that it is appropriate to read the WN as embracing a particularized extension of the arguments of the LJ and the TMS, the fact that the problem could have been thought to exist does highlight an aspect of Smith's theory of human agents and agency that cannot be ignored. The appearance of *different emphases* within the complex make-up of human nature in the TMS and the WN should be accounted for explicitly in any complete interpretation of his project in such a way as to sustain its unified status.

In the TMS, Smith was intent upon showing that, as a matter of principle, individual human nature is such as to make possible an autonomous social harmony and stability through an appropriate balancing of the moral virtues. The pursuit of prudent self-interest, to the extent that it generates any disturbances to the accepted state of collective welfare, is able to be counterbalanced by the existence of moral rules and conventions that are derived from the primary sentiment of sympathy and reflect the desire to uphold the virtues of benevolence and natural justice in intersubjective relations. As we saw above, this is all conditional upon the assumption that the virtue of self-command is of sufficient strength to ensure conformity to such informal rules in the face of the juxtaposed primary drive to serve the self. Smith's lack of complete confidence in the operation of this principle of immanent social harmony in the real world stemmed initially from his recognition of the potential for failure of the implementation of natural justice. As already suggested in the previous chapter, a society can survive without the passive virtue of benevolence, but it cannot do so without the protection and security afforded to individual agents by justice. So it was in respect of the latter that any weakness in the agents' powers of self-command became vital and called for the acceptance of constructivist intervention in the form of a system of administered justice as an additional balancing force in the systemic generation and maintenance of harmony.

What came to Smith's attention was that natural justice is most likely to break down in that most fundamental and pervasive sphere of human activity in which agents pursue their material provisioning needs. When situated so as to serve this objective, human agents confront imperatives and constraints that elicit from them a dominant drive of self-interest. They must operate in a physical environment where most natural resources prove to be relatively scarce and in which maximum efficiency in the production of the consequently delimited flow of needed goods and services demands that the process be organized through division of labour and specialization. As a result, agents must depend essentially upon one another in the realization of their material provisioning needs. That is, within the set of more general social relations, there exists a complex of inter-agent relations that are the manifestation of purely economic motivations and activities. These constitute for individual human agents a prestructured set of modes of participation in the operations which are directed towards collective material provisioning.

Smith focused his political economy on these human dimensions of the material provisioning process, with the tenor of his inquiry already apparent in the LJ as an immediate reflection of his deliberations on the problem of upholding the virtue of justice when self-interest imperatives become so prominent. He realized that the particular nature of the inter-agent dealings in the commercial sphere should be precisely defined if we are to comprehend the balance required between autonomous and constructivist bases for the emergence of socioeconomic harmony and stability. It was readily apparent to him that the human relations involved are characterized by a considerable remoteness in an intersubjective sense as a consequence of their essentially functional rather than personal nature. This was perhaps the most significant of the shifts of perspective that emerged in the WN when compared to the TMS. Agents were now to be represented as dealing with each other much more anonymously, more at arm's length, as it were. So not only was the economic sphere dominated by the self-interested objectives of agents, but also the reliance on sympathy-based sentiments as a compensation for the negative effects of this self-interest could no longer be sustained to any meaningful extent. As will become apparent, a central objective of the WN was to show that human agents dominated by self-interest in a 'commercial' economy could be *volitionally* contained and constrained by other, more structured means to act in ways that are consistent with the maximum of collective material well-being per capita.

Smith's position on the economic aspects of human agency as it was initially presented in the LJ and developed in the WN represented an extension of the depiction of agents in the TMS to take particular account of their economic situation and its effect on their character, conduct and relations with others. Most importantly, it needs to be emphasized that these aspects of human existence were shown by Smith to have specific features which became the basis of both the positive and normative political economy exposited in the WN. His perception of human nature itself was largely the subject of the TMS. In that work he also provided some analysis of the effects of agents' situations on their character and conduct generally, touching on specifically economic matters only in passing. The objective in the LJ was to situate the individual agent within a system of justice as a means of mitigating the specific limitations of the sympathy-based sentiments that would otherwise hold societies together. In particular, it was apparent to Smith that certain characteristics of the involvement of agents in the process of material provisioning made it of immediate concern in relation to the delivery of justice. This concern is the theme of the next section.

4.2 Justice and political economy

Individual human agents, if they are collectively to constitute an harmonious economy and society, must exist in a state of balance between opposing psychological and emotional forces. For individuals, the balance to be struck which delivers peace of mind is between the pressures of self-interest and those from the existence of sympathy feelings for others. Each agent is at the centre of his/her own universe, so to say, with others revolving in orbits around at varying intersubjective distances which reflect the degree of sympathetic concern involved in the relationships. A dominance of sympathy would centripetally pull all others in towards the agent and he/she would find it difficult to establish a set of relations which allows sufficient scope for even the basic necessities of self-interest to be pursued without mental anguish. By contrast, were self-interest to overwhelm entirely any sympathy for others, the agent would be at war with the world and his/her set of relations would explode centrifugally. In most social arrangements in which agents live, this would render life impossible because of the dependence of one agent upon many others in a variety of ways and to varying degrees.

In this immediate need for internal sentimental balance within the psyche of individual agents is to be found the potential for balance that facilitates the existence of economic and social collectives that serve, inter alia, their functional needs. These collectives evolve in a range of sizes, scopes and bases for bonding, from the nuclear family to national societies. Memberships of such collectives are part of the structure of the mediating situations in which each individual agent operates. Such mediations direct his/her pursuit of self-interest, largely unconsciously, towards the more or less balanced well-being of all agents who are its members. To this end, there exist within the collectives, and thus in the economy and society as a whole, first, sets of moral rules and obligations; secondly, the established order and ranks of agents according to some concepts of function and relative status; and thirdly, an appropriate set of institutions, including the systems of justice and government. All of these facilities, most of which evolve spontaneously over time without conscious agent design, act to contain and constrain, without destroying, the agents' inclinations to pursue self-interest. They also act so as to harness as far as possible the natural virtues of the agents, the balanced operation of which ensures social harmony. Their design must be such as effectively to promote prudent self-interest as the driving force which delivers the material potential for collective well-being, while minimizing the scope for the abuse of this drive and the harm it can do to others by distorting the distribution of that well-being relative to what is deemed socially acceptable.

To a significant extent, Smith expected the maximum of welfare and the minimum of harm to be delivered by some 'ideal', so-called natural state of economy and society. However he was realist enough to recognize the potential in all facets of human existence for one individual to do harm to others through insufficiently controlled pursuit of self-interest. The viability and maintenance of an harmonious and stable social order depends necessarily upon suppressing this potential as far as possible. Where there is scope for breakdown to occur, the institution of government which evolves to represent, in some way or other, to one degree or another, the collective interest of all society's constituent agents can be expected to act. There was, of course, no pretence by Smith that this representation was even close to equitable, given the highly restrictive political franchise which applied at the time. Be this as it may, the government was charged with the responsibility to establish and enforce a body of laws and sanctions which would, ideally, capture and reinforce the autonomous inclinations of individuals to deliver natural justice to their fellows. The idea was, though, to render this delivery in a manner no longer dependent in any ultimate sense upon the unreliable sentiments of the agents concerned by means of the mediation of a formalized structure of directives which guide proper conduct in a wide range of inter-agent dealings. These comprise the system of laws and sanctions which will largely reflect the dominant ethical values and the norms of socioeconomic justice of the era. They do so, in particular, with due regard to what is defined as constituting harm to another, together with the hierarchy of significance ascribed to the different categories of harm and the sort of sanctions that apply for doing harm so defined.

It is not my intention here to probe too far into Smith's history and theory of jurisprudence as recorded in the two similar sets of student notes which comprise the LJ (LJ(A), pp. 1ff and LJ(B), pp. 395ff). However it is pertinent to note that, in Smith's era, the academic subject called Jurisprudence covered a wide range of particular themes. Its primary focus was on the theory and practice of justice both as a natural and as a constructivist phenomenon. To a significant extent, this inquiry involved detailed historical and contemporary investigations of the principles and precedents upon which the administration of justice by governments is founded. Smith summarized his subject most broadly thus: 'Jurisprudence is the theory of the rules by which civil governments ought to be directed'; or, less normatively, it is 'the theory of the general principles of law and government' (LJ(A), p. 5; LJ(B), p. 398). As to the precise scope of the subject, put in the language of the day, 'the four great objects of law are Justice, Police, Revenue, and Arms' and Smith specified the respective concerns of the first two, that will be of most concern below, as follows: 'The object of *Justice* is the security from injury, and it is the foundation of civil government'; while the 'objects of *Police* are the cheapness of commodities, public security, and cleanliness .... Under this head we will [also] consider the opulence of the state' (LJ(B), p. 398). These themes deal expressly with aspects of the human foundations of political economy which were not dealt with as fully in the WN and/or were more appropriately treated in their close relation to the theme of justice. Justice and Police combine to promote and to protect the material welfare of the nation through the appropriate control and direction of human agency. If opulence is to be assured, agents must be able to create and accumulate wealth in the form of property with the guarantee of security from any personal or material injury. And the creation of wealth itself will be assisted by the institution of properly designed promotions and regulations of Police which ensure the unimpeded operation of free trade and hence 'the cheapness of provisions, and having the market well supplied with all sorts of commodities' (LJ(A), p. 6).

At the most basic level, Smith's theory of justice specified that to injure another in particular sorts of ways under particular conditions could be considered to constitute a crime. He set out three general areas of potential injury and defined justice on that basis: 'The end of justice is to secure from injury. A man may be injured in several respects. 1st, as a man 2dly, as a member of a family 3dly, as a member of a state'. Focusing only upon the first of these, we find Smith arguing that an agent 'as a man, ... may be injured in his body, reputation, or estate', each aspect being linked to a set of rights that warrant protection (LJ(B), p. 399). Essentially, then, a 'crime is always the violation of some right, natural or acquired, real or personal' (LJ(B), p. 476). It is apparent that the key concept here is that of a *right*, or some attribute of an agent's situation that he/she is entitled to have protected against loss: that is, 'those rights that belong to a man as a man, ... [which] generally can be considered without respect to any other condition' (LJ(A), p. 8). As indicated, some rights are natural and personal: 'These rights which a man has to the preservation of his body and reputation from injury are called natural' (LJ(B), p. 399). Moreover 'That a person has the right to have his body free from injury, and his liberty free from infringement unless there be proper cause, no body doubts' (LJ(B), p. 401). Other rights are acquired by virtue of the agent's situation and cumulative biographical experiences. They may be personal or real, but, as Smith notes, 'acquired rights such as property require more explanation' in respect of their acceptance and protection under the law (LJ(B), p. 401). But, most particularly, whatever is nominated as a right under the law is the subject of jurisprudence, for 'the end proposed by justice is the maintaining of men in what are called their perfect rights' (LJ(A), p. 5).

In these introductory words about the notion of justice is to be found the central concept which links justice most directly with police, that is, for our purposes, into the world of capitalist cum commercial political economy, namely that of *property* or *estate*. Smith sensed that this right required some particular justification as the object of protection under the law because it could not be considered to be a natural one. He proceeded to inquire into the terms that could provide a raison d'être for it (LJ(B), pp. 401, 459). He listed 'five causes from whence property may have its occasion', but we will only be concerned with the first of these, which encompasses the notion of the acquisition of newly created property – the others refer to the possession and transfer of already existing property. This first he called 'Occupation, by which we get any thing into our power that was not the property of another before' (LJ(A), p. 13). As a matter of general principle, he sought, in passing, to justify property acquisition by this means in terms of the established ethical standards of 'commercial' society as they had been argued in the TMS: 'Occupation seems to be well founded when the spectator can go along with my possession of the object, and approve me when I defend my possession by force', an additional point of justification being that 'if I have gathered some wild fruit it will appear reasonable to the spectator that I should dispose of it as I please' (LJ(B), p. 459). It is to be noticed immediately that the basis for property creation and acquisition referred to here was the actual exercise of labour effort. At another time in his lectures, recorded in the 'Anderson Notes' discussed and reproduced by Ronald Meek (1977, pp. 57ff) and most probably dating from the early 1750s, Smith put this point more explicitly: 'To deprive a man of the beast or fish he has caught, or of the fruit he has gathered, *is depriving him of what cost him labour and so giving him pain*, and is contrary to the laws of the rudest society' (ibid., p. 82, emphasis added).

With good reason, Smith treated it as more or less self-evident that a 'commercial' system could only be harmonious and stable, and generate the maximum possible production and growth of per capita material provisioning, if the right to accumulate and possess property is protected by law. Indeed 'the foundation of civil government' is the establishment and maintenance of justice as the delivery of 'security from injury' (LJ(B), p. 398) so that 'The first and chief design of every system of government is to maintain justice; to prevent the members of a society from incroaching on one anothers property, or seizing what is not their own. The design here is to give each one the secure and peaceable possession of his own property' (LJ(A), p. 5). It followed for Smith that it is because 'a man may be injured in his estate' comprising, inter alia, real property, that one of the crucial judicial functions of governments is to protect such property: 'Property and civil government very much depend on one another. The preservation of property and the inequality of possession first formed it [*sic*], and the state of property must always vary with the form of government' (LJ(B), pp. 399–400, 401).

It is appropriate to recall at this point that property and the inequality of its distribution have been referred to in the TMS as being behind the self-interested motivation of agents who act with industry and frugality. Agents were there shown to be driven by the desire to possess property for reasons that go beyond the utility value of the items involved to include the approbation and admiration by others that possession brings. Thus, added to the direct and absolute desire to have and use property, is the drive from the desire to emulate those who are rich in order to attain the sociopsychological satisfaction that derives from a more elevated status in the 'distinctions of ranks and the order of society'. A proper structure of property rights completes this argument, in that agents can rest assured that their aspired to possessions will be protected once obtained. The notion was reiterated in the WN, where Smith stated quite explicitly that his thesis was that 'the acquisition of valuable and extensive property ... necessarily requires the establishment of civil government' (p. 710). The rationale for this belief was to be found in the limitations of human moral sentiments:

> But avarice and ambition in the rich, in the poor the hatred of labour and the love of present ease and enjoyment, are the passions which prompt to invade property .... Wherever there is great property, there is great inequality. ... The affluence of the rich excites the indignation of the poor, who are often both driven by want, and prompted by envy, to invade his possessions. (pp. 709–10)

It is to be noticed, though, that the argument here not only depends upon the natural foibles of human agents, but also is given added weight by the relativistic outcome of the inequality in the distribution of wealth that characterized mercantile capitalism. Thus 'Civil government, so far as it is instituted for the security of property, is in reality instituted for the defence of the rich against the poor, or of those who have some property against those who have none at all' (p. 715). Under the circumstances, Smith's conclusion in the WN was quite clear: 'It is only under the shelter of the civil magistrate that the owner of ... valuable property, which is acquired by the labour of many years, or perhaps of many successive generations, can sleep a single night in security' (p. 710).

According to Smith's ideas as recorded in the LJ, the relationship between jurisprudence and political economy went further than concerns about the protection of property. Of most particular interest in the present context is the way in which he related economic activity and its results to the tenets of justice by emphasizing the fact that these things are essentially functions of the mode of organization of human agency. A crucial point to recall immediately is that, in matters of material welfare, as in other matters, Smith reflected his era, in that he was no advocate of immediately egalitarian principles as the basis for justice. That this was so is indicated by his continued tacit acceptance in the WN, as in the analysis of the TMS, of the mass of the poor alongside minority wealth, together with its defence by means of an institutionalized structure of economic and social subordination and deference, as facts of life in a 'commercial' system. Heilbroner refers in this respect to the 'order bestowing principle of subordination' as a 'crucial element in the socialization of man', concluding that '*in this way the social fact of inequality, potentially the source of social disruption and unrest becomes itself the reinforcing agency of cohesion and order*' (1982, pp. 433–4, original emphasis). For Smith, it was rather the case that individual agents should have *free access to the opportunities* to acquire material possessions to the extent allowed by their respective functional positions in the social and economic distinctions of ranks and order of society. It was their right to be able freely to try to improve their material positions by means of their own acquisitive self-interest, industry and frugality. Justice is served when those who, by one means or another, have already acquired real wealth and economic power are prevented from impeding the efforts of those aspiring legally to emulate the possession of such things.

It was also evident to Smith that the mode of organizing production in the 'commercial' economy brought with it the potentially problematical requirement that it rendered each agent dependent upon a range of others for the realization of his/her material ambitions. This represented an extension of the more general fact of the necessarily social nature of human being given prominence in the TMS: 'man, who can subsist only in society, was fitted by nature to that situation for which he was made'. In society, the mutual interdependence of agents renders them vulnerable as individuals to the harm that can be caused by the actions of others. However he was sanguine that,

even though 'the necessary assistance should not be afforded from ... generous and disinterested motives, [and even] though among the different members of society there should be no mutual love and affection, the society,
though less happy and agreeable, will not necessarily be dissolved' (pp. 85–
6). In this context, where the pressures of the moral rules of natural justice
may be ineffectual, the rationale for such optimism was the notion of the
mutual functional utility of social arrangements: 'Society may subsist among
different men, as among different merchants, from a sense of utility, ... and
though no man in it should owe any obligation, or be bound in gratitude to
any other, it may still be upheld by a mercenary exchange of good offices
according to an agreed valuation' (p. 86). The potentially injurious effect of
dependence upon others remained, though, and was made more specific in
the argument of the WN. There individual agents were rendered as potentially vulnerable to the conspiratorial endeavours of common interest groups
of others to whom they must relate. These groups strive to create barriers
against the free access of agents generally to the potential material benefits
that could accrue to their unimpeded industry. So, whereas commercial intercourse and trade 'ought naturally to be, among nations, as among individuals,
a bond of union and friendship, [it] has become the most fertile source of
discord and animosity' (WN, p. 493). So it was, then, that one of Smith's
major preoccupations in the WN was to seek out all mercantile impediments
to free participation in the economy, inspired by 'the mean rapacity, the
monopolizing spirit' and 'the interested sophistry' of merchants and manufacturers, and to recommend legal and institutional reforms which would
bring about their destruction (WN, pp. 493, 494). As I shall argue in the next
chapter, Smith's advocacy of conscious and planned reform in the face of
such mercantile distortions required him to establish an 'ideal' logic for the
structure and operations of a 'commercial' economy with the intention of
ensuring that any systemic renewal would conform as closely as was practi-
cable to it. He began this inquiry by arguing out the essentials of efficient
human organization of the production process, a theme taken up in the
following section.

4.3 Human agency and the organization of production
In the LJ, Smith broached some of the ideas that provided foundations for,
and partially foreshadowed the theses of, his economic magnum opus, *An
Inquiry into the Nature and Causes of the Wealth of Nations* (WN), when he
extended the themes of jurisprudence to include economic analyses. Such an
extension was considered to be a logical one in the teaching of moral philosophy in his era. Here we meet the second of the objects of jurisprudence that
was referred to above as Police, the main themes of which were the best
means of promoting and defending the material opulence of the society as a

collective of human agents, the plenty and cheapness of commodities which comprise that opulence and the operational effectiveness of measures to ensure the security of agents and their property (LJ(A), pp. 331ff; LJ(B), pp. 486ff). More particularly, a crucial object of Police was to elucidate 'the proper means of introducing plenty and abundance into the country, that is, the cheapness of goods of all sorts …[, where] these terms plenty and cheapness are in a manner synonimous, as cheapness is a nec<e>ssary consequence of plenty' (LJ(A), p. 333). It would then be an integral part of the ensuing inquiry to establish the nature of the plenty to be produced: 'to consider what opulence and plenty consist in, or what are those things which ought to abound in a nation … [and] to consider what are the naturall wants and demands of mankind' (LJ(A), pp. 333–4). An appropriate interpretation of the rationale for these concerns is to be found in the fact that, of all the activities in which human agents engage, the most immediately dominant and imperative are those which constitute the material provisioning processes which meet the 'naturall wants and demands of mankind'. For the vast majority of agents, some form of participation in economic activities is an absolute necessity which dominates their life-world and is the precondition for doing anything else.

The particular manifestation of the primacy which human agents give to the material provisioning demands of their existence was perceived by Smith in the LJ to arise most essentially from the fact that they are distinct in the quality of their natures and needs from other animals. For most animals, the processes of satisfying material needs do not involve anything which could be regarded as agency in the complex sense implied here. Most especially, animals generally do not engage in the mediation of production between the raw materials of the natural environment and the physical means of satisfying their needs. There are, of course, exceptions to this, for example the weaving of webs by spiders, the building of dams by beavers and the storage of food by squirrels. But what sets human agents apart ultimately, as far as we can be sure, is that these animals cannot articulate the plans for and processes of their activities; that is, they lack self-consciousness and discursive capacities in this and other respects. Smith recognized these facts as the essential foundations and distinguishing marks of the character of human life and of the search for material opulence by human agents. Several peculiar characteristics of human nature were to be given due recognition in his investigation into the nature and causes of the wealth of nations. For the most part, these peculiarities were those which he found to separate humankind from animals generally, evidently a theme of some philosophical interest and concern in his era (see Spiegel, 1979, pp. 103ff). The importance of these characteristics for any understanding of Smith's political economy is that they comprise the particular and constant aspects of human nature which he saw as the logically prior foundations of the situated human agency that is manifested as the phenomena of the 'commercial' system. Just how the inherited situational environments in and through which agents, so characterized, must operate gave rise to the actually realized form of that system was the central theme of Smith's analytical endeavours. The actual mercantilist form on which he focused his critical insights was then arraigned against the ideal of a 'system of liberty' in order to espouse the latter as a viable alternative for contemporary society that would deliver a greater degree of opulence for all people.

The first evolutionary peculiarity with which human agents must contend is that, compared to other animals, the contemporary human agent is 'in a much more helpless and destitute condition with regard to the support and comfort of his life' in the sense that, with some limited exceptions, 'All other animalls find their food in the state they desire it ... [whereas] man, of a more delicate frame and more feeble constitution, meets with nothing so adapted to his use that it does not stand in need of improvement and preparation' (LJ(A), p. 334). Food production is joined by the need for produced clothing and shelter in order to avoid the exigencies of the weather that have little or no effect on other animals (LJ(A), pp. 334–5).

A second aspect of human nature which is closely linked to the biologically determined basis of material subsistence concerns the capacity of reproduction. In this respect, human agents were akin to other animals in that their reproductive process is integrated with a natural sexual drive. And, moreover, they also confront, according to Smith, an effective reproduction rate that is a function of the extent to which their material provisioning needs are met. That is, in times of material prosperity, the combination of good individual health and high infant survival rates brings an upswing in the rate of population increase, while in lean times the opposite effect is evident. In the case of human agents in a 'commercial' society, the above process is dominated by the mediation of the level of real wages paid to workers as a consequence of the state of supply and demand in the labour market. The means by which this mechanism operates is the confrontation of changing demand for labour with the existing pattern of supply. The response is assumed to be on the supply side, but Smith did not give due recognition to the relatively long-term nature of such adjustment and to the consequent need for an interim short-term mechanism in which demand elasticity could be expected to play a role. As he went on to explain, in any case, if the demand for labour is on the increase, 'the reward for labour must necessarily encourage in such a manner the marriage and multiplication of labourers, as may enable them to supply that continually increasing demand by a continually increasing population'. As a result, 'the demand for men, like that for any other commodity, necessarily regulates the production of men; quickens it when it goes on too slowly, and stops it when it advances too fast' (WN, p. 98). It is appropriate, though, to draw attention to Smith's sensitivity to the social complications that are involved in the above mechanism. His focus was on the 'inferior ranks' of people in isolation, for it was they who, relative to the wealthier classes, suffered the burden of producing relatively greater numbers of children. Also it was they for whom periods of poverty caused more distinct fluctuations in the fertility and infant mortality rates (WN, pp. 96–7).

Then, as a third peculiarity, human agents make things even more complex for themselves in the process of material provisioning by making demands on the provisions that go beyond their immediately operational and practical utility. What Smith pointed to here was the third peculiarity that 'man alone of all animalls on this globe is the only one who ... [gives regard to] the differences of things which no way affect their real substance or give them no superior advantage in supplying the wants of [his] nature'. For example, 'even colour, the most flimsy and superficiall of all distinctions, becomes an object of his regard' (LJ(A), p. 335). He went on to conclude more generally, and with some considerable perceptiveness for his day, with respect to the human foibles of consuming behaviour that the 'four distinctions of colour, form, variety or rarity, and imitation seem to be the foundation of all the minute and, to more thoughtfull persons, frivolous distinctions and preferenc<e>s in things otherwise equall, which give in the pursuit more distress and uneasieness to mankind than all others' (LJ(A), p. 336). The significant impact of this peculiarity was to turn the material provisioning process into the pursuit of wealth per se, for the want of such wealth knows no bounds in human agency, according to Smith. In the TMS, we find him dealing with this human trait in some detail, citing the purpose of 'all the toil and bustle of this world ... [and] the end of avarice and ambition, of the pursuit of wealth, of power, and preheminence' as the vain rewards of parading our riches and struggling to emulate those who are even richer (p. 50). As he went on to put it in the WN: 'The desire of food is limited in every man by the narrow capacity of the human stomach; but the desire of the conveniencies and ornaments of building, dress, equipage, and household furniture, seems to have no limit or certain boundary' (p. 181). Once again here, Smith drew attention to this peculiarity as a most fortunate one in the evolution of humankind. What he saw as the deceptive and false rewards of material riches brought with them the exceptional stimulus to the inventiveness and industry of some human agents which raises the quality and quantity of all classes of goods and services available to all people.

A fourth peculiarity of human nature was the one probably responsible for much of the above complexity of the material provisioning process, but, at the same time, for the ability of agents to meet the challenge posed by such complexity in the face of a natural scarcity of resources. This was the claim that 'Man has received from the bounty of nature *reason and ingenuity, art, contrivance, and capacity of improvement* far superior to that which she has bestowed on any of the other animalls' (LJ(A), p. 334, emphasis added). Smith discovered the most immediate evidence of these 'primal' abilities (cf. Heilbroner, 1982, p. 430) in the development of specialization and division of labour in the process of production as the essential basis for satisfying the complex needs of agents and for the progressive increase of their material welfare. More will be said about this centrepiece of the WN analyses in a moment, after we have considered three further peculiarities of human nature which, according to Smith, are intimately connected with its establishment and ongoing development.

As a fifth peculiar characteristic of human nature, Smith adopted the widely accepted and, as we shall see in later chapters referring to J.S. Mill, enduring Humean principle that all humans are born with roughly equal innate abilities. Taylor observes that 'one of the beliefs prevalent in his epoch, which Smith shared, was the optimistic environmentalism which holds that in native endowments most men are substantially alike or equal ... and that most human differences result from differences of environmental influence, opportunity, education, and experience' (1960, p. 98). The import of this belief in the present context was that the ultimate destiny of agents in their economic life, at least, was a matter of exposure to and learning from the situations in which they grow to maturity. Heilbroner treats this theme in Smith's work as providing a deeper understanding of the unity of the TMS and WN representations of the human agent. Thus it is 'the transformation of what I shall call "primal human nature" into socialized man, the actor who inhabits and activates the moral and economic world with which Smith is concerned' (1982, p. 429). The details of the 'primal' dimensions of human nature were pursued in Chapter 3 above and will not be repeated here. The essence of the matter is summarized by Heilbroner when he cites reason and the passions as the two key concepts: 'The capacity for reason, which plays its complicated duet with the passions, permeates the process of socialization, but must be rooted in presocialized human nature' (ibid., p. 430). That is, the influence of the passions on human character and conduct is modified by the existence of reason applied to the agent's situation.

Smith illustrated all this in a more specific and pointed way in the WN with his example of the street porter and the philosopher (cum scientist), the thrust of which was that the 'difference of natural talents in different men is, in reality, much less than we are aware of', so that 'the very different genius which appears to distinguish men of different professions ... is not upon many occasions so much the cause, as the effect of the division of labour' (WN, p. 28; cf. LJ(A), p. 348). So it was that the origin of the different modes of participation of agents in the material provisioning process could not be accounted for by merely citing innate variations in individual characteristics.

Rather the inherited institution of specialization and division of labour allows agents to develop different skill patterns, largely independently of their in-born talents. Such differences, then, 'arise not so much from nature, as from habit, custom, and education' (WN, pp. 28–9). More generally the principle to which Smith drew attention here was that some inherited institutional environmental context must be invoked as the moulding and directing force if we are to account for the observed forms of human agency in the economy. He referred in particular to the fact that an essential part of the socioeconomic system into which human agents are born comprises a structured organization of labour functions within which they choose their line of specialization. To quote Heilbroner again, 'the complex conditioning apparatus of society creates not only moral man, capable of entertaining sentiments that refine and alter his judgements, but *economic man* whose social activities have been altered in the manner specifically necessitated by commercial society' (1982, p. 432, emphasis added). The former concern with 'moral man' was the subject of Chapter 3 above. My present focus is on the notion of an 'economic man' as far as, and in the form that, such a character was pertinent to Smith's arguments in the WN. It will be emphasized continuously below that, in the WN, this notion embraced the broad image of human agents as conditioned and constrained by their economic situation to exhibit that character and conduct which proves appropriate to maximizing their own individual well-being.

A sixth peculiarity of human nature to which Smith drew attention from time to time in his work is appropriately invoked at this point to reinforce the above argument. It is a necessary condition for the pursuit of wealth per se that human agents have the desire to improve their position and status amongst other members of society by whatever means they think apt. In the TMS, Smith posited the most general form of this characteristic: 'To deserve, to acquire, and to enjoy the respect and admiration of mankind, are the great objects of ambition and emulation'. As the means to realize such desires, Smith recognized immediately that 'the acquisition of wealth and greatness' would win out over any 'study of wisdom and the practice of virtue' (p. 62). In the context of political economy, the specific pursuit of wealth, and hence of greatness, became the key motivating force of agents' actions in the guise of their desire to 'better their condition':

> a desire which, though generally calm and dispassionate, comes with us from the womb, and never leaves us till we go into the grave. In the whole interval which separates those two moments, there is scarce perhaps a single instant in which any man is so perfectly and completely satisfied with his situation, as to be without any wish of alteration or improvement of any kind. (WN, p. 341)

And, Smith continued, 'an augmentation of fortune is the means by which the greater part of men propose and wish to better their condition', means which he saw as 'the most vulgar and the most obvious'. More than this, though, 'the uniform, constant, and uninterrupted effort of every man to better his condition, [is] the principle from which public and national, as well as private opulence is originally derived' (WN, pp. 341–2, 343). The unstated mediation here was, again, none other than the development of specialization and division of labour in production and its continued improvement by means of those other aspects of the character and conduct of human agents designed to 'better their condition', namely, the propensity to save and accumulate additional capital in conjunction with the ability to invent and innovate in order to apply that capital through ever more efficient machinery. With respect to the propensity to save by human agents, Smith was sanguine that, on balance in any period, their inclinations to prodigality in spending, 'the profusion or imprudence of some', would 'always [be] more than compensated by the frugality and good conduct of others'. For he believed that, 'with regard to profusion, the principle which prompts to expence, is the passion for present enjoyment; which, though sometimes violent and very difficult to be restrained, is in general only momentary and occasional' (WN, p. 341). It followed, then, that 'Though the principle of expence ... prevails in almost all men upon some occasions, and in some men upon almost all occasions, yet in the greater part of men, taking the whole course of their life at an average, the principle of frugality seems not only to predominate, but to predominate very greatly' (WN, p. 342). Smith's analyses of the optimal mode of bringing these potentials of human agency to fruition in an 'ideal' economy are taken up in the next chapter.

What has become increasingly apparent in the above outline of the peculiarities of human nature to which Smith referred is that, while it was his initial focus on the requirements for efficient material production that led him to realize the importance of specialization and division of labour, he gave an immediate emphasis to the human origins and consequences of these requirements. Indeed he went so far as to suggest that the ultimate causal origin of this phenomenon of production is to be found in a seventh peculiarity of human nature itself: 'This division of work is not ... the effect of any human policy, but is the necessary consequence of a naturall disposition altogether peculiar to men, viz. the disposition to truck, barter, and exchange' (LJ(A), p. 347; cf. LJ(B), pp. 492–3). Thus, in the WN, 'it is this ... trucking disposition which originally gives occasion to the division of labour' (p. 27). The basis for this claim was that the agents concerned recognize this propensity in others: 'Thus it is that the certainty of being able to exchange the surplus produce of their labours in one trade induces them to seperate themselves into different trades and apply their talents to one alone' (LJ(A), p. 348; cf. WN, p. 28).

Three observations should be made about this argument. First of all, it is to be noted that Smith did not always maintain a clear distinction between the idea of inter-trade specialization and that of intra-trade division of labour. In this respect we should read his seminal endeavours so as to allow for this limitation. What is readily apparent, with the benefit of our hindsight, is that it was the *specialization* aspect to which the above-claimed propensity of human agents should have been attached. As Smith realized, the separation of specific lines of material production can only be viable if it is integrated with some system of post-production commodity distribution. In the 'commercial' stage, this is dependent upon a market exchange mechanism which is a manifestation of this trucking and bartering predisposition. On the other hand, the introduction of the *division* of labour takes place in the context of particular technically organized production arrangements in which the transfers of the material outputs of each stage to the next do not depend on any such propensity.

Secondly, the above ideas concerning *both* the specialization and division of labour originated in Smith's further distinction of humankind from other animals, this time with respect to the inclination of human agents consciously to develop a dependence upon others. Only rarely do animals exhibit such tendencies: 'In almost every other race of animals each individual, when it is grown up to maturity, is entirely independent, and in its natural state has occasion for the assistance of no other living creature' (WN, p. 26). And in such rare cases as do occur, the apparent cooperation and dependence stem from a coincidence of individual behaviours and in no way reflect any, even implicit, contract regarding the anticipated results (LJ(A), p. 347; cf. LJ(B), pp. 492–3 and WN, pp. 25–6). Moreover any constructed contact between animals, and between animals and humans, most often has its origins in the apparently emotion-like behaviour of the animal: 'When an animal wants to obtain something either of man or of another animal, it has no other means of persuasion but to gain the favour of those whose service is required', and the only overt sign of this endeavour will be some sort of 'fawning', 'flattering' or 'adulation'. In effect, the animal appeals to the emotional responses of the other, including its human contact (WN, p. 26; cf. LJ(A), p. 347). Now, while human agents may at times adopt a similar strategy for appealing to others, this was not Smith's concern in the context of seeking out the basis for specialization of labour. As he put it, the immediate import of an agent's dependence on others from this perspective is that 'man continually standing in need of the assistance of others, must fall upon some means to procure their help'. Such inter-agent relations as arise here, he went on to realize, are predominantly functionally oriented as they most essentially involve the operational implementation of production and of the subsequent processes of exchange, and are of a largely anonymous and distant nature as a result. In the context of the LJ, Smith expressed the solicitation of material help by one agent from another in terms derived from the argument of the TMS: 'This he does not merely by coaxing and courting; he does not expect it unless he can turn it to your advantage or make it appear to be so. Mere love is not sufficient for it, till he applies in some way to your self love' (LJ(A), p. 347). Here he foreshadowed that famous passage in the WN where this argument received its final form:

> In civilized society ... [man] stands at all times in need of the co-operation and assistance of great multitudes, while his whole life is scarce sufficient to gain the friendship of a few persons. ... But man has almost constant occasion for the help of his brethren, and it is in vain for him to expect it from their benevolence only. He will be more likely to prevail if he can interest their self-love in his favour, and show them that it is for their own advantage to do for him what he requires of them. Whoever offers to another a bargain of any kind, proposes to do this. ... It is not from the benevolence of the butcher, the brewer, or the baker, that we expect our dinner, but from their regard to their own interest. We address ourselves, not to their humanity but to their self-love, and never talk to them of our own necessities but of their advantages. (pp. 26–7)

It is the impersonal nature of human relations in the economic sphere to which our attention is drawn in this piece and it suggests, I would argue, that something more than an innate 'propensity' is involved in the development of the specialization phenomenon.

This brings me to the third of the observations about the source of *specialization* of labour per se in this so-called 'propensity to truck, barter, and exchange'. In the LJ, this human trait was simply cited as 'naturall'. However, in the WN, Smith was prepared to entertain the notion that it may not be so readily accounted for: 'Whether this propensity be one of those original principles in human nature, of which no further account can be given; or whether, *as seems more probable,* it be the necessary consequence of the faculties of reason and speech, it belongs not to our present subject to enquire' (p. 25, emphasis added). In spite of Smith's disclaimer here, a little further inquiry suggests that, once human reason is allowed to prevail, the logic of the emergence of specialization cannot be summed up by merely arguing that it arose as a 'necessary consequence' of the existence of this propensity. It is more appropriate to attribute specialization to applied reason; that is, to the coincidence and mutual reinforcement of the practical realization that concentration upon one specific line of production improves agent productivity, and thus leaves a surplus over personal needs, with the recognition that exchange by means of mutually advantageous bartering with others is possible. These are learned manifestations of that very 'reason and ingenuity' which, as noted above, Smith cited as lifting humans out of the animal world, and thus do not require the evocation of any particular innate 'propensities' at all. Indeed his own illustrative examples suggest that specialization comes with the progressive realization by human agents of just such a coincidence (WN, p. 27; cf. LJ(A), p. 348). Most importantly, once the specialization of labour becomes established, individual agents are socialized into it as one of the many institutions which they inherit and with which they cooperate in their own interest and thereby reproduce for future generations.

As to the origins of the *division* of labour within any process of production itself, we are left to speculate that these are lost in the trial and error of human evolution. The grounds for this are that it would have taken little but the innate 'reason and ingenuity' of human agents to realize that such division brings great increases in manual dexterity and in the speed of operations and handling in production. From there, but a short extension of applied intelligence was required to work out that with this division comes simplification and increased specificity of production operations and the consequent scope for the application of machine functions to replace manual functions. The rather obvious effect of this reorganization of production was to raise the productivity of labour within specializations and thus give agents the opportunity further 'to better their condition'. In its operational form, then, the division represented but a more finely tuned development of the specialization principle. Apropos the claimed causal status of the above-cited propensity 'to truck, barter, and exchange', though, it is quite evident that the effectiveness of the *division* of labour in raising productivity does not depend at all upon any post-production bartering. Although Smith did not make the distinction as clear as he might have, the operation of such a division is internal to the production unit and its benefits are accrued pre-market and without the mediation of a relative value concept or an exchange strategy. Quite clearly the so-called propensity, whatever its origin and status as a human trait, is not a necessary condition for the emergence of the division of labour, even though it is such for trade specialization. In this respect, Meek and Skinner conclude that 'the division of labour properly so-called only exists where there is *specialization* both in terms of area of employment and process of manufacture. For Smith, such *specialization* was the characteristic of the fourth ["commercial"] socio-economic stage *alone*' (in Meek, 1977, pp. 48–9, original emphasis).

Already in the lectures recorded in the LJ during the 1760s, then, Smith had recognized the importance of specialization *and* the division of labour as means of simultaneously increasing the productivity of labour time, of raising the consequent aggregate of production or opulence and of reducing the cost of production which makes commodities potentially cheaper. (See Meek and Skinner, in Meek, 1977, pp. 33ff for the full story of the development of these ideas in Smith's thought.) The key contributing factors in these phenomena were those suggested above and, in the WN, Smith set out more formally the same ideas as had been adumbrated in the LJ:

> This great increase in the quantity of work which, in consequence of the division of labour, the same number of people are capable of performing, is owing to three different circumstances; first to the increase of dexterity in every particular workman; secondly, to the saving of time which is commonly lost in passing from one species of work to another; and lastly, to the invention of a great number of machines which facilitate and abridge labour, and enable one man to do the work of many. (WN, p. 17; cf. LJ(A), p. 345)

What is to be noticed in this passage is that the means of improving labour productivity cited are common to the development of both specialization and the division of labour. However, in the case of the latter, they comprise effectively institutionalized ways of containing and directing the actual exercise of working time within an already specialized trade or production facility which maximize the standard and use made of the innate and learned skills of human agents. The common level of potential talent with which each individual is born can be turned into a commercially useful skill much more readily and effectively the simpler and more delimited are the production tasks to be performed. Having inculcated the particular skills needed in the workers, it is then important that they be applied for the maximum effective time during the working day. In this respect, Smith noted first of all that 'it is impossible to pass very quickly from one kind of work to another; that is carried on in a different place, and with quite different tools' (WN, p. 18). And, just as importantly, it needs to be recognized that human agents suffer from certain limitations which slow down the application of multiple skills:

> A man commonly saunters a little in turning his hand from one sort of employment to another. When he first begins the new work he is seldom very keen and hearty; his mind, as they say, does not go to it, and for some time he rather trifles than applies to good purpose. The habit of sauntering and of indolent careless application ... renders ... [the worker] almost always slothful and lazy, and incapable of any vigorous application even on the most pressing occasions ... [and] this cause alone must always reduce considerably the quantity of work which he is capable of performing. (WN, p. 19)

Evidently what the division of labour delivers in order to overcome such human foibles is the elimination of the opportunity to saunter and the need to break into the continuity of the productive tasks that workmen perform. The increased effectiveness of the delivery of labour inputs then raises the productivity of each worker. These increased skills and the effectiveness of their application are magnified even further through the replacement of some power-dependent and speed-related functions by machinery invented for the specific purpose, referred to by Smith as the abridgment of labour, and by then linking the performance of work to the machine-determined and -paced production environment, which he referred to as the facilitation of labour (WN, p. 19).

Smith's ideas about the invention and innovation processes which provide the machines needed for extensive division of labour dominated his initial discussion of the issue, but it also focused upon the way that human agents are involved. In particular, he argued that the origin of the machinery may be traced to the division of labour itself: 'the invention of all those machines by which labour is so much facilitated and abridged, seems to have been originally owing to the division of labour' (WN, p. 20). One of two sorts of circumstances may be involved in the stimulus to invent and innovate. First, some machinery is developed by the workers or artisans who actually perform the functions to which the machine is to be related: 'A great part of the machines made use of in those manufactures in which labour is most subdivided, were originally the inventions of common workmen, who, being each of them employed in some very simple operation, naturally turned their thoughts towards finding out easier and readier methods of performing it' (WN, p. 20; cf. LJ(A), p. 346). Thus, in this respect, as he had noted earlier, 'that the originall invention of machines is owing to the division of labour is not to be doubted' (LJ(A), p. 351). Secondly, though, there are some inventions of a more general applicability which are the result of such inspired and profound insight that they are usually only the work of those agents with particular scientific talents to whom Smith referred, in the style of his day, as philosophers (LJ(A), pp. 346–7). He concluded in the WN that these latter sorts of inventions had a twofold source, both of which involve extensions of the specialization principle: 'Many improvements have been made by the ingenuity of the makers of machines, when to make them became the business of a peculiar trade; and some by that of those who are called philosophers or men of speculation, whose trade it is not to do any thing, but to observe every thing' (WN, p. 21). Smith did not go on to explore further these aspects of human agency that are so vital to the realization of the gains from division of labour. The dynamics of invention and innovation were thus simply left as an implicit part of the general industry exercised by agents.

In addition to these particular sources of improvement to production, Smith also drew attention to the idea that the scope for the benefits of the division of labour to be realized is limited by the extent of the market for what is to be produced. This, he reasoned, is due to the fact that, as the degree of the division increases, so must the number of workers employed and hence the minimum viable scale of operations. The market must increase at least concurrently if the additional production is to be disposed of profitably, with such an increase being very dependent upon the facilitation of transport in Smith's era (LJ(A), pp. 355–6; LJ(B), p. 494; and WN, pp. 32ff).

What emerges from this section is the image of the individual human agent conceptualized by Adam Smith in the process of constructing his political economy. We have seen that he worked from a general understanding of human nature and chose to give emphasis to the characteristics which he believed were dominant in the particular imperative of agents wresting their material provisioning needs from an often stringent natural environment. It was Smith's immediate concern with this human agent-centred approach to political economy which inclined him to perceive of the wealth of a nation as primarily composed of the periodic flow of the real commodities that could be made available to satisfy the material needs of people. These needs themselves were complicated by certain features of human nature, as we have just seen. However the important aspect of Smith's approach to political economy which is to be carried forward for further development below is the predominant focus of his analyses on *production* as the foundation of all other economic structures and operations which mediate between it and the ultimate act of personal consumption by agents. It should be added, though, that this foundation status demanded only that the other economic functions be more or less consistent with it. Certainly no determinism was implied.

In the next chapter, the elucidation of these characteristics of human agents is shown to have provided Smith with the necessary foundation for his exposition of the *logic* of the 'commercial' economic system in which he found himself and all the other agents to be historically situated. I emphasize that my immediate concern is with the logic of the system in order to foreshadow the very real distinction that we will find Smith to have drawn between this *potential* mode of operation of the system and its actual operation as the mercantilist product of historical evolution.

5 Human agency in a 'commercial' economy

5.1 Introduction

In the WN, Adam Smith drew an analytical contrast between two representations of the contemporary economic system. On the one hand, he sought to describe the most significant of the actual characteristics of the empirical 'commercial' system which he observed around him, replete with all its mercantilist trappings and distortions; on the other hand, he distilled out the logical construction and operation of the essentials of that system, in what he suggested constituted its strictly natural form, and gave them a formal discursive representation. The latter may effectively be thought of as an 'ideal' version of the system, characterized by complete agent freedom and resource mobility, against which its contemporary mercantilist manifestation was to be arraigned.

The objective of establishing the 'ideal' of a secure 'system of liberty' was argued out by Smith around what Hans Jensen has called a model of 'conceptualized reality'. It was a 'reality' in the sense that the WN contained a body of hypothetical–theoretical analysis that was devised, not only from Smith's understanding of extant theories of situated human agency in economic doctrines, but also from his own observations of the empirical manifestations of the human agency phenomenon itself (Jensen, 1984, pp. 194ff). This systematic positive analysis of the political economy of an idealized vision of the 'commercial' stage of development served as the foundation and justification for his ultimate advocacy of reforms to mercantilism directed at extending and reinforcing the institution of economic liberty. As Nathan Rosenberg notes, while the WN 'provided the first systematic guide to the manner in which the price mechanism allocated resources in a freemarket economy', at the same time Smith 'was very much preoccupied with establishing the conditions under which this market mechanism would operate most effectively' (1984, p. 117). The actual realization of these conditions would not be any straightforward task in the face of existing vested interests and Smith accepted that the 'system of liberty' could never be a 'pure' one, as it were: there would always be 'defects in the natural order, even when left to take its own course' (Viner, 1984a, p. 154). Jerry Evensky has pursued this theme in Smith's work and concludes that there is a 'duality' in his thought involving a distinction between 'the ideal world – the [natural] Design – and the real world' so that, while Smith 'would assert that the former should be the goal of the latter, ... he recognizes that the full achievement of this goal is impossible owing to human frailty' (1987, p. 457; cf. p. 462 and 1989, pp. 125ff, 136).

It is in this respect that it is worth emphasizing that Smith's analysis was not built around any idealized version of human agents. On the contrary, as we shall see, the object was to show how systematic reforms could *contain and properly direct the complex actual exigencies of contingent human nature,* as they were set out in the previous chapter, a point also recognized by Rosenberg (1979, *passim,* 1984, *passim*). For these reasons it is important to assess what Smith's espousal of the 'ideal' could be expected to deliver with some care: in particular, to be mindful that, in the process of conceptualizing it, he maintained his ever-present sensitivity to the foibles of real human agents whose actions could never be fully insulated from the drives of individual economic self-interest. Smith chose to represent human agents always as they really are by virtue of their nature and nurture and ultimately to situate them in an analytical 'ideal' tempered by the realities of its practical implementation and operation.

For Smith, then, the analytical focus was strictly on the implications of *situational conditions* for the character and conduct exhibited by agents, keeping to the fore the fact that those conditions are themselves, to a large extent, the conscious or unconscious products of the actions of collective agents themselves. Consequently it also needs to be recognized that situations are not only constraining for agents but also facilitating. That is, just as a particular situational environment can constrain the self-interested actions of agents or groups, it is also possible that it could be so constructed as to exacerbate the opportunity for such actions. The balance of this dual effect on situated agents warrants particular consideration in understanding what determines the individual form and collective outcomes of their participation in economic activities. For, as we shall see below, the extant mercantile system was interpreted by Smith as one which actually facilitated the exercise of collusive self-interest. What his 'ideal' revealed was that an appropriate redesign of some of the key structural–institutional features of the system could just as readily constrain these practices. The crucial preconditions for such a redesign were that agents should be induced to act as self-interested *individuals* in their choices and decisions within free and competitive markets for resources and commodities.

The one intellectual defence of his approach which Smith found then extant in the political economy literature comprised the Physiocrats' theoretical reactions to the extremes of mercantile sectoral privileges and restraints instituted by Colbert in France. He devoted a chapter of the WN to a critique of 'this very ingenious system'. The intention was to extract what he could from it, *on his own theoretical terms,* in order to give more cogent support to its espousal of a 'system of natural liberty' as the optimum environment for

commerce (WN, pp. 663ff). His study of the system, and his sometime
contact with its most important advocates while in France, led Smith to
conclude of it that '*with all its imperfections, [it] is, perhaps, the nearest
approximation to the truth that has yet been published upon the subject of
political oeconomy* ... [and] its doctrine seems to be in every respect as just
as it is generous and liberal' (WN, p. 678, emphasis added). I will omit the
well-known details of his perceived imperfections of the Physiocrats' conception of the economy, with its excessive orientation towards the exclusive
productivity of agricultural capital and labour, for in the present context it is
what Smith found to admire in their work which is significant. Some of these
things remained implicit in the theoretical exposition of his 'ideal' commercial economy, but two stood out when he considered their doctrine as such.
First, Smith shared their idea of 'representing the wealth of nations as consisting, not in the unconsumable riches of money, but in the consumable
goods annually reproduced by the labour of the society' (WN, p. 678).
Secondly, he found wholly defensible their 'representing perfect liberty as
the only effectual expedient for rendering this annual reproduction the greatest possible', for 'every violation of that natural distribution, which the most
perfect liberty would establish, must, ... necessarily degrade ... the value and
sum total of the annual produce' (WN, pp. 678, 673). These crucial theoretical premises were for Smith the two ends, as it were, of his entire political
economy of reform. The WN began with the first as its ultimate foundation
piece, reflecting his rejection of that key theoretical assumption upon which
the whole of the mercantilist doctrine had misguidedly been based. The
second emerged as a consequence of his inquiry into and representation of
free and competitive markets as the 'ideal' means of resource allocation. The
maximum of agents' liberty, the opportunity for agents freely to compete in
the supply of commodities, the resulting natural distribution of resources and
the maximum periodic flow of real production from a given resource base
that such conditions ensure, became the core ideas around which he constructed his 'conceptualized reality' in the WN. This construction is the focus
of the next section.

5.2   The 'ideal' operation of a 'commercial' economy

The analytical construction of the WN reflected the unified interdependence
of the four operational categories which comprise any economic system.
Production is the foundation of the material provisioning process and personal consumption by human agents is its end objective. Neither has any
rationale without the other. In developed societies, real wealth production is
characterized by the specialization and the division of labour discussed in the
previous chapter (section 4.3). The crucial focus of the WN was set out at the
very beginning: 'The annual labour of every nation is the fund which origi-

nally supplies it with all the necessaries and conveniencies of life which it annually consumes, and which consists always either in the immediate produce of that labour, or what is purchased with that produce from other nations' (p. 10). The same emphasis was carried in the title and foreshadowed contents of Book I of the work: 'Of the Causes of Improvement in the productive Powers of Labour, and of the Order according to which its Produce is naturally distributed among the different Ranks of the People' (p. 13).

It is apparent from this short summary that the provisioning process requires that some system of exchange and commodity circulation be developed in order to mediate between production and the consumption needs of diverse participating agents. Thus, 'when the division of labour has been once thoroughly established, it is but a very small part of a man's wants which the produce of his own labour can supply' and he then 'lives by exchanging, or becomes in some measure a merchant, and the society itself grows to be what is properly a commercial society' (WN, p. 37). This mediation was sufficient in itself 'in that early and rude state of society which precedes both the accumulation of [capital] stock and the appropriation of land' (WN, p. 65): that is, in the period before the predominance of the institution of private property in the means of production and the employment of wage-labour as the mode of their operation. In the fully 'commercial' stage of economic development, 'as soon as stock has accumulated in the hands of particular persons, some of them will naturally employ it in setting to work industrious people, whom they will supply with materials and subsistence' (WN, pp. 65–6). This separation of the ownership of the stock of means of production from most of the labour required for its productive operation added a further dimension to the economic process. It meant that some system had to be worked out for distributing the sales revenues, net of material and amortization costs, which accrue in the first instance to owners of property, amongst all those agents deemed to have contributed to their generation.

The ambiguous nature of the interdependent relations between commodity value forms and income distribution as they were presented in the WN will not be critically considered here. Smith's analyses raised a number of conundrums that have been the focus of theoretical controversy since they first appeared. To this day, there is no broadly agreed solution to the problems which he explicitly or implicitly posed (cf., for example, Bowley, 1973; Dobb, 1973; Hollander, 1973; Meek, 1973; O'Donnell, 1990). Rather than add to, or even try to represent, an already vast and variegated literature, my concern with the issue will be confined to the way Smith handled the involvement of human agents in the characteristic value and distribution processes and outcomes of the 'commercial' economic system.

It was, for Smith, a self-evident fact that any fixed means of production stock, including land, is inert in and of itself and unable to produce without its expansion to include raw materials, and more crucially, without the appropriate complement of labour activity. For the present purpose, the important point is that:

> The most useful machines and instruments of trade will produce nothing without the circulating capital which affords the materials they are employed upon, and *the maintenance of the workmen who employ them.* Land, however improved, will yield no revenue without a circulating capital, *which maintains the labourers who cultivate and collect its produce.* (WN, p. 283, emphasis added)

There was, then, in Smith's perception, a legitimate sense in which the sole source of value added in production, through the transformation of inputs into useful outputs, could be attributed to the exercise of labour, albeit with the immediate need somehow to recognize the different qualities of such labour. Labour quality varied most obviously in its output productivity, as measured by the value of revenue generated per unit, and in its burden of disutility experienced by the worker (WN, p. 65). But, leaving these differences aside, Smith made labour, one way or another, the foundation of the *existence* and *measure* of value in exchange and thus focused the value problem sharply on the cost of production determined solution (WN, pp. 47ff, 65ff). Most directly put, 'labour was the first price, the original purchase money that was paid for all things' and 'the real price of every thing, what every thing really costs the man who wants to acquire it, is the toil and trouble of acquiring it'. Thus it is that ' labour ... is the real measure of the exchangeable value of all commodities' (WN, pp. 47–8).

It was equally apparent to Smith, though, that, once economic development had proceeded beyond 'that early and rude state of society', the high level of productive capacities achieved by workers is only made possible by the preparedness of the class of owners to act as 'the undertaker of the work who hazards his stock' in the production venture. Especially was it the 'intention of the [use of] fixed capital to increase the productive powers of labour, or to enable the same number of labourers to perform a much greater quantity of work', on the condition that 'every fixed capital ... requires to be continually supported by a circulating capital' (WN, pp. 287, 283). Such an undertaker, then, because of the risks to be taken, '*could have no interest to employ [labourers], unless he expected from the sale of their work something more than what was sufficient to replace his stock to him*' (WN, p. 66, emphasis added). Then, 'in this [advanced] state of things, the whole produce of labour does not always belong to the labourer. He must in most cases share it with the owner of the stock which employs him'. More specifically, 'The value which the workmen add to the materials, ... resolves itself in this case into two parts, of which the one pays their wages, the other the profits of their employer upon the whole stock of materials and wages which he advanced'

(WN, pp. 67, 66). Indeed, as we saw above, Smith realized that this was the only rationale for making the advances in the first place.

Although Smith developed his famous pin manufacturing example to illustrate how the division of labour operates, it also enabled him to show how the surplus of net revenue can occur as a result of the organization of the production process itself. In this case, the productivity of labour time is raised to such an extent by the introduction of the division of labour that the cost of each pin falls to a fraction of its previous level and can thus be sold at a fraction of its price. Ignoring any concerns about the relevant demand elasticity, the example assumed that revenue from sales would increase sufficiently to enable workers to be paid more and to leave a surplus that is assumed to accrue to the master who owns and commands the stock of means of production (LJ(A), pp. 341ff; cf. WN, pp. 14–15). These masters, then, are those to whom the surplus net revenue is due, in the first instance, as gross profit. Then, when Smith came to define the concept of productive labour in Book II of the WN, the source of the capacity for the payment of profit could not have been more clearly stated. Quite categorically, he asserted what must have appeared to him to be the obvious empirical fact that 'whatever part of his stock a man employs as capital, he always expects it to be replaced to him with a profit' and he 'employs it, therefore, in maintaining productive hands only' (WN, p. 332). He posited productive labour as that which 'adds to the value of the subject upon which it is bestowed', but the added value is to be, for the labourer, sufficient for 'his own maintenance, and ... *his master's profit*': thus, though the worker 'has his wages advanced to him by his master, he, in reality, costs him no expence, the value of those wages being generally restored, *together with a profit, in the improved value of the subject upon which his labour is bestowed*' (WN, p. 330, emphasis added).

Similar reasoning was used to account for the appearance of a third component of income distribution as rent paid for access to the productive capacities of land. In this case, the share of revenues generated by the market realization of the value-adding power of labour effort was to be paid to the owner of the landed property. In Smith's words: 'As soon as the land of any country has all become private property, the landlords, like all other men, love to reap where they never sowed, and demand a rent even for its natural produce' (WN, p. 67). A fourth form of income to be accounted for was apparent to him as well. The interest paid on stock advanced in money form, but not applied directly to production by its owner, draws a share of the profit which accrues as a result. This 'interest or the use of money ... is always a derivative revenue', for 'It is the compensation which the borrower pays to the lender, for the profit which he has an opportunity of making by the use of the money' (WN, p. 69).

Three interrelated matters concerning income distribution are of importance for our understanding of the role of human agency in the analyses of the WN and each of these will now be considered in turn. First, as already suggested above, Smith found the explanation for the payment of various income forms to follow from the mode of organization of production and its requirements in terms of the categories of participation among which the agents were distributed by inheritance, socialization and/or choice. It was specialization and division of labour that meant that the production base of the provisioning process comprised an evolved allocation of individual human agents to particularly defined and delimited functional roles which, when correctly coordinated, maximize the rate of commodity output. The agents who inherit, as it were, and more or less choose to fill these functional positions thereby have the form, character and results of their mode of participation in the economy largely predefined for them.

In order to ascertain the nature of the relations into which agents enter with others in the economic sphere of their life-world, consider a *typified* individual born into and growing to maturity in a 'commercial' society. For argument's sake, let us assume the agent is male. On reaching working age and facing economic independence from his family, our young agent moves into the world of work. He carries with him some legacy of his domestic socialization in the form of an inclination and/or opportunity to enter into a particular vocational mode of participation in the economic system which he confronts as a given in its form and demands. Most importantly this world comprises a set of relations with others which pervade every dimension of his life concerned with the realization of his material provisioning needs. Once he leaves the confines of his adult home, the human environment within and through which he must work on a daily basis consists of a vast number of others upon whom he depends more or less directly. In a varying pattern of contacts, some regular and some more random in nature, all the agents concerned, including our individual, will be expected to serve certain functions without the need for any significant or enduring degree of personalized interaction. That is, the essential form of any relationship is always predesigned and has variable degrees of transitoriness, depending upon the part of his life-world in which it appears. The most significant point to be stressed is that the successful completion of the agent's daily round of transactions, at least as a matter of formality, does not depend upon the establishment of any relationship that is psychologically or emotionally based. In the sphere of economic transactions, he was soon made aware that the typical relationship is of a form quite different from that between family members and close relatives. In particular, the effect is to render relations in the world of work and commerce immune to the psychological retributions that would be suffered if the agent pursued his own exclusive self-interest in dealings with those close to him in the sympathetic sense. The need to sustain the same sort of 'moral balance' that is important to the agent as a family member or friend is removed once he enters into the more distant relations which are required of him as a participant in the economy.

A fundamental fact of economic existence involved here is that, in order to be a legitimated consumer, an agent must take up some mode of participation that is recognized in the distribution system as contributing to production, leaving aside the potential for a limited number of agents to opt out or be forced out in various ways into an idleness which is wholly unconnected with productive activity per se (WN, p. 71). Most probably by means of his observations of the operations of the 'commercial' economy, Smith provided a typified structure of the most essential functional roles that were filled by agents in order to facilitate production. This framework of human agency can be identified only from widely scattered remarks in the WN (but see, for example, pp. 362ff). Agents allocate themselves by inheritance, choice or implicit coercion *predominantly* to one of the following operational categories: worker manufacturer, master owner–manufacturer, landlord, gentleman farmer, tenant farmer or farm worker. In addition to these functions, some agents devote their participation to the facilitation of commodity circulation as either wholesale or retail merchants. In Smith's era, with the usual exception of the landlords, these functions all involved some actual exercise of what he termed productive labour time 'which adds to the value of the subject upon which it is bestowed' (WN, p. 330). It was also the case, though, that some rights to consume a share of the value of the material product could be acquired as non-labour incomes by recognized forms of participation in production *other than immediate labour contribution*. Smith was adamant, too, that *this* share does not accrue as a result of any 'labour of inspection and direction' of the master *in and of itself* (WN, p. 66). Rather, as we have seen, Smith argued that the necessary condition for the effective division of labour was the accumulation of the stock in the hands of individual agents who are prepared to set wage-labour employees to work. Then, by associating increased productivity with the advancement of the stock, he resolved the problem of linking his labour-based concept of exchange value to the existence of a non-labour profit share in revenues.

Smith was very well aware of the idea of the separation of ownership and productive control of the stock (WN, p. 66) and it is clear that he intended to confine the receipt of profit to the function of owning stock per se, just as the landlord received rent for the mere ownership of productive land. However, as he noted, it was an empirical matter that, in his era, the overlap of functions and incomes received by individuals was quite common: masters who owned stock frequently provided the labour of inspection and direction, landlords and their tenant farmers often accrued part of their respective incomes as profits of the stock they had advanced to improve the land, and independent artisans, merchants and other self-employed persons could be considered to have incomes jointly comprising wages of labour and profits on their stock-in-trade (WN, pp. 69ff, 160). But the existence of such coincidence of functions in individual agents did not interfere with the principle that income forms and shares were linked to the mode of the participation of the agent in production and/or circulation, even where agents engaged in more than one mode at the same time.

The second matter of significance here is that the efficient single-period allocation of resources to the various categories of material production was shown to be integrally dependent upon the relations which intervene to distribute the value produced and the revenue realized in the market. One of Smith's most significant and lasting contributions to the development of economic thought was his formal recognition of this allocative role for income distribution. His concern with the nature and causes of the wealth of nations always emphasized that it was per capita material consumption which was ultimately to be maximized, albeit as qualified by a socially acceptable distribution of income in the first place. From the beginning of his thought on this theme, as it was recorded in the LJ, he referred to the need for the pursuit of cheapness and plenty in the supply of commodities (LJ(A), p. 333; LJ(B), p. 487). How this was to be achieved was the central problem of the mixture of positive and normative analysis which comprised the WN. The idea that cheapness flowed from plenty within the context of market exchange was now supported by a recognition that the former is also the result of efficiencies deriving from specialization and division of labour in production, facilitated by an appropriate accumulation and allocation of wealth in the form of capital investments in means of production. So it was, then, that Smith wrote the WN with the object of establishing the necessary conditions under which accumulation and hence the scale and efficiency of production would be maximized, along with the minimization of the natural prices around which market prices centred. For this to be so, he argued, the basic conditions were the free mobility of all productive resources, including labour power, in order to ensure their most effective allocation in terms of productivity, and unimpeded competition between producers, in order to ensure that the market-induced movements of commodity production and price levels were in no way restricted.

These unrestricted free-market conditions were an integral part of the 'ideal' economy which, for Smith, amounted, in effect, to the natural order of things economic. Thus it is 'the natural effort of every individual to better his own condition, when suffered to exert itself with freedom and security, [that] is so powerful a principle, that it is, alone, ... capable of carrying on the society to wealth and prosperity' (WN, p. 540; cf. Viner, 1984a, p. 143). The key to this 'wealth and prosperity' was the proper allocation of capital on the basis of the maximum advantage perceived by individual agents. It was

Smith's argument that such pursuit of agent self-interest would, in the free-market context, deliver the maximum aggregate social welfare: 'the study of his own advantage naturally, or rather necessarily leads him to prefer that employment [of his capital] which is most advantageous to the society' (WN, p. 454). Or, as Smith put the matter more specifically in a well-known passage, the essence of which, including the reference to an 'invisible hand', had been adumbrated in the TMS in the context of a natural distribution of produced commodities (pp. 184–5; see above, section 3.3):

> As every individual ... endeavours as much as he can both to employ his capital in the support of domestic industry, and so to direct that industry that its produce may be of the greatest value; every individual necessarily labours to render the annual revenue of the society as great as he can. *He generally ... neither intends to promote the public interest nor knows how much he is promoting it.* ... He intends only his own gain, and he is in this, as in many other cases, *led by an invisible hand to promote an end which was no part of his intention.* (WN, p. 456, emphasis added)

It was in Book I, Chapter VII of the WN that Smith provided the essentials of his analysis of the single-period optimum allocation of resources between sectors and lines of production by means of this 'invisible hand' in an 'ideal' free market. This equilibrium optimum, dependent as it was on the perfect mobility of resources, would be signalled by a particular matrix of quantitative and qualitative input–output relations in production. Its realization depended upon the recognition by agents of the existence of one or more differentials between the market and the natural prices of commodities which could be corrected by a reallocation of their resources. For individual agents, this market state would be indicated by the fact that the rates of return to their particular input factors of production are different from the established natural rates. These latter 'ordinary or average' rates, for 'every society or neighbourhood', are 'naturally regulated ... partly by the general circumstances of the society, their riches or poverty, their advancing, stationary, or declining condition; and partly by the particular nature of each employment' (WN, p. 72). It is significant to note that the latter point implies a *structured pattern* of natural rates of factor incomes rather than any simple uniformity. Smith went to great lengths in the WN to elaborate upon this insight and ended up devoting a substantial chapter to outlining the sources of the cross-sectional structure and the sustained temporal pattern of the relativities involved (pp. 80–81, 116ff). Most importantly for my purposes, Smith distinguished between relativities due to 'the nature of different employments' and those due to 'the different laws and policy of the society in which they are carried on' (WN, p. 80; and see pp. 116ff and 135ff respectively, for details). It was, of course, the latter differentials which he would concentrate upon in his proposals for reforming the mercantile system.

In the case of any particular line of production, when the wages of labour and the allocation of the surplus realized in the market to means of production owners results in just these natural rates of return, then the commodity price must have also been at its natural level. Such a price also clears the market, given the existence of that effectual demand which Smith defined specifically as the 'demand of those who are willing to pay the natural price of the commodity' (WN, p. 73). The emergence of a condition of deficient or excessive demand relative to the periodic supply would generate competitively driven changes in the market price actually realized. Ignoring the complexities of the actual timing and patterns of adjustment involved, as Smith himself did, the result would be experienced by participants in the production process as a similarly competitively driven change of their income rates relative to the natural rates established in equilibrium. These changes would arise as the pattern of demand for their services shifted as a result of the commodity supply response to the price change. It was as a consequence of these income changes that Smith envisaged the corrective shift of resources would occur to bring the affected supply back into line with effectual demand (WN, pp. 73–5; see O'Brien, 1975, pp. 79ff).

It is possible, as Smith realized, for conditions to be such as to maintain the supply-effectual demand misalignment for some extended period of time, most usually in the direction which raised market prices above the natural prices. However he stressed that, with free-market competition and mobile resources, the nascent tendency to bring back the price and factor returns to their natural levels would always be present. He adopted the well-known analogy of the force of gravity to convey his point here that, once the conditions sustaining an excess demand, most especially, are removed, a natural force, indeed an 'invisible hand', would ensure a reallocation of resources to restore the natural outcomes (WN, pp. 75, 77, 79, 456). Thus he wrote later in the WN that 'the private interests and passions of men naturally lead them to divide and distribute the stock of every society ... as nearly as possible in the proportion which is most agreeable to the interest of the whole society'. To this piece he added the empirical qualification that 'all the different regulations of the mercantile system, necessarily derange more or less this natural and most advantageous distribution of the stock' (p. 630). It was also these conditions that he would strive to have eliminated, especially where they could be shown to be the result of restrictive or collusive practices by agents, with or without the sanction of commercial law or policy.

The third of the points to be made in the present context is that income distribution was linked by Smith to the all-important process of capital accumulation upon which the growth and development of the wealth of a nation depends. The rationale for the theoretical construction of his 'ideal' free-market economic system was to expose the necessary conditions for optimizing the allocation of resources, so as to provide both for the maximum of current real welfare per capita, and for the maximum possible rate of its growth through saving and accumulation. What he came to realize was that the consistency of these objectives depended essentially upon the appropriate design and maintenance of the distribution mechanism and its particular consequences from the perspective of the income categories of agents involved. One of the main driving forces behind the economic decisions and actions of agents was cited by Smith to be the pursuit of the means to 'better their condition', specifically by increasing their wealth and generally by raising their socioeconomic status in the ranks and orders of the society. For the most part, access to such opportunity could come only from the capacity to save out of current incomes and to increase the value of stock accumulated and applied to production (WN, pp. 337ff). Smith was inclined to the view that it was largely the master manufacturers who had the will, the opportunity and the means to accumulate, although he made little of the idea explicitly. At the same time, he held agriculture in very high regard for what he saw as its very substantial productivity relative to industry generally, albeit not to the extremes espoused by the Physiocrats (WN, pp. 363–4, 674ff), but the immediate potential for its increase through stock accumulation was limited by the life style of the landlords, which was not conducive to parsimony, and by the lack of scope for increasing the division of labour in its production processes (WN, p. 16). For these reasons it was the masters of manufacturing upon whom he focused as having the greatest incentive and capacity to apply accumulated funds to profitable undertakings and thereby continuously to 'better their condition'.

The argument which Smith presented concerning the process of saving and capital accumulation hinged first of all on the distinction he drew between productive and unproductive labour. Whatever may be the ambiguities of this distinction, the message that he intended to convey is quite clear. *His* definition was couched so that the effect of the exercise of productive labour was embodied as value added to a product, whereas the performance of unproductive labour served only the immediate convenience of its employer (WN, p. 330). The import of this distinction between productive and unproductive labour was, for the present purpose, that the proportion between them in a nation was an indicator of its actual and potential prosperity, in that the former is employed by accumulated capital to generate revenue and the latter by revenue already generated. And, in any nation, 'Wherever capital predominates, industry prevails: wherever revenue, idleness. Every increase or diminution of capital, therefore, naturally tends to increase or diminish the real quantity of industry, the number of productive hands, and consequently ... the real wealth and revenue of all its inhabitants' (WN, p. 337). Quite clearly, according to Smith, the economic growth and development of a nation, measured by the increase in its per capita annual real income, depends in the first instance upon the accumulation of capital through saving out of net revenues. The key aspect of human agency involved here was that of parsimony, for 'capitals are increased by parsimony, and diminished by prodigality and misconduct'. What followed from this was the surprising fact that 'parsimony, and not industry, is the immediate cause of the increase of capital [in that] whatever industry might acquire, if parsimony did not save and store up, the capital would never be the greater' (WN, p. 337). Overall, what emerged from Smith's discussion of the involvement of human agents in the processes of saving and accumulation was a highly sanguine image of the prospects for the growth of wealth of a nation. The drive to save and to preserve the capital stock, the opportunities for profitable investments in productive capital, and the talent of the agents as entrepreneurs, were all claimed and presumed to be more or less predominantly positive natural characteristics of a free-market 'commercial' economy.

A further issue considered by Smith regarding the prospects for ensuring the maximum production and growth of real wealth per capita was to which categories of economic agents the larger proportions of net revenue should accrue in order for this to be realized. This required some judgement about the impact that the free pursuit of self-interest by these groups would have on aggregate production, saving and accumulation. The particular real effect that the pattern of distribution has would then appear in the allocation of capital and other resources, both in total and at the margin of accumulation, to particular sectors of production which experience different degrees of productivity in their use of inputs. By this connection, the distribution of incomes becomes the means by which the gross productivity of the use of resources, and the consequent level of production per capita, is determined. Any form of impediment to the free operation of markets which allocate resources to where they accrue the best possible yields would, in Smith's view, reduce real output below its potential. His ultimate concern was with the extent of the potential for contrived monopoly power over resources to be created by particular mercantile groups by means of the intervention of both private collusions and public regulations.

He tackled the issue first of all from the income distribution perspective by reflecting on the relation between the interests of 'the three great, original and constituent orders of every civilized society', the categories of landowners whose income is rent, of labourers whose income is wages, and real capital owners whose income is profit, and the material well-being of the whole society (WN, p. 265 and pp. 264ff). According to Smith, the landowners and labourers were of little or no concern in the matter of the way incomes are distributed. Although his argument on the theme varied, there was a sense in which both rent and wages were predominantly incomes accruing to essentially passive groups of agents. What was at issue here was the limited capacity of these agents to affect their incomes by virtue of the constraints imposed on them by the institutions of distribution. Rent was depicted as largely the residual paid out to landlords after ensuring that wage and profit rates were sufficient for production to be ongoing (WN, p. 162). Wage determination was dominated by the push by masters to sustain the minimum necessary for an assured continuous supply of workers, with all efforts by workers to improve on this being firmly resisted (WN, pp. 82ff). The picture which Smith painted of these two great 'orders of every civilized society', then, was a very particular one in the light of his intentions in the WN. What we have before us is an image of the vast majority of participants in the economic processes of 'commercial' capitalism as more the *subjects* of collective material outcomes than in control of them. The real income shares of landowners and of workers in the prosperity or decline of an economy are more or less synchronized with those events and there is little that they can do as individuals to win any disproportionate returns for their services. The ultimate point of his argument, then, was that neither of these categories of agents has the potential, by any collusive or legally created commercial practices, to increase their own prosperity out of line with what is happening to the economy generally. This was not so in the case of the third of the 'original and constituent orders' of a 'commercial' economy, the industrial or merchant owners of financial and real capital.

There can be little doubt that, for Smith, members of this third order of participating agents were the driving force of the contemporary economy: 'Merchants and master manufacturers are ... the two classes of people who commonly employ the largest capitals, and who by their wealth draw to themselves the greatest share of the publick consideration.' It was they who owned 'the stock that is employed for the sake of profit, which puts into motion the greater part of the useful labour of every society' and it was their 'plans and projects [which] regulate and direct all the most important operations of labour' (WN, p. 266). The extent and strength of this economic power, of course, gave them a privileged political situation which Smith found them to have exploited to the full in their own self-interest, assisted by the effective complicity of the landed aristocracy. In the case of these mercantile groups we can begin to form an idea of the roots of their actual position of economic dominance in the mercantilist version of the 'commercial' stage which Smith was to arraign before his 'ideal'. In the next section, I consider how the characteristics of the mercantile system of Smith's era can be understood as the collective consequence of the self-interested motives and activities of these dominant categories of economic agents. The challenge for him was to argue a reform analysis in which the character and motivations of the capitalists was accepted as natural. Yet, at the same time, he wanted to ensure that they were so situated, and thus contained and constrained, as to render the detrimental effects of their conduct on aggregate and per capita material welfare minimal, given the essential premiss of maintaining agent liberty.

5.3   Human agency in the operations of a mercantilist economy

Smith's observations of the actual 'commercial' system made it plain that it was replete with 'a hundred impertinent obstructions with which the folly of human laws too often encumbers its operations' (WN, p. 540). All of these effectively impeded individual liberty so that even the most basic conditions for the ideal functioning of an economic system based on capital in the means of production did not exist. Smith reminded his readers of the 'perfectly self-evident' premiss that 'consumption is the sole end and purpose of all production; and the interest of the producer ought to be attended to, only so far as it may be necessary for promoting that of the consumer' (WN, p. 660). Reality was, of course, quite different. The impediments to agents' freedom in fact took the form of a bias in the system towards the immediate interests of producers of commodities to the exclusion of the interests of consumers: 'In the mercantile system, the interest of the consumer is almost constantly sacrificed to that of the producer; and it seems to consider production, and not consumption, as the ultimate end and object of all industry and commerce' (WN, p. 660). Smith was in no doubt, too, that such a situation had been engineered by the collusions and influence of merchants and manufacturers (WN, p. 661). What disturbed him first and foremost about this constructivist bias in the system in favour of producers was that it was intellectually founded upon what he considered to be a false doctrine about the *nature* and the *causes* of the wealth of nations.

Right from the beginning of the WN, Smith had emphasized that his conception of wealth comprised a flow of real commodities measured on a per capita basis. His single-minded imperative was to promote the cheapness and plenty of domestically available consumer goods. This was in stark contrast to contemporary mercantilist doctrine in which real commodities were but a means to the accumulation of wealth as a stock of money, largely in precious metal form, in the hands of a minority of rich merchants. Put simply, a 'rich country, in the same manner as a rich man, is supposed to be a country abounding in money; and to heap up gold and silver in any country is supposed to be the readiest way to enrich it', and it seemed to follow that 'to multiply those metals ought, ... upon that account, to be the great object of its political oeconomy' (WN, pp. 429, 430). Smith rejected such notions as patently unrealistic: 'It would be too ridiculous to go about seriously to prove,' he argued, 'that wealth does not consist in money, or in gold and silver; *but in what money purchases, and is valuable only for purchasing*'

(WN, p. 438, emphasis added). He drew a satirical and homely, but, at the time, probably a very cogent, analogy to emphasize this essential point:

> To attempt to increase the wealth of any country, either by introducing or by detaining in it an unnecessary quantity of gold and silver, is as absurd as it would be to attempt to increase the good cheer of private families, by obliging them to keep an unnecessary number of kitchen utensils. As the expence of purchasing those unnecessary utensils would diminish instead of increasing either the quantity or goodness of the family provisions; so the expence of purchasing an unnecessary quantity of gold and silver must, in every country, as necessarily diminish the wealth which feeds, cloaths, and lodges, which maintains and employs the people. Gold and silver, whether in the shape of coin or of plate, are utensils, it must be remembered, as much as the furniture of the kitchen. (WN, p. 440)

Not only did this cleverly devised passage convey the pointless nature of monetary wealth accumulation in and of itself, but it sustained the fact that gold and silver money was an essential and very useful *component* of the nation's capital, just as *some* utensils were essential to furnish a kitchen. But, he went on, just as the availability of utensils would be taken care of by the exigencies of kitchen activities, the needs of production and/or trade would take care of the provision of the correct amount of the money commodities (WN, pp. 435ff, 447). It may well be that these assertions, along with other aspects of Smith's representation of the doctrine, drew only a caricature and neglected some of the more sophisticated writings of the period, but the fact was that it was this naive version of the mercantilist arguments which was popularly understood and instrumental in the practical and detrimental effects of their propaganda (WN, pp. 449–50; and see La Nauze, 1937).

The most obvious manifestation of the influence of mercantilist notions became an extensive complex of regulations, some de jure and some de facto, reaching into most aspects of production and trade so as to influence the balance of trade with other countries. The important twist that Smith gave to his critique of these regulations was that, 'without taking much further notice of their supposed tendency to bring money into the country', he proceeded to consider 'chiefly what are likely to be the effects of each of them upon the annual produce of its industry'. His primary objective was to show that, 'according as they tend either to increase or diminish the value of this annual produce, they must evidently tend either to increase or diminish the real wealth and revenue of the country' (WN, p. 451). Most generally put, his concern was that:

> No regulation of commerce can increase the quantity of industry in any society beyond what its capital can maintain. It can only divert a part of it into a direction into which it might otherwise not have gone; and it is by no means certain that this

artificial direction is likely to be more advantageous to the society than that into which it would have gone of its own accord. (WN, p. 453)

Smith believed that, almost inevitably, the constructivist direction of re-sources by agents themselves would have a negative impact on aggregate real production: 'I have never known much good to be done by those who af-fected to trade for the publick good' (WN, p. 456). The message of his reasoning about agents situated in the 'ideal' commercial state was that 'without any intervention of law, ... the private interests and passions of men naturally lead them to divide and distribute the stock of every society, among all the different employments carried on in it, as nearly as possible in the proportion which is most agreeable to the interest of the whole society' (WN, p. 630). By contrast, 'all the different regulations of the mercantile system, necessarily derange more or less this natural and most advantageous distribu-tion of stock', for their effect 'can only be to force the trade of a country into a channel much less advantageous than that in which it would naturally run of its own accord' (WN, pp. 630, 506).

The evolution of an economic system in which minority groups of human agents were able to further their interests at the expense of the majority was consistent with Smith's perception of the particular characteristics of human nature that dominate in the material world. Agents base their market conduct on the fact that their economic relations with others are functionally rather than personally based and, therefore, independent of the bonds and concerns of sympathetic sentiments. Self-interest, pursued in this case in the form of mercantile conspiracy and collusion, leaves the agents involved untroubled by any of the established moral rules that influence closer, more intimate human relations. These rules remain intact, but the actions of agents in matters economic are very largely beyond their reach. This emphasis on self-interest is combined with the agents' imperative of bettering their condition in the drive by each individually to appropriate as much of the value of the net revenue generated in any period as possible, with the minimum outlay of material resources and human effort. That is, each mercantile agent sets out to secure a position of economic advantage through appropriate manipulation of the inherited system. The means by which this could be assured involved the adoption of a collusive approach towards participation in the economic process in order to avoid the exigencies of competition with other agents who have like interests. In the case of manufacturers, joint control over production and marketing was sought and, in the case of merchants, joint control over conditions of commodity sales.

In the WN, Smith first confronted the potential for contrived economic malpractice along these lines when he considered the theoretical possibility of the exercise of monopoly power in the operations of the markets for resources and commodities. As he was to put it at one point concerning its practical relevance, although 'monopoly ... is a great enemy of good management', it was still the case that 'monopoly of one kind or another, indeed, seems to be the sole engine of the mercantile system' (pp. 163, 630). The centrepiece of his analysis of this phenomenon was the concept of a natural price for each commodity, itself dependent upon the concept of a natural rate of return to the owners of each category of resource input. As a matter of principle, the market price of a commodity or resource input could be expected to settle at the natural level over time, were it not for deviations induced by the continuation of accidental and/or contrived conditions in the market-place which impede the work of the 'invisible hand'. As mentioned earlier, Smith likened the market price–natural price relation to a gravitational tendency which would only be realized under the ideal and sustained conditions of human agency comprising 'perfect liberty' for agents in all their economic operations, including the perfectly free mobility of their resources.

This is a significant assertion, for, ironically, it provides the basis for understanding the means by which agents could conspire to raise and maintain prices above the natural level and thereby redistribute incomes in favour of themselves. The theoretical mechanism here specified the potential for some agents to charge a monopoly price for their resource, either directly or, most often, indirectly through the restricted supply of the commodity they produce. Smith granted that the basis for sustaining the market price for a significant time above the natural price could be some accidental or natural advantage enjoyed by the producer. Here he included such situations as one of high levels of effective demand for a particular commodity which a producer can keep secret, at least for some period of time, and, meanwhile, enjoy the supra-natural profits. Also a producer who discovers and keeps secret some cost-reducing technique will enjoy above-normal profits, although in this case the gain can be obtained at the natural price and does not need any restriction of supply at all. A further case that he cited was the return of supra-natural rents from scarce land with special advantages for raising produce for which there is always an excess of effective demand, such as fine wine. This represents what may be called a natural monopoly and is sustainable for indefinite periods. But monopoly power could also be attributable to some externally determined 'particular regulations of police' which apply to the operations of some specific lines of production or trade: 'A monopoly granted either to an individual or to a trading company has the same effect as a secret in trade or manufactures' (WN, pp. 77, 78). The general principle which Smith posited on the basis of these examples was that 'the monopolists, by keeping the market constantly under-stocked, by never fully supplying the effectual demand, sell their commodity much above the natural price, and raise their emoluments, ... greatly above their natural rate. The price of monopoly is upon every occasion the highest which can be got' (WN, pp. 78–9). He recorded that the mercantile agents had the power to affect and control both ends, as it were, of their economic well-being. They did so by means of contrived measures to ensure the minimization of costs of production flowing from labour and raw material inputs and to ensure the maximization of commodity sales revenue through exports and domestic consumption at the highest possible prices (cf. WN, p. 353).

At the cost end, they conspired to ensure that real wages were kept to the absolute minimum consistent with the sufficient short-term and long-term supply of labour services. The wage rate was set nominally, given the current price of provisions, by means of a bargained contract between a worker and a master employer. Smith was quite frank about the realities of this bargaining process as they involve and affect the two parties. To begin with, 'the workmen desire to get as much, the masters to give as little as possible [, with the] former ... disposed to combine in order to raise, the latter in order to lower the wages of labour' (WN, p. 83). In practice, the operation of these principles was very heavily biased towards the interests of the masters in Smith's era. The outcome of the bargain depended on the relative strengths of positions which the parties hold in the negotiations. For workers, gaining such collective strength was fraught with difficulties due essentially to the formal proscribing of combinations for this purpose. At times, he noted, workers were prepared to combine locally under especially strained circumstances of high priced provisions or where the profit return of masters was known and considered to be so excessive as to incite a degree of resentment which led to organized agitation for higher wages. The result was frequently a violent confrontation which could only result in notorious publicity for the workers and the intervention of the legal authorities to punish the leaders. There was little hope ever that their wage position could be improved by such confrontation (WN, pp. 84–5; cf. pp. 157–8).

The view from the perspective of the masters was in radical contrast to this and they, 'upon all ordinary occasions, have the advantage in the dispute, and force the other into a compliance with their terms' (WN, p. 83). Masters operate with the distinct advantage that their smaller numbers enable them to combine more readily and with greater secrecy in order to resist any upward pressure on or to effect any downward adjustment in wages. Their combinations were not illegal and, indeed, 'whenever the legislature attempts to regulate the differences between masters and their workmen, its counsellors are always the masters'. Masters had the generalized support of a bevy of statutes introduced specifically to regulate conditions of particular trades. These enabled them to 'enter into a private bond or agreement, not to give more than a certain wage under a certain penalty' and had the effect of enforcing 'by law that very regulation which masters sometimes attempt to establish by such combinations' (WN, pp. 84, 157–8). Individually, masters were also under some moral pressure to conform to the set wages: 'To violate this combination is every where a most unpopular action, and a sort of reproach to a master among his neighbours and equals' (WN, p. 84). And, in spite of the fact that they are, at least, 'always and every where in a sort of tacit, but constant and uniform combination', they received little publicity 'because it is the usual, and one may say, the natural state of things which nobody ever hears of' (WN, p. 84). In comparison with workers, what is more, the masters have the economic advantage of being able to sustain themselves materially for a substantial period of time without active production by means of running down their wealth. Employment for workers was a much more immediate imperative. So, while 'in the long run the workman may be as necessary to his master as his master is to him, ... the necessity is not so immediate' (WN, p. 84). All in all, then, under the terms of the organization of 'commercial' capitalism, the owners of means of production could be assured that, in other than boom times when labour became scarce, the cost of this most pervasive of inputs to production would be largely under their control and as close to the subsistence minimum as was socially and politically acceptable.

At the other end of the total process of production and realization of commodities through their sale, although Smith's analysis lacked precision on the matter, it must be assumed that the mercantile agents colluded on the matter of price. Their objective was to ensure that the wholesale and retail market prices they received were as high as possible and yet consistent with the maximization of revenues, given the constraints of effective demand patterns and elasticities in domestic and export markets. Expressed in very general terms, the situation was such that 'people of the same trade seldom meet together, even for merriment and diversion, but the conversation ends in a conspiracy against the publick, or in some contrivance to raise prices'. Moreover, Smith went on, 'it is impossible indeed to prevent such meetings, by any law which either could be executed, or would be consistent with liberty and justice' (WN, p. 145). Such was Smith's own socialization that he apparently failed to notice the irony of this statement vis-à-vis his earlier implicit acceptance of the Draconian anti-combination laws affecting workers. Presumably, by the standards of the period, these laws were 'consistent with liberty and justice' and presented little problem of enforcement. He was of the view, though, that a main source of exacerbation of mercantilist misconduct was the opportunity for and protection of it afforded by a complex web of formalized and unformalized institutional and regulatory structures and practices which comprised the operational situations of the agents concerned.

From this point onwards, the approach adopted by Smith in the WN was to seek out all the potential sources of constructed monopoly power in the mercantile economy. His intention was to expose these sources and to set about formulating a strategy of reforms which would remove them by destroying or constraining their means of operation.

The contemporary mercantile system observed by Smith was one in which the functional form of the participation in the economic process by all agents was in some way affected by contrived characteristics of the situations in which they had to operate. For the most part, these situations comprised formalized and/or unformalized institutional structures which had evolved or been constructed for the purposes of controlling these agent functions. The impact on each category of participant varied, but with an inevitably either positive or negative bias in terms of the share of material welfare enjoyed by the group. Already, from the above arguments, it is apparent that it was the capitalist owners of the means of production and commodity distribution, most especially the manufacturers and merchants, whose inherent and contrived situations were such as to give them positive monopoly power to pursue their economic self-interests to the disadvantage of the society as a whole, especially the vast majority of agents whose only possession is their capacity to provide labour services from day to day. These mercantile orders of agents had a continuing interest in restricting the opportunity for and the effects of competition, contrary to the interest of the domestic public: 'to narrow the competition must always ... serve only to enable the dealers, by raising their profits above what they naturally would be, to levy, for their own benefit, an absurd tax upon the rest of their fellow-citizens' (WN, p. 267). Such inclinations by mercantile groups led Smith to express the caveat that 'The proposal of any new law or regulation of commerce which comes from this order, ought always to be listened to with great precaution ... . It comes from an order of men, ... who have generally an interest to deceive and even to oppress the publick, and who accordingly have, upon many occasions, both deceived and oppressed it' (WN, p. 267).

Indeed, from time to time, the WN contains a stringent critique of and a hostile stance against the conduct of all mercantile agents who exercised their contrived powers within the system to advantage themselves. Recall how any meeting of mercantile groups was claimed to end 'in a conspiracy against the publick, or in some contrivance to raise prices' (WN, p. 145). This accusation was a reflection of the sort of *obiter dicta* which occur from time to time throughout the WN slighting the character and conduct of mercantile agents. Some of these derogatory asides are listed below (cf. Rosenberg, 1979, p. 21):

- 'the clamour and sophistry of merchants and manufacturers' (p. 144);

- 'The sneaking arts of underling tradesmen' (p. 493);
- 'the impertinent jealousy of merchants and manufacturers' (p. 493);
- 'the mean rapacity, the monopolizing spirit of merchants and manufacturers' (p. 493);
- 'the interested sophistry of merchants and manufacturers [which] confounded the common sense of mankind' (p. 494);
- 'the passionate confidence of interested falsehood' of merchants and manufacturers (p. 496);
- the 'mean and malignant expedients' of merchants and manufacturers (p. 610);
- the laws 'which the clamour of our merchants and manufacturers has extorted from the legislature, for the support of their own absurd and oppressive monopolies ... like the laws of Draco, ... may be said to be all written in blood' (p. 648).

This hostile, even at times vituperative, attitude towards the mercantile groups represents rather an irony, if not a paradox, in Smith's work for at least two reasons which are worth noting. First of all, it was the rise of these mercantile agents to dominance with the development of towns that began and furthered the emergence of the bulk of people from the dark ages of feudal servitude and rural poverty. This particular process was well described by Smith in Book III of the WN. While it is evident that, for most of these people, the improvement of social and material welfare was only a matter of degree, Smith was sanguine that the economic development process under an 'ideal' free-market capitalism would ultimately benefit all people absolutely, albeit not with any great advances towards any simple equality in the relativities of income and wealth distribution. The agents who must be responsible for this advance were those very manufacturers and merchants he chose to subject to the sort of harsh abuse cited above and whose pecuniary incentives to participate in the development process he wanted to curtail.

Secondly, and relatedly, it was doubly ironic that he accepted the exigencies of human nature as given, and recognized the significance of situations in affecting actual conduct, while at the same time being prepared to denigrate the mercantile agents for, so to say, doing what came naturally. Anyone who could write that 'such, it seems, is the natural insolence of man, that he almost always disdains to use the good instrument, except when he cannot or dare not use the bad one', could have perhaps been less inclined to condemn the *systemically induced* opportunism of these agents (WN, p. 799). At one point, Smith showed more sympathy for agents who face situational conditions which enable them to serve their own interests first: 'It is the system of government, the situation in which they are placed, that I mean to censure; not the character of those who have acted in it. *They acted as their situation naturally directed*' (WN, p. 641, emphasis added). The generalized implications of this passage are given extra weight when we recall that, for Smith, human agents born as essentially equal beings are then the subjects of their developmental environment (WN, pp. 28–9; cf. Rosenberg, 1984, p. 111 and n.27). The clue here for any viable reforms to the mercantile system that were to be founded on the principle of liberty was to ensure that the volitional containment of agents by their situations harnessed their self-interest for the public benefit.

The more apparent of the contrived institutional structures which dominated the situationally directed economic activity of human agents in the mercantile era were many and varied. Smith devoted a significant proportion of the WN, especially in Book IV, to detailing these and their effects on the state and progress of cheapness and plenty of consumer commodities. Leaving aside such details here, it remains clear that the essential thrust of his critique was that this complex body of regulations and institutions, which he referred to generically as 'the Policy of Europe', had been constructed largely at the collective behest of the mercantile groups operating through the parliament of the day, necessarily with the imprimatur or acquiescence of the ruling landed aristocracy. He referred on several occasions to the ability of these groups to 'extort' the legislative support for industry and trade from the members of parliament so that it was 'the industry which is carried on for the benefit of the rich and the powerful, that is principally encouraged by our mercantile system' (WN, p. 644; cf. pp. 643, 648). His observation of the situation led him to conclude that the reason for the success of these 'extortions' was to be found in the intellectual propaganda perpetrated by the mercantilists on the basis of tendentious arguments, albeit in a sense innocently, given the accepted dogma of the era (WN, p. 434). Reinforcement for this propagandist approach by mercantile groups was ensured by the fact that any 'member of parliament who supports every proposal for strengthening ... monopoly, is sure to acquire not only the reputation of understanding trade, but great popularity and influence with an order of men whose numbers and wealth render them of great importance'. By contrast, such was the influence of these groups that any parliamentarian who attempted to thwart their monopolistic endeavours, however well-intentioned and whatever his rank, could not protect himself from 'the most infamous abuse and detraction, from personal insults, nor sometimes from real danger, arising from the insolent outrage of furious and disappointed monopolists' (WN, p. 471).

The ultimate effect, then, of these intellectually contrived political constructs was to facilitate the conspiratorial and collusive practices of mercantile interests and to ensure their control over their own economic destiny. The regulations and institutions concerned reached into the organization and operations of most aspects of the production and the domestic and overseas exchange of commodities, with the result that market uncertainties and contingencies that would be generated by unrestricted entry and competition were reduced through the existence and exercise of monopoly power. More specifically, the effect was to direct the allocation of resources, especially the capital stock and the labour which it pulled along with it, towards those sectors of production and trade in which such power was established and which thus ensured the greatest and most secure rate of return. An integral part of this process was the restriction of output in order to maintain upward pressure on the price and sales revenue combination received by the owners of capital. The key consequence which followed from such a controlled economic environment was a differential structure of wage and profit rates which was not in accordance with the natural differences of the employments themselves as they would emerge in a system of perfect liberty (WN, pp. 135ff, 452ff).

Throughout his extended exposé of the specific measures to control domestic and international trade which the mercantile groups had been able to have established, Smith's stance was very predominantly critical. As already indicated in the *obiter dicta* concerning the conduct of these categories of agents quoted earlier, most of which were in fact elicited in the context of his critique of mercantilist controls, at times his remarks bordered on the vituperative. It is to be suspected that such expressions of outrage were designed to give maximum propaganda effect to the call for reforms to the system which pervaded the whole argument. In the next section, Smith's reform strategy is considered briefly from the perspective of its implications for the conduct of human agents.

5.4 Containing human agency by reforms

The general requirement for effecting the reform strategy to be found in the WN was the enforced revision of the various dimensions of the situations and conditions which agents confront in their participation in the economic process. What it is important to recognize is that, in deliberating about his reforms, *Smith took the intrinsic character and natural conduct of all economic agents as given.* His inspiration was to realize that the significant core of agents' economic conduct is ultimately a product of the inherited situation in and through which they are initially socialized and educated as youngsters. Similarly, in their adult lives, they are effectively coerced, perhaps with a degree of volitional cooperation, to operate in such predetermined situations. At all stages of human life, then, the situational environment in which agents live acts reflexively to affect their character and conduct. It is worth noting, in passing, that it was for this reason that Smith was so conscious of the need for a properly designed and publically funded education system. He argued for it on the grounds that it would prepare people to become more effective employees and masters, as well as mitigating against some of the otherwise stupefying effects of the day-to-day drudgery of labour that afflicted the majority of them. In the case of the latter ground, he asserted that an educated populace would have the added advantage of being more politically reliable and stable because of their more discerning responses to any advocacy of rebellion (WN, pp. 781ff). As a consequence of these sensibilities, the most viable reform measures were perceived by Smith to be those which direct attention to the social and economic system rather than to the characteristics of agents themselves; that is, towards measures which appropriately contain, direct and constrain, as well as facilitate, the natural inclinations of egoistic human agents in such a way that each individual's character and the conduct through which it is manifested are brought into coincidence with that which serves the collective interest.

Some care is needed in order accurately to represent the nature of Smith's critical onslaught against the regulation of commercial activity, for it is all too easy to portray him as simply a single-minded arch libertarian. There can be no doubt about his essentially laissez-faire credentials, for the key mode of reform which he advocated comprised the removal of all impediments to free entry to and effective competition in industry and trade. But, as we shall see below, his reforms were cautiously tempered by a recognition that some containment and direction of the excesses of mercantile self-interest through formal interventions remained a necessary condition for the maximum social benefit from real wealth creation and growth to be assured.

The thrust of all mercantile collusive endeavours to cajole and conspire in their own commercial interests was the reduction of competition within trades and the facilitation of monopoly power controls over the costs of production and purchases and over the prices and quantities of commodities on sale. These controls also extended to the division of commodity sales between domestic and foreign markets and to the sale of foreign commodities in domestic markets. In all such cases of controls, Smith's critique and espousal of their removal was guided by what he believed to be the 'ideal' alternative of a free market regime, a 'system of liberty', in which manufacturers and merchants would be induced to operate as individual independent agents. His objective was to show how agents situated in this alternative commercial environment could be led voluntarily to conduct their business in a way that would ensure the maximum collective interest of all people. As we saw in the previous section, the crucial mechanism here was the allocation of their resources according to free-market signals which centred around the natural rates of return to input factors. The allocation process related especially to capital as the operationally primary input from an organizational and control perspective. It was capital which facilitated the employment of labour and land, and provided the financial advances to purchase the raw materials and machinery used in production. It also funded the establishment of merchant stocks and provided other necessary advances required for engaging in trade.

Smith's objective was to see the removal of all sorts of regulatory structures designed to impede the operation of free production and trade by redirecting resources in a way which served only the interests of the mercantile agents. He inferred that such removal would, *by itself*, restore an adequately competitive market structure as the natural alternative (WN, p. 687). The principle upon which this claim depended was quite clearly that the collective outcome of the pursuit of self-interest by individual agents was not a product of such conduct per se. Rather the collective results were determined by the situational conditions in which those interests were pursued. However, although his more pragmatic arguments on this point remained ambiguous, the one thing which interpreters generally agree upon is that, whatever comprised the substance of the laissez-faire doctrine so often attributed to him, he never intended to espouse the concept of perfect competition (see especially McNulty, 1967; Richardson, 1975; Jensen, 1984). What seemed to matter more to Smith in the reform of market conduct was that the *spirit of competition* between participating agents be restored, with the precise number of competitors this carried with it being of lesser importance. A basic principle which he so astutely recognized as pertinent to the whole issue of the nature of competition was that the stable number of competitors in a market segment was ultimately delimited by the condition that each be economically viable in terms of at least yielding natural returns to the resources used. Consequently the number was determined primarily by the effectual demand scale of that market, and by the associated degree of technical division of labour that this made possible, with the lower limit being just two participants. He envisaged that, in some market situations, a duopoly could well be the only *potentially* competitive condition possible (WN, pp. 361–2). Then, whatever the merits of expanding the number of competitors might be, there was an upper limit to that number which any size of a particular market segment could support. This was something free agents would have to sort out through their operations: 'Their competition might perhaps ruin some of themselves; but to take care of this is the business of the parties concerned, and it may safely be trusted to their discretion' (WN, p. 362; cf. pp. 144–5). Clearly there is no evidence here of a notion of competition whose effectiveness is dependent upon agent numbers per se.

For Smith, competition was a *process* involving agents' decisions and actions: that is, a process of human agency in which they pursued the maximum returns to their input factors, guided by market price signals. The response mechanism, as we have seen, comprised the reallocation of resources under an agent's control when the realized price was different from the established natural price. The equilibrium result towards which the system would thereby naturally gravitate, he claimed, was one in which, for all commodities, supply equals effectual demand. But competition was not adequately represented by such a *state* of equilibrium. Rather, its existence was manifested as the process by means of which markets tend towards it as a result of the freedom of agents to respond to price signals. For Smith, innocent of the profound abstractions designed to restrict the scope and complexity of agent conduct, and of the associated mathematical developments which were to follow, the inelegance and imprecision of this presentation of a free market 'ideal' was of no concern. Indeed it is most apt to describe his theory of competition as a theory of disequilibrium-induced tendencies.

Free and effective, if imperfect, competition was, then, the crucial condition which would ensure the maximization of the flow of real per capita wealth in any period of time and its growth over time. This was the objective which underpinned all of Smith's analyses which were directed towards his advocacy of reforms. The belief behind the analysis in the WN appears to have been the sanguine, and rather naive, one that, if the *contrived opportunities* for agents to conspire and collude were dismantled, then this effective competition between them would be the natural result, even when the number of competitors was severely circumscribed by the conditions for economic viability. So it was, he reasoned, that the specific reform measures to be recommended in order to achieve his pragmatic 'ideal' economy and society comprised largely the removal of situational opportunities for the exercise of mercantile monopoly power.

As a matter of strategy, what Smith realized all too clearly was that his *advocacy* of a reform programme which would establish a perfect 'system of liberty' *could not make it so*. There would remain limits to the degree of liberty possible within any 'commercial' system consequent upon the implementation of the reforms proposed, as a matter both of reasoned and of practical necessity. On the former count, he wrote that some

> regulations may, no doubt, be considered as in some respects a violation of natural liberty. But those exertions of the natural liberty of a few individuals, which might endanger the security of the whole society, are, and ought to be, restrained by the laws of all governments; of the most free, as well as of the most despotical. (WN, p. 324)

And, concerning the practicalities of liberal reforms, he concluded that

> to expect, indeed, that the freedom of trade should ever be entirely restored in Great Britain, is as absurd as to expect that an Oceana or Utopia should ever be established in it. Not only the prejudices of the publick, but what is much more unconquerable, the private interests of many individuals, irresistibly oppose it. (WN, p. 471)

What was at issue in these qualifications to the ideals of reform was first and foremost a matter of principle. While Smith may have formulated an economic 'ideal' which would appropriately contain and direct self-interest so as to maximize social welfare, he paid some limited attention to the *political* dimensions of the implementation process, too. According to George Stigler, though, Smith left us with a major paradox by not providing a sufficiently developed political theory based on self-interest which is compatible with his economic 'ideal' (Stigler, 1975, *passim*). Stigler's particular concern is that the dominance of egoistic motives and calculations concerning action was not elicited in the political context as the most reliable principle upon which to found the contemporaneous reforms needed at that level. Without the cooperation of the parliamentarians, the removal of mercantile impediments to free trade could not proceed by legislative means. What Smith did not establish was how this cooperation was to be assured through containment and direction of the self-interest of these political human agents within the parliamentary system. A.W. Coats's response to this alleged paradox in Smith is to suggest that the dominance of self-interest, on the basis of which human agents calculate and act in the economic sphere, is not immediately transferable to the political context (Coats, 1984, *passim*). Especially is this one area of human agency where the nature of the choices and decisions to be made, and the social relations which influence them, rule out the exclusive rationale of self-interest. If Smith realized this, as a full appreciation of his model of the human agent would suggest he did, then Stigler's critique is misdirected. However the problem to which he drew attention did remain without due attention in the WN.

Perhaps in recognition of the need for active political involvement, in espousing the removal of all possible impediments to the free mobility of resources and to free trade in commodities domestically and internationally, Smith remained conscious that the process of reform would have to be a gradual one, as well as one which could never be complete. The reason for this was given as the significant disruption to existing trade, and to the agent interests concerned, that would follow the removal of mercantile regulations and protections. Smith referred to situations where, because long-established mercantile privileges were involved, 'humanity may ... require that the freedom of trade should be restored only by slow gradations, and with a good deal of reserve and circumspection' in order to avoid depriving 'all at once many thousands of our people of their ordinary employment and means of subsistence' (WN, p. 469; cf. p. 606).

Overall, Smith was certain that some of the regulations which were the manifestations of the interventions by government in the commercial sector would have to remain as an integral part of the reform outcomes. To begin with, all monopoly power could not and should not be ruled out completely by whatever means were to be used to restore competition in markets. In the case of undertakers prepared to be involved in high-risk ventures, he accepted that 'it may not be unreasonable to incorporate them into a joint stock company, and to grant them, in the case of their success, a monopoly of the trade for a certain number of years' (WN, p. 754). Also the provision of certain commercial support services was considered to be appropriately carried on through joint stock companies because, for them, all of their operations 'are capable of being reduced to what is called a routine, or to such a uniformity of method as admits of little or no variation', leaving little scope for the realization of monopoly power (WN, p. 756; and ff). Included here were banking, commercial insurance, canal services and water supply services. Smith also saw in the regulation of imports some possibility for the retention of protective measures even in an environment of predominantly free trade. These were essentially designed to ensure the effective continuation of domestic industry in particular lines of production (WN, pp 463ff).

In Smith's 'system of liberty', then, government would remain active, despite his firmly held conviction that, in the general course of its economic history, 'the profusion of government must, undoubtedly, have retarded the natural progress of England towards wealth and improvement' (WN, p. 345; see Viner, 1984b; Rosenberg, 1984; and R.H. Campbell and Skinner, 1976, pp. 34ff). However the activities directed by parliament on behalf of the sovereign were mostly to be confined to the performance of 'three duties of great importance, ... plain and intelligible to common understandings' (WN, p. 687). These were the provision of defence and justice, along with the more open-ended 'duty of erecting and maintaining certain publick works and certain publick institutions, which it can never be for the interest of any individual, or small number of individuals, to erect and maintain'. Most of such public facilities could not be left to private-sector operations because the pecuniary rate of return that could be secured was insufficient to ensure the required investments, even though the social returns might be considerable (WN, pp. 687–8). Smith devoted the very long Part V of the WN to the economic and other issues raised by the maintenance of an active government sector in an otherwise private free-enterprise commercial system. The important general conclusion that can be gleaned from this extensive inquiry is a confirmation that he remained committed to a properly designed and circumscribed structure of government intervention and participation in the economy of a 'system of liberty'. He argued that this would ensure a sustained and growing maximization of material wealth per capita, albeit with little concern for other than its 'natural', socially acceptable distribution.

6 Human agency and Smith's methodology

The purpose of this chapter is to draw together the important facets of Smith's representation of human agents and agency in political economy and to summarize the extent to which this representation can be shown to have shaped the methodological legacy implicit in his work. Beyond some early comments on the methodology of the natural sciences, Smith did not provide any more detailed or specific treatment of the issue, especially as it applied to political economy. What degree of methodological awareness directed his composition of the WN must be gleaned by implication. It is apparent from the nature of the work, though, that any methodological preconceptions which he held as a result of his early ventures into the philosophy of science were not allowed directly to determine the analytical design or strategy of the WN. The methodological bases of his treatise were rather those which Smith found it most appropriate, more or less consciously, to adopt for each particular dimension of its wide and varied substantive coverage of economic, social and historical material.

At a quite fundamental level, Smith carried forward the empiricist tradition of Locke and Newton, especially by way of his critical respect for the work of Hume. The basis of all knowledge was observation, experiment and experience. The world comprised a set of systems which worked by mechanisms about which human analysts could learn by probing their hidden logic. We should recall the analogy of the fob watch, the workings of which were exposed by prising off its back cover. Moral philosophers believed that much the same could be done in order to explain human and social phenomena as the product of the 'machinery' of society, as it were. They drew especially on the idea that something equivalent to gravity must be acting to ensure the cohesion of societies, especially once the work of Hobbes and Mandeville had outraged the conservative intellectuals and theologians with their claims that human agents were dogged egoists and little more. For Hobbes in particular, humankind needed to be controlled by extensive artificially devised institutional constraints. Sentimentalist reactions sought an alternative binding force. They found it in the innate moral virtue which derived from sympathy and benevolence towards others and claimed it to be a sufficient sentimental counterweight to keep self-interest under control. Their arguments stood Hobbes on his head by asserting that the human malevolence which flowed from egoism was environmentally generated rather than innate. The idea dawned that the character and conduct of human individuals was determined by the situations in which they were placed. Social reform could thus ensure individual well-being and social harmony by removing the causes of economic disadvantage and counteracting the dominance of inherited privilege, both of which contributed to the brutish state in which the poor lived.

It was at this point that Smith entered the intellectual lists and took up his inquiries into these issues. He set out to rewrite moral philosophy by adopting and adapting the particular threads of antecedent work which he found congenial. His essential premiss was that moral science could only proceed from a thorough understanding of human nature. As a consequence, his life's project began with the TMS, the objective of which was to examine how much of the general cohesion of the complex life-world of human agents could be accounted for by the balancing of moral sentiments. His studies, along with his own observations and introspections, made it clear, that outside the immediate family group, self-interest was the dominant motivation for human action. As societies did not explode into Hobbesian ego-driven chaos, it was equally evident that some sympathetic sentiment must be keeping people from destroying each other in the struggle to maximize returns to their egos. Smith's inquiries in the TMS largely confirmed this state of moral balance. The sentimental make-up of human agents was such as to ensure that, to a significant extent, social harmony and stability could depend upon moral rules for their maintenance. However, following out the implications of the gravity analogy as it was argued by Hutcheson and Hume, Smith also accepted the application of a sort of inverse square rule to the degree of sentimental centripetal force between two agents as their intersubjective distance increased. He reasoned that, although the sentiment of self-interest was ever-present as a dominant motivating force for human agents, as their relations with others became increasingly functional and anonymous, and thus distant, the impact of sympathetic sentiments on their conduct decreased rapidly. For close relations with family and friends, the intersubjectivity was of a purely sentimental nature. For the relationships that facilitated the fundamental processes of material provisioning in a world of specialization and division of labour, the interdependence was purely functional. Their rationale was some reciprocal material benefit with no expectation of emotional returns. Benevolence and like sentiments had no role at all to play and some other explanation for the social cohesion of economically interdependent agents was required. To a limited extent, it was necessary to invoke the institutions of justice to account for this cohesion. The basic conditions for the protection of rights and property could only be established by a constructivist system of laws and sanctions. It was this dimension of social life which was to be addressed by Smith in the unfinished project on Jurisprudence of which the LJ reports are the only extant remains. In that context already it was apparent to him that, to account for the involvement of human agents in the economic extensions of moral philosophy covered by the rubric of Police, more than self-interest plus justice would be needed.

The consequent intention of the WN was to reveal how the contemporary economy operated as a human system by adapting and extending the theories of the TMS and the observations of the LJ. Primarily this involved a shift of emphasis to one particular facet of human existence, albeit a most fundamental one. Smith's focus was now on a system whose phenomena are direct functions of a complex aggregation of individual human agent relations and actions that are directed by the physical, social and institutional situations through which they are realized. We should recall that the ultimate purpose of the inquiry into the nature and causes of the wealth of nations was to provide the understanding which would justify and facilitate systemic reform. Fundamental to Smith's analyses in this context was his belief that it was the functional and relational dimensions of their environment that could act to contain and constrain any negative consequences of encouraging and perpetuating the vital mobilizing force of economic self-interest. As he observed the burgeoning system of market capitalism that surrounded him, he found that its situational structures operated to exacerbate rather than mitigate the undesirable tendencies of mass egoism. It had provided a commercial environment replete with opportunities for the collusive pursuit of material self-interest by particular economic groups to the detriment of the collective welfare outcome for human agents generally. Smith emphasized that it was material wealth generation per capita which really measured the essential welfare consequences of production. The overwhelming and unrestrained pursuit of self-interest, which Smith referred to as the legitimate and omnipotent drive by agents 'to better their condition', was exercised within the systemic situation that we now generally refer to as mercantilism.

The system was characterized by a myriad of formal and informal, de jure and de facto, impediments to the free and natural operation of the markets of the capitalist economy. In particular, manufacturers and merchants had engineered a network of economic structures and institutions by manipulating the political system on the basis of the successful promotion of a false doctrine about the nature and causes of the wealth of nations. These constructed interventions in the economy were designed to ensure that the mercantile agents accrued a degree of monopoly power over their trading environment which promoted and secured their specific interests to the maximum possible extent, independently of the individual and collective consequences for the material welfare of others. Smith argued that it was the false and misleading mercantilist economic theory, so effectively used as the basis of pamphlet and other propaganda, which persuaded parliamentarians over the years to encourage the evolution of the system. Its negative economic consequences included the reduction of aggregate wealth production below its potential, or natural, level, by distorting the distribution of resources, the distortion of the distribution of the realized outputs away from that considered to be optimal, and a reduction of the rate of growth of real wealth below its inherent potential.

As far as Smith was concerned, the empirically observed economic system was able to be reduced by a process of simplifying abstraction to an essential and minimal logic of structure and operation in which the pursuit of self-interest by individual human agents could be shown to result in the maximum per capita production and growth of material wealth. In adopting this procedure, it was not his intention to apply an abstract methodology in any a priori, axiomatic form. The assumptions from which he argued, especially those relating to human agents and agency, were to be derived by induction from observation and introspection. For the purpose of modelling this abstracted 'ideal', the operation of the markets through which resources are directed to input sites and commodities are distributed to consumers had to be the manifestation of the choices and actions of free and independent agents acting purely in their own individual self-interest. The mobility of resources and commodities was assumed to be unimpeded and there was fully effective competition between the agents in all markets in which they participated. Under these conditions, commodity prices, along with the incomes of all agents with some claim to share in the revenues generated by virtue of their function in the social organization of production, would all 'gravitate' to their natural levels by means of the 'invisible hand' of competition operating in either the static or dynamic context. For Smith, then, it was this free-market, effectively-competitive capitalism which represented the 'ideal', and natural, version of the extant mercantilist economy. It might be added here that he realized quite clearly that this model was of a limited epistemological status. It could not be subjected to any *direct* test of its veracity because it had no empirical manifestation. Even were it to be effectively implemented as the result of a reform process, its actually observed operations would always be complicated by the existence of 'disturbing causes'.

This 'ideal' model of market capitalism, as it was constructed in Books I and II of the WN, was presented in a logical form that derived from the emphasis Smith put on the essential role of human agency in the generation of its object phenomena. Political economy was a moral science concerned with a crucial and major part of the total life-world and activities of human beings, as they are in observed reality. In this context, he chose to give heavy emphasis to the pursuit of self-interest by individual agents, the one dimension of the human character and conduct that he found to be *empirically* and pervasively the most relevant. Any intellectual representation and consequent understanding of economic phenomena had to be seen to be consistent with the self-interest premiss. Smith's analyses gave the impression that this premiss was to be considered axiomatic, but its status was far from being simply a priori. It had been shown to be logically connected with the total image of human nature worked out in the TMS and was consistent with what Smith believed he observed as underpinning the operations of the mercantilist system. The one thing that is evident, as far as we are able to tell from the construction of the argument of the WN, is that he put this empirically oriented requirement before any preconceived demands that particular epistemological expectations or methodological conformity may impose upon the exposition. There was simply no hint of such dogmatism anywhere in Smith's writings. The pluralist tenets of methodology which guided the construction of the WN were permitted to vary from time to time in accordance with the demands of the particular analytical object in focus and the expositional objective that Smith was seeking to achieve. Throughout the WN, there was no endeavour by Smith to introduce a strictly 'one-dimensional' and perfectly rational egoistic, maximizing human agent as the sole economic decision maker and actor. In order to support a purely axiomatic deductive methodology, this would have been the most tractable assumption to adopt, so that the human–behavioural facet of the logic of any argument was uniquely directed and wholly reliable. That is, the human agency in the analysis would appear as merely a behavioural equation or an objective function with a mechanistic form. There is little indication that Smith would have found such a naively rationalistic model of man congenial as a representation of human agents, even in those parts of the WN where his methodology came closest to using deductively reasoned logic to develop the 'ideal' version of the economy. It is, as a consequence, quite inaccurate to read into Smith's argument any methodologically preconceived model of the human agent along the lines that would ultimately be taken in formulating the concept of a 'classical economic man'. The agents represented in all of Smith's economic analyses were characterized by a complex of active attributes, with the effect that their egoistic pursuits in endeavouring 'to better their condition' were tempered from the outset. Their conduct was always contained and directed by the competitive market situation, backed up by an effective system of justice, in which they were conceived to operate.

So it was, then, that, even in the use of what most approximated the deductive methodology, Smith remained conscious of the complex nature of the origins in human agency of even the abstracted versions of capitalist phenomena. The outcome of this was a rather 'soft' deductively logical form of argument in which the conclusions were not tied back uniquely to the somewhat loosely expressed premises. Indeed, throughout much of the WN, the methodology was intentionally historical and empirical, although it should be added that there is no evidence that Smith considered that he had derived any generalized conclusions in the sense that a strictly demonstrative inductive logic would demand. He was not an historicist in this sense. His application of the historical methodology in the WN was confined to eliciting a descriptive representation of the evolution and contemporary character of the mercantile economy, especially in Books III and IV. The objective in these parts of his exposition was to establish the empirical form of the system of manufacturer and merchant privilege and distortion that was to be the target of his reform programme.

Essentially Smith's idea was that the existing system could be emasculated by the removal of its institutional supports. The reform process which was to be implemented was shown to be predominantly non–constructivist in nature. He posited the argument that the renovated system should be consistent with the previously established immanent logic of the extant, but distorted, version of itself. That logic, he envisaged, was to be made operationally effective by the *removal* of distortions rather than the addition of anything. The theoretical process by means of which the 'ideal' had been exposed was to be replicated in practice as far as actual conditions would allow. Smith had no delusions that he could be an effective 'man of system', setting out to show how to construct a new political economic order: he was no revolutionary in this respect. The 'system of liberty' was, for him, a natural state in which the contemporaneously constructed elements of intervention were able to be at a minimum, especially in the economic life of individual agents. The reforms would leave the inherent character of agents as they are within the system, but contain and redirect their voluntary actions so that collectively they optimize its material potentials.

In the next chapter, which opens Part II, devoted to the work of John Stuart Mill, I will explore the consequences that this imprecise and mixed methodological legacy left by Smith had for the subsequent evolution of political economy after the turn of the nineteenth century. Inevitably some took up and developed exclusively the nascent abstract–deductive approach to economic reasoning which they claimed to have identified in the WN and which they perceived as the only means by which their doctrine could achieve widespread respect as scientifically justified. For others, the dissenters as things turned out, Smith became the source of inspiration for inductively oriented historical methodology. The ultimate outcome of this ambiguous legacy for economic science is well known. 'Economic man' became the foundation of a body of abstract-deductive analyses presented with the maximum of rigour whatever the cost in terms of its failure to maintain contact with reality. But, as I will argue in some detail below, in the middle of all the subsequent methodological machinations consequent upon variable readings of the WN, John Stuart Mill should be given due weight as an accomplice in what happened. However this accusation of complicity needs to be tempered by the fact that he remained the one outstanding figure whose own philosophical erudition, and consequent methodological circumspection, rivalled that of Adam Smith. Mill's intellectual scope and sophistication ensured that he revealed an acute awareness of the implications of human agency for the methodology of political economy. What we will find, though, is that, compared to Smith, he was less concerned with the moral foundations of human agency and more concerned with its implications for the proper logical design of economic argument.

PART II

JOHN STUART MILL

7 'Economic man' and the formation of classical methodology

7.1 Introduction

My theme in this chapter is the rise to dominance of a classical methodology in which 'economic man' was the exclusive representation of the human agent in economic analyses. I intend to argue that this rise was due in the main to the intention of some of the key writers of the early nineteenth century to promote political economy as a science in the definitive sense that applied to the physical sciences. If deductive logic applied to axiomatic premises was to be the methodological form which economic arguments and explanations were to take, the troublesome subjectivism and contingency of human sentiments as the bases for action somehow had to be represented by an objective behavioural function. The motivations and responses of human agents had to be rendered uniquely directed and reliable. Any divergence from the hypothesized conduct and its origins were to be perceived as disturbances to what remained the essentially dominant forces affecting human economic agency.

When the writers of the nineteenth century reflected upon the legacy of Adam Smith in order to guide their deliberations about political economy, they found his message far from methodologically precise. In earlier chapters we have considered the origins of this legacy. In particular, those seeking to secure a scientific status for their ideas could not rely on the undisputed authority of the WN for the defence of their claims. What was missing in particular was any attempt by Smith to specify a rigorously reliable model of economic man which could be entered as an axiom in formal reasoning. The consequence was that his use of deduction was 'soft' and, as well as being intermixed with much historico-inductive argument, it lacked the definitude of conclusions that his successors sought. The methodological strategies subsequently defended ranged from what was soon to become the orthodoxy of treating the subject as a purely deductive science whose conclusions could be relied upon as essentially true to reality, leaving aside the particulars of any 'disturbing causes' that apply from time to time, to the heterodox critiques of such a position coming from the school of historicist and inductivist writers.

My specific objective in this chapter is to sketch in the substance of these interim controversies in classical methodology, with particular reference to the problem of representing human agency in analyses and to the rise to dominance of 'economic man' as the ultimately successful solution. It is intended that this sketch should form the backdrop to my deeper inquiry into John Stuart Mill's reactions to the state of economic methodology that he inherited.

7.2 The transition to classical methodology

The political economy of the nineteenth century began with the appearance of Say's *Traité d'Economie Politique*, published in 1803. Say took up and formalized the WN, a work that he found was in need of a more definitive substantive structure and a more logically continuous and rigorous methodology in order to give its doctrines the maximum impact (1964, p. xix). He went on a little later to reinforce this opinion: 'In many places the author is deficient in perspicuity, and the work almost throughout is destitute of method' (ibid., p. xliii). At one point, though, he found it appropriate to praise Smith for his careful attention to seeking out empirical truth in the inductive parts of the WN: 'he has applied to political economy the new mode of scientific investigation, namely, of not looking for principles abstractedly, but by ascending from facts the most constantly observed, to the general laws which govern them'. By means of 'a succession of demonstrations, ... [he] has elevated many propositions to the rank of indisputable principles' (ibid., p. xxxix). This praise turned out to be wholly consistent with Say's own strongly inductivist inclinations, even though it ignored the more deductive parts of Smith's treatise. He wrote of the merits of applying the methodology of Bacon to political economy: 'The excellence of this method consists in only admitting facts carefully observed, and the consequences rigorously deduced from them'. Political economy was at one with '*experimental*' natural science in this respect, for it went beyond the '*descriptive*' method of statistics to 'unfold the reciprocal action of substances on each other, or in other words, the connexion between cause and effect, as [in] chemistry and natural philosophy'. The science, then, 'does not resort for any ... explanations to hypothesis', but instead, working 'from facts always carefully observed' it makes known the '*general facts*' concerning wealth (ibid., pp. xvii–xviii, original emphasis).

The important message that Say conveyed was one which attempted to transcend the usual limits of the inductive approach: 'like others who have followed the same path in method, [he] promptly got into difficulties in explaining how economists, who cannot make experiments, are to isolate essential and constant facts from the unessential which they observe' (Bowley, 1949, p. 36). No satisfactory strategy for this requirement was ever made explicit by Say. Nevertheless he went on to amplify his perception of the appropriate methodology by claiming a degree of certainty for the conclusions usually confined to deductive reasoning from axiomatic premisses. The full implications of assertions such as the following only found their ultimate destiny in the abstract–deductive modelling of James Mill and Ricardo. Political economists, he claimed, 'as certainly proceed from the nature of things as the laws of the material world'. In their general facts, they 'do not imagine them; they are results disclosed ... by judicious observation and analysis' (Say, 1964, p. xxv). Thus 'A perfect knowledge of the principles of political economy may be obtained, ... [and] whenever the principles which constitute its basis are the rigorous deductions of undeniable general facts, [it] rests upon an immoveable foundation' (ibid., pp. xix–xx). As a consequence of such faith in the powers of reasoning that was at least based upon inductive observations, Say was able to foreshadow the notion of the 'disturbing cause' which the deductivists would adopt in future (ibid., p. xx). And, as if to provide a recipe for the writing of James Mill's starkly abstract–deductive *Elements of Political Economy* (1966a), he advised that '[a] treatise on political economy will ... be confined to the enunciation of a few general principles, not requiring even the support of proofs or illustrations' (Say, 1964, p. xxvi; cf.p. xlv).

However, to do complete justice to Say, it must be added that his consciousness of the ontological nature of the phenomena with which political economy deals led him to delimit the logical rigour which could legitimately be applied in its analyses. In particular, he argued that mathematical methods would take the science beyond the boundaries of legitimate representation into what amount to misleading degrees of abstraction, even though the quantitative nature of the subject matter may appear to lend itself readily to such treatment (cf. 1964, p. xxvi n). What he noticed here was that the reason for adhering to this limitation is to be found in the fact that economic phenomena are ultimately rooted in the exigencies of human agency: 'The *values* with which political economy is concerned ... being ... subject to the influence of *the faculties, the wants and the desires of mankind* [emphasis added], they are not susceptible of any rigorous appreciation, and cannot, therefore, furnish any *data* for absolute calculations' (ibid., p. xxvi, original emphasis). Those who were to follow did not immediately use mathematical techniques, but their obsession with logical rigour and analytical certainty caused some of them to overlook Say's wise methodological caveat, nonetheless. Later editions of the *Traité* gave recognition to this when Say expressed his misgivings about the methodological direction in which Ricardo's *Principles* was taking political economy. He noted that it was 'a well founded objection to Mr. Ricardo, that he sometimes reasons upon abstract principles to which he gives too great a generalization ... [and] pushes his reasonings to their remotest consequences, without comparing their results with those of actual experience'. What Say's most influential successors ultimately failed to give credence to was that 'The science of political economy, to be of practical utility, should not teach, what *must necessarily* take place, if even deduced by legitimate reasoning, and from undoubted premises; it must [rather] show, in what manner that which in reality does take place, is the consequence of other facts equally certain' (ibid., p. xlvii, original emphasis). The challenge here was to keep the 'disturbing causes' of actual empirical phenomena more to the fore in political economy as Adam Smith had done. This was to be largely ignored in the subsequent methodological developments because of the high cost in terms of the precision of conclusions foregone, although it hovered just in the background of Ricardo's 'strong case' analyses (cf. Hollander, 1985, pp. 15ff).

James Mill's Scottish intellectual origins exposed him to the idea that history could provide observers with the means to construct a Newtonian science of man as a science of mind and action, the laws of which would facilitate an understanding of the nature of human progress. Mill's inclination was to be a didactic expositor and this, combined with a belief in the idea of progress, 'helps to explain his taste for sweeping generalisation and, to a certain extent, his dogmatism' (Winch, 1966b, pp. 5, 6). He had a dedicated belief that the power of reason, proper education and good government could secure the continuous improvement of human welfare. To this end, he became a Utilitarian propagandist and infected all those around him to some degree with the same ultimate purpose, including Ricardo and his son, John Stuart Mill (ibid., pp. 11ff, 22). Writing propaganda with a faith in reason called for the presentation of argument in the most logically rigorous form possible in order to convince readers of the definitude and certainty of its conclusions. Loose ends and 'disturbing causes' could only divert their attention from the essential message, so these were not for Mill or for those under his tutelage. He may have found in Adam Smith the origins of a scientific political economy, but it was to become something quite different in his hands. The most cursory comparison of the WN with James Mill's *Elements of Political Economy* (1966a) make this quite apparent. Both works had their propagandist intentions, but the latter conveyed its arguments with a consciously abstract and even geometric tenor: 'It was Mill who ... introduced for the first time into the language of political economy the Euclidean metaphor, which is even more audacious than the Newtonian metaphor' (Halévy, 1972, p. 272). And Hutchison has Mill explaining to Ricardo 'how a treatise on the principles of political economy should be set out ... like a text book of geometry' (1978, p. 35). Further to these views, Hutchison's summary of Mill's relation to Smith generally is apt:

> Mill drastically and decisively sharpens and hardens Smith's theories, putting them in a much starker and more unqualified form, imbuing them with his own particular confident dogmatism, and giving them a much more definite cutting-

edge in terms of policy applications, to the extent of making them new and different doctrines. (1978, p. 29)

While Hollander has little objection to the classification of Mill's methodology as being at the starkest abstract end of the deductive–inductive spectrum, he does dissent from the view that this is such an obvious contrast with Smith's endeavours. For Hollander, as for some others before him, it was really Smith who pioneered the abstract–deductive methodology and Mill more or less followed his lead (Hollander, 1985, pp. 8–9, 36ff). However it is not possible to deny the difference between the representations of the conduct of human agents upon which their respective deductions were based: in Smith's work, human agents were always much less objectively portrayed than in Mill's.

In addition to the above restrictions, James Mill's enthusiasm for inquiry into the intricacies of the human mind, which ultimately manifested itself in his long exposition of associationist psychology, *Analysis of the Phenomena of the Human Mind* (1967), published in 1829, was not permitted to intrude into the understanding of matters economic. The human psychological essence of political economy, so evident in the methodology and substance of Smith's work, was allowed virtually to disappear, although, as I will note below, in Mill's study of other subjects in the humanities it remained prominent. It is of interest to note in this respect that Mill's biographer, Alexander Bain, summed up the *Analysis* in terms which exposed its pretensions: 'His account of the Intellectual faculties is meagre in the extreme; and, in dealing with Abstraction and Reasoning, he discusses rather the logical than the psychological aspects. Indeed, a considerable portion of the work should have gone to make up a treatise on Logic' (1967, p. 413). That is, at least Mill's general approach to the laws of human nature was consistent with what remained in political economy, for in that context, it was merely the homunculus of 'economic man' whose conduct was treated as a matter of logic alone, being uniquely and reliably determined by the unmitigated pursuit of maximum wealth with the minimum of cost.

As an economic methodologist, James Mill made some ostensible endeavour to preserve that aspect of Say's approach in which even the starkest of reasoning was to be based on experience. He claimed that abstract theory was but the scientific reflection of real phenomena: 'good abstract principles are neither more nor less than the accumulated results of experience, presented in an exceedingly condensed and concentrated state' (quoted in Winch, 1966c, p. 367). Here there is much that might suggest a methodological perspective akin to Adam Smith's. However the 'test' of a theory which finally secured its veracity, once it had been logically established as a cogent explanation of a phenomenon, was its conformity to the demands of logical reason rather than its consistency with observation. Bain made the following reference to the tenor of a piece Mill wrote on education around 1818 and published in the *Supplement to the Encyclopaedia Britannica*: 'the *a priori,* or deductive handling is here exclusively carried out. The author hardly ever cites an actual experience in education; far less has he a body of experience summed up in empirical laws, to confront and compare with the deductions from the theory of the human mind' (Bain, 1967, p. 247). The same sort of methodology pervaded Mill's massive work, *History of British India.* This may appear incongruous, but it is evident that his perspective on history was philosophical in that it, too, should take an abstract form and seek to argue general laws of motion and progress on the basis of the laws of human nature. Halévy puts together some illustrative *obiter dicta* from the Preface to the work that focus on this theme:

> History for him is not a recital, but a methodological description of social phenomena and the laws which regulate them. The historian needs 'the most profound knowledge of the laws of human nature, which is the end as well as the instrument of everything', 'the most perfect comprehension of the principles of human society, or the course into which the laws of human nature impel the human being, in his gregarious state'. (1972, p. 271)

Hutchison similarly points out that the *History* was concerned with 'determining "laws of society", "laws of human nature", "stages of social progress"' (1978, p. 38). There is much in all this about education and history that could also be written about Mill's methodology in political economy, albeit, as I suggested above, without the due emphasis on the importance of a complete understanding of human nature and conduct which he could have sustained for *any* inquiry into human phenomena. Somehow, though, he saw political economy as different in that it demanded a degree of formal analytical precision that precluded any inclusion of psychological contingencies.

Winch summarizes the sort of methodological stance James Mill took by noting that 'he puts forward no "external" criteria for the establishment of truth, in terms, say, of empirical evidence; the truth seems to be simply what right-minded, qualified economists believe it to be' (Winch, 1966c, p. 370). That remarkable piece of Millian hyperbole entitled 'Whether political economy is useful' (J. Mill, 1966b), published in 1836, was indicative of his position on the completeness and certainty of political economic truths as they were to be found in his *Elements.* Ultimately, Mill's son, John Stuart, in his *Autobiography* (AUT), was to conclude of his father's work that 'all his modes of thought' carried the defect of 'trusting too much the intelligibleness of the abstract, when not embodied in the concrete' (p. 27). And, in spite of a degree of softening of the stark methodological image of James Mill suggested above in some more recent comment by Neil de Marchi (1983),

Hollander remains convinced that it was Mill who espoused such 'a defective methodology'. And he concludes that it was one 'with which Ricardo took issue and which J.S. Mill was to repudiate' (1985, pp. 14–15). The extent and sense of this repudiation by the young Mill will be considered in the chapters to follow.

7.3   David Ricardo

There can be little doubt that David Ricardo's links with James Mill were very strong and that they jointly gave political economy its pronounced degree of abstraction in an endeavour to ensure its effect as a propaganda weapon in the fight for free trade. Hutchison's summary of their project gives it just the right balance:

> [The] main meaning and intention of the Millian–Ricardian theories and methods can be found in the nature of the policy conclusions derived from them ... and [they] depended on, with great exactness and rigidity, ... 'strongly' simplified assumptions or theories. The Millian–Ricardian abstract, deductive method started from starkly unqualified assumptions (or 'strong cases') based on *no systematic observation of the behaviour and knowledge of buyers and sellers, savers and spenders, parents and wage earners.* They led immediately and inevitably to sharply *laissez-faire* policy doctrines. (1978, p. 45, emphasis added)

Indeed, as I have already touched on above, the crucial thing which the emerging political economy lacked by virtue of its methodology, and this applied as much to Ricardo's *Principles* as to Mill's *Elements,* was a properly extensive consciousness of the empirical conduct of human agents. It was quite evident that Adam Smith had realized in the WN that the minimal representation of the *realities* of human agency ruled out the advocacy of such strictly free-market policies as those which were now being reached by pure deduction from the most abstract of assumptions (see section 5.4 above). Ricardo was the worst offender in this respect and it is claimed that he 'is not merely the *only,* but outstandingly the *most,* thoroughgoing advocate of *laissez-faire* among the major British economists' (Hutchison, 1978, p. 51, original emphasis).

In his endeavours to defend this advocacy, Ricardo was prepared *publically* to turn political economy towards the most humanly sterile of methodologies. His use of 'abstract models, rigid and artificial definitions, syllogistic reasoning' meant that 'the historical, the institutional, and the empirical faded into the background, and explicit social philosophy shrank to a few passing remarks' (Sowell, 1974, p. 113; cf. pp. 120, 122). At this cost, political economy claimed to have been shown to be a real science in the sense that its methodology replicated that of the natural sciences *and* in the sense that its conclusions were logically certain. Apropos the latter quality,

Sowell has gathered for us 'some of the more exuberant statements of the Ricardians' which demonstrate their conviction: 'some conclusions in economics were "as certain as the principle of gravitation" [Ricardo], "established beyond all question" [McCulloch], "perfectly conclusive" [James Mill], and "unanswerable" [J.S. Mill], ... [and] they possessed "all the certainty of a mathematical demonstration" [J.S. Mill]' (1974, p. 118). The inclusion of J.S. Mill here as a 'Ricardian' in the sense implied will be subjected to some critical inquiry later on.

Now the narrow interpretation of Ricardo as an extreme deductivist obviously stemmed from the very limited access which earlier doctrinal historians had to his unpublished writings. The case of John Neville Keynes, writing in 1890, is indicative. Even though he was essentially a defender of the abstract–deductive methodology (Blaug, 1980, p. 82), he was moved to observe that, 'while Ricardo's writings contain some of the most brilliant and instructive examples of close deductive reasoning to be found in the economic literature, ... his manner of employing the deductive method is not free from grave faults' (Keynes, 1973, p. 237). These faults were several, but they centred upon the *degree* of abstraction which Ricardo resorted to. Keynes complained that his premises were 'never explicitly formulated ... probably because they seemed to him [to be] in no sense arbitrary abstractions, but patent facts to which it was unnecessary specially to call attention' (1973, p. 294). He was prepared to concede, though, that the premises were originally suggested by observation, albeit with too narrow a perspective (cf. 1973, pp. 238–9, 294–5). The effect remained, however, that 'neither the subsidiary postulates, nor those that underlie the greater part of the reasoning, are explicitly indicated' (ibid., p. 237). Keynes was equally critical of the status of the conclusions which were reached by Ricardo's reasoning. The 'explanations and qualifications, which are continually necessary in the interpretation of his results, have usually to be supplied by the reader himself' and the 'tone adopted by Ricardo suggests ... an undue confidence in the absolute and universal validity of the conclusions reached' (ibid., pp. 237–8).

A more severe critique of Ricardo's legacy, contemporary with that of Keynes, came from Walter Bagehot, writing in 1895. At times, his remarks were rather too extreme to be justifiable, such as when he asserted that Ricardo 'had no large notion of what science was ... [and, to] the end of his days, indeed, he never comprehended what he was doing'. Equally improbably, he accused Ricardo of dealing 'with abstractions without knowing that they were such [so that he] thought he was considering actual human nature in its actual circumstances, when he was really considering a fictitious nature in fictitious circumstances' (Bagehot, 1973, p. 205). This said, though, a reader of the *Principles* in isolation probably could reasonably be expected to agree with Bagehot's assessment that political economy appeared to deal 'with an unreal and imaginary [human] subject ... which in the existing world cannot be found ...' in much the same way as purely theoretical mechanics dealt 'with physical materials ... which no one ever expects to find in reality' (ibid., p. 97). Thus it dealt 'not with the entire real man as we know him in fact, but with a simpler, imaginary man', so that, in particular, the 'abstract man of this science is engrossed with one desire only – the desire of possessing wealth, not of course that there ever was a being who always acted as that desire would dictate' (ibid., pp. 97–8). Bagehot granted that there was a sense in which this desire was 'the greatest of industrial desires' and that there was a sound rationale in science for the use of abstractions of this form. But the result was that it should be considered 'as a science of "tendencies" only' because in the 'science of society, ... the forces are ... very various and difficult to perceive' (ibid., pp. 98, 100). His critical insight here was that, although the deductions of political economy 'may be incontrovertible, and its results precisely true, whenever its assumptions are true, ... these results will be very imperfect guides, wherever those assumptions are impaired by contradictory matter' (ibid., p. 103). What was missing from Ricardo's exposition, and others of its ilk, was a due recognition that political economy could, at best, provide 'a convenient series of deductions from assumed axioms which are never quite true, which in many times and countries would be utterly untrue, but which are sufficiently near to the principal conditions of the modern world to make it useful to consider them by themselves'. In this sense, then, Bagehot's critique of Ricardo was not that the deductive methodology was wrong, but rather that its results could only serve as a preliminary, or heuristic guide to understanding economic phenomena and preparing policy (ibid., pp. 205–6). Adam Smith might well have concurred.

What emerges from the above argument is the prima facie case that 'Ricardo's method ... essentially ... involved taking hypothetical premises, deducing conclusions from these premises, and making no attempt to verify the results' (O'Brien, 1975, p. 69). But, as Sowell notes in regard to this 'verification' problem in classical methodology as a whole, 'economics was generally conceived of in the classical period as *having a scientific core'*, although it was 'universally understood that most individual economic principles had not been, and could not be, subjected to controlled experiments and so lacked the degree of certainty of conclusions in the natural sciences'; moreover, 'for the Ricardians the complexities and uncertainties of the real world were precisely the reason for *not* relying on direct "experience" *as a source of explanatory hypotheses*' (1974, p. 144, original emphasis).

The importance of these observations for Ricardian scholarship is that they hint at a rationale for the starkly abstract–deductive methodology of the period which transcends the dominance of the merely propagandist objectives cited above. It has been Samuel Hollander who has led the push for a

revision of the narrow interpretation of Ricardo's methodological predilections, but it was perhaps Robert Torrens who first hinted at the need for it. In
his *Essay on the Production of Wealth* from 1821 (1965), Torrens started out
as a critic of Ricardo. His line was the common one that Ricardo's use of
abstraction was too extreme, causing a loss of adequate contact with empirical reality for his theories to be immediately meaningful. By contrast, Torrens
cited Malthus as a writer guilty of the opposite sin of formulating insufficiently coherent theory in his concern to stay in touch with reality. He
concluded, perhaps a little harshly, that 'as presented by Mr.Ricardo, Political
Economy possess [*sic*] a regularity and simplicity beyond what exists in
nature; as exhibited by Mr.Malthus, it is a chaos of original but unconnected
elements' (1965, p. v). Later on, though, he was to write in his *Budget* of
1844, with somewhat more penetration, that Ricardo's 'Political Economy is
presented as an abstract science. All his reasonings are hypothetical. *His
conclusions are necessary truths ... under the premises assumed'*, but we can
still proceed, if we wish to 'make the necessary corrections for the difference
between the hypothetical circumstances and the circumstances which actually exist, *to arrive at conclusions practically true under the varying conditions of society'*. The key consequence of Torrens's reading here was that the
'impression that his [Ricardo's] conclusions are at variance with the facts ...
involves a misconception'. Rather it was the case that his 'conclusions are in
strict conformity with the facts which he assumes; and, modified by the
proper corrections, on account of the difference between the assumed and the
existing facts will be found to be in tried conformity with the existing facts'
(quoted by O'Brien, 1975, pp. 69–70, my emphasis added). O'Brien uses this
quotation to exemplify his own view that 'the whole tenor of Ricardo's
approach was opposed to verification' because what was argued in his theories was not immediately able to be isolated in any accessible 'test data'.
Thus, O'Brien continues, the 'message which his [Ricardo's] successors took
from his procedure was that if a conclusion was reached logically from
plausible premises it was correct even if the data contradicted it' (1975, p.
69; cf. Blaug, 1980, p. 58).

   The thrust of Hollander's revisionism is that the sort of arguments which
we have just been considering suggest that Ricardo was a rather more subtle
and sophisticated methodologist than some received readings, based largely
on his published works, would indicate. Especially is it evident that Ricardo
should not be aligned so readily with James Mill's starker expositions, as has
been the practice of some interpreters (Hutchison, in particular). Hollander's
challenging and provocative summary of Ricardo's methodological position
is worth quoting in full.

His understanding of the historical relativity of the behavioural and technological axioms of his models is impressive. He rejected oversimplified models on empirical grounds. He was keenly aware of the specifically pedagogic role played by his strong-case assumptions. He was conscious to a high degree of the clash between the short-run and the long-run implications of policy proposals; and also of the *ceteris paribus* conditions upon which his models were constructed rendering them inappropriate as predictive engines and unambiguous guides to policy. (1985, p. 15)

It is not possible here to expound or challenge with any justice Hollander's lengthy and cogent defence of these radical theses (1985, pp. 15ff; cf. 1987, pp. 325ff). He probes the backdrop to Ricardo's published, albeit implicit, methodological pronouncements by means of a detailed reading of the unpublished private and other material, both theoretical and policy-related. His objective is to seek out all of Ricardo's mitigating comments affecting the apparent severity of his abstract–deductive approach. I will focus here on the correspondence with Malthus, which turned out to be so indicative of just the points that Hollander wishes to make.

For example, he cites the early letter to Malthus from 1811 in which the distinction that he saw between behavioural axioms and 'disturbing causes' is made clear: 'It would be no answer to me to say that men were ignorant of the best and cheapest mode of conducting their business and paying their debts, *because that is a question of fact not of science, and might be urged against almost every proposition in Political Economy*' (Ricardo, 1951, VI, pp. 63–4; quoted by Hollander, 1985, p. 17, my emphasis). That is to say, even though there 'can be no doubt that the maximization of money returns reflected, for Ricardo at least, a close first approximation to contemporary business reality' (Hollander, 1985, p. 20; cf. p. 24), and that this appeared in the form of the axiom of exclusive maximum wealth pursuit by 'economic man' in Ricardo's theories, he did not preclude the potential for agents to be ignorant and make mistakes in reality. Hollander also quotes the well-known letter to Malthus in which Ricardo emphasized that his work was never intended to be immediately relevant to the comprehension of actual economic phenomena: 'Our differences, may in some respects, I think, be ascribed to your considering my book as more practical than I intended it to be'. It was rather, he wrote, his objective 'to elucidate principles, and to do this I imagined strong cases that I might shew the operation of those principles ... undisturbed by any other operating cause'. To this he added the all-important claim: 'I think that I have reasoned correctly from ... [my particular] premises' (Ricardo, 1951, VIII, p. 184, quoted in part by Hollander, 1987, p. 331). However, on the theme of seeking to obtain empirical confirmation of his theories, Ricardo had already written to Malthus earlier that, 'if I am too theoretical *which I really believe is the case,* – you I think are too practical. There are so many combinations, – so many operating causes in Political Economy, that there is great danger in appealing to experience in favour of a particular doctrine, unless we are sure that all the causes of variation are seen and their effects duly estimated' (Ricardo, 1951, VI, p. 295; quoted by Hollander, 1985, pp. 34–5, my emphasis). Be this as it may, the 'strong-case' assumption was nonetheless further defended by Ricardo on the grounds that he was representing the long-run empirical core of the economy. It was in this vein that he wrote to Malthus that

> one great cause of our difference in opinion ... is that you have always in your mind the immediate and temporary effects of particular changes – whereas I put these immediate and temporary effects quite aside, and fix my whole attention on the permanent state of things which will result from them. Perhaps you estimate these temporary effects too highly, whilst I am too much disposed to undervalue them. (Ricardo, 1951, VII, p. 120; quoted by Hollander, 1985, pp. 28–9)

What remains as an unresolved puzzle in these and other ideas that Hollander posits about Ricardo's methodological consciousness is the fact that Ricardo himself did not respond publicly to the misinterpretation of his position that Malthus and other commentators had made so apparent. He could have readily taken action to enter some qualification to his stance by adding a methodological note to the later editions of the *Principles*, but chose not to do so. Perhaps even more curiously, when writing his unpublished *Notes on Malthus*, he made no comments at all on the methodological exposition that Malthus presented in the Introduction to his own *Principles*. Malthus's work was expressly written as a rebuttal to the abstract–deductive strictures of Ricardo's *Principles*. And yet, even though Ricardo and Malthus appeared to be almost diametrically opposed on matters of methodology, and even though Ricardo had intended to publish the *Notes*, it seems that he just let this opportunity to set the record right pass him by. It remained the case, then, that the *public* impression given by Ricardo to his contemporaries and immediate successors was that he espoused a severely abstract–deductive methodology as the one most appropriate to political economy. The subtle qualifications to which Hollander refers were left unknown and it was this *public* Ricardo whose methodology achieved and sustained its dominance over the science in its classical era.

7.4   Reactions to Ricardo

It was certainly Ricardo's public methodological position against which the dissenters reacted and which his disciples were called upon to defend. In the era of consolidation of the classical school that led up to the 1840s, when John Stuart Mill became the authority, several figures stand out as having made some methodological contributions that are significant for my argument here.

Thomas Malthus, as the above references to his correspondence with Ricardo suggest, stood out as a dissenter from the Ricardian orthodoxy because of his concerns about the incongruency between its methodology and what he saw as the complex ontological nature of the human phenomena with which political economy set out to deal. Ricardo's methodological influence also came under concerted attack from the group who became known as the 'Cambridge Inductivists'. It is not possible to pursue this latter episode here in any detail, so I will confine my treatment of it to a few indicative references to one of the founding critics in the group, Richard Jones. The others who were involved included, most significantly, William Whewell, but, while his initial writings on the theme date from around the early 1830s, their real impact, along with that of his later work, overlaps with J.S. Mill's contributions and will thus belong in that context below. Finally, among the defenders of the mainstream classical doctrine, it was John McCulloch and Nassau Senior who stood out as having some explicit consciousness of what they were doing methodologically. McCulloch's passing comments on the issue were limited but significant, whereas Senior, almost alone, provided some formal explication of the methodology of the doctrine and thus laid the groundwork for the younger Mill's subsequent endeavours. Each of these writers warrants some brief consideration in turn.

In his Introduction to *The Principles of Political Economy,* published in 1820, Malthus concluded by alluding to the fact that his implicit target in setting out his methodological alternative had been Ricardo's *Principles.* Although he recognized 'the ingenuity and consistency of the system which it maintains and develops with so much ability', and even though he 'sometimes felt almost staggered by ... [Ricardo's] authority', he 'remained unconvinced by his reasonings' because 'some of the fundamental principles of' the work 'appeared ... to be erroneous' (1936, p. 18). Malthus's central point of contention was that Ricardo had adopted a methodology which evaded the true complexity of the object phenomena which he purported to explain. Malthus simply could not accept the idea that all such complexity was legitimately handled by the ex post addition of its complicating consequences to core 'strong cases', where the conclusions of the latter were claimed to be securely certain and generally relevant by virtue merely of their logical construction.

It was first and foremost the human ontology of economic phenomena to which Malthus referred when he rejected any mathematical–geometric analogy in political economy: 'we should fall into a serious error if we were to suppose that any propositions, the practical results of which depend upon *the agency of so variable a being as man,* and the qualities of so variable a compound as the soil, can ever admit of the same kinds of proof, or lead to the same certain conclusions, as those which relate to figure and number'

(1936, p. 1, emphasis added). He conceded that there may well be observed principles of economic conduct and events which have a secure degree of generality and continuity, but his misgivings remained at the ontological level in that 'even these, when examined, will be found to resemble in most particulars the great general rules in morals and politics founded upon the known passions and propensities of human nature'. As a consequence, he continued, 'whether we advert to the qualities of man, or of the earth he is destined to cultivate, we shall be compelled to acknowledge, *that the science of political economy bears a nearer resemblance to the science of morals and politics than to that of mathematics*', and, consistently, he added that this was a conclusion 'which could hardly fail to be formed merely from *a view of the subjects about which political economy is conversant*' (ibid., pp. 1–2, emphasis added). Confronted with these 'variable and complicated phenomena', political economists have insisted on proceeding with 'a precipitate attempt to simplify and generalize', which is 'indeed the desirable and legitimate object of genuine philosophy, whenever it can be effected consistently with truth'. As far as Malthus was concerned, it was the 'first business of philosophy ... to account for things as they are', but this could not be the case in political economy, with the complex and shifting nature of its underlying causalities, and the result had been the construction of 'crude and premature theories' (ibid., pp. 8, 5). These theories had this quality because the political economists failed in three crucial senses: first, by usually ascribing a single cause to an event, they were unable to represent other, often interacting causal factors that may be empirically relevant; secondly, it was difficult for them to make due allowance for limitations and exceptions in actual phenomena; and finally, there was their disinclination, because they were so secure in the logic of their theories, to attempt to test their conclusions for consistency with the facts (ibid., pp. 5–6, 8; cf. pp. 10–11).

For Malthus, there was no legitimate alternative to an approach to political economy in which the limitations of theories, consequent upon the complex nature of its object phenomena, were confronted from the outset. His rather 'soft' methodological conclusion was summed up thus: 'In many cases ... it may not be possible to predict results with certainty, on account of the complication of the causes in action, the different degrees of strength and efficacy with which they may operate, and the number of unforeseen circumstances which are likely to interfere' (ibid., p. 13). It was Malthus's objective in his own work to posit 'some of the most important rules of political economy for practical application' and, in order to do so, he undertook to 'make frequent reference to experience ... [and] to take a comprehensive view of all the causes that concur in the production of particular phenomena' (ibid., p. 16). In this ambitious endeavour he was quite well aware that he should not give too much credence to the inductive alternative of forming explanatory generalizations because of the potential for spurious correlations to appear and be mistaken for causal relations. Rather he leaves us with the hope that he will be able to find a 'just mean' between the extremes of pure deduction and pure induction, and, thereby, 'to approach, as near as I can, to the great object of my research – the truth' (ibid., p. 17). That he ultimately believed more in the pertinence of the deductive methodology, though, is suggested by some revealing correspondence he had with William Whewell over the latter's mathematical papers on political economy. Malthus was prepared to grant that 'mathematical calculations may in some cases be introduced with advantage into the science of Political Economy', adding that he had 'long thought that there are many of the results in political economy which have some resemblance to the problems *de maximis et minimis*' (de Marchi and Sturges, 1973, p. 387; quoted by Hollander, 1985, p. 18n).

Richard Jones proclaimed himself to be a dedicated inductivist critic of the insufficiently realistic premises and the deductive methodology around which the Ricardian orthodoxy had been constructed. It is of interest here that one of his critical passages in *An Essay on the Distribution of Wealth* (1956), dating from 1831, referred explicitly to the human ontological roots of the difficulties confronted by the abstract–deductive methodology. His inductivist stance dictated that 'the principles which determine the position and progress, and govern the conduct, of large bodies of the human race, placed under different circumstances, can be learnt only by an appeal to experience'. In contrast to this:

> He must, indeed, be a shallow reasoner, who by mere efforts of consciousness, by consulting his own views, feelings and motives, and the narrow sphere of his personal observation, and reasoning *a priori,* from them expects that he shall be able to anticipate the conduct, progress and fortunes of large bodies of men, differing from himself in moral or physical temperament, and influenced by differences, varying in extent and variously combined, in climate, soil, religion, education and government. (1956, p. xv)

Jones had here hit on the really problematical precondition of any human science, that of discovering how adequately to represent the situated human agents whose conduct generates its observed object phenomena. We will, in due course below, find J.S. Mill confronting the problem in just these terms. Jones himself pursued the issue no further in the present context except to proceed to recommend and defend as wholly viable ever more extensive observations and to let the facts speak for themselves, so to say. In this procedure, though, he warned of the danger of jumping to conclusions about revealed principles too soon. The process could only proceed by, perhaps slow and laborious, steps from simple and limited to more comprehensive and correct theories (ibid., pp. xix–xx, xl–xli).

In his own exposition on rent, Jones asserted that his object was 'to get a sight of the principles, which govern the distribution of the wealth annually produced by the lands and labour of the human race; and of the effects produced by the action of those principles among bodies of men existing under different circumstances'. He not only had a strong faith in induction as a reliable source of the actual creation of these principles, but he was also sanguine about their efficacy in the role as bases for prediction. His claim was that 'the experience of the past and present, can alone, on such a subject, afford any sure foundations for anticipations as to the future' (ibid., p. xxiv). Having so stated his principles of methodology, however, there is a body of scholarly opinion which suggests that he was unable fully to practise them in his own work. Among his contemporaries, Whewell (1964, pp. ixff, *passim*) was convinced of Jones's inductive bona fides. By contrast, Torrens foreshadowed the modern view that he ended up with an ad hoc mixture of induction and deduction, at times merely applying Ricardo's theories with some situationally relevant 'disturbing causes' attached (Hollander, 1985, pp. 41, 43). The upshot was that, whatever may have been the merits of Jones's critical insight into the ontological problematics of constructing economic theories which flow from the human origins of their objects, it seems that his own alternative behaviourist strategy could not be so readily put into practice.

Although he was a wholehearted supporter of Ricardo's doctrines, John McCulloch proved to be more explicitly conscious of the claims that they were making about human agency as it was represented in their theories. This is noticed by Marian Bowley, who aligns McCulloch with Adam Smith's similar consciousness (Bowley, 1949, pp. 38–9). She quotes from McCulloch's *Principles of Political Economy* (1965), which first appeared in 1825, to the effect that he believed the axiomatic treatment of the human agent therein to reflect 'a part of the original constitution of man' which was able to be identified 'by the aid of observation and analysis'. He emphasized that 'the principles which determine the production and accumulation of wealth are inherent in our nature, and exert a powerful, but not always the same degree of influence over the conduct of every individual'. As a consequence, 'the theorist must, therefore, satisfy himself with framing rules which explain their operation in the majority of instances, leaving it to the sagacity of the observer to modify them so as to suit individual cases' (quoted by Bowley, 1949, p. 39). Bowley's comments on McCulloch's caution then draw attention to the fact that, while he 'was the only one to make the slightest attempt to state the premises relating to human behaviour' upon which the laws of economics were founded, he did not go on to undertake the inquiry that would have been required to establish the empirical bases for the assumptions made about the conduct of human agents. It is incorrect, though, to assert, as Bowley does, in this respect that the classicals in general were simply satisfied to accept Smith's legacy regarding the representation of human agency (1949, pp. 38–9). As should be apparent from above argument, Smith's treatment was much more comprehensive than any of the models of 'economic man' resorted to by the Ricardians or their critics. It was only J.S. Mill who among the classicals had a sufficiently extensive intellectual perspective to probe the issue to the depth that it warranted.

Throughout his life, Nassau Senior maintained an interest in political economy that extended to explicit concerns about its methodology. In the period prior to the work of J.S. Mill, two of his works are of interest: the 'Introductory Lecture on Political Economy' (1966), delivered in Oxford University in 1826 and published the following year; and the book, *An Outline of the Science of Political Economy* (1938), first published in 1836. A further significant contribution to methodology was made in the 'Four Introductory Lectures on Political Economy', delivered during Senior's second period in Oxford and published in 1852. However these took account of Mill's writings and will not be considered here.

The 1826 'Lecture' comprised largely an exposition of the distinction to be made in political economy between its theoretical and practical branches. Senior attributed much of the difference of opinion in the science to a failure to keep this separation clear (cf. 1938, pp. 3ff). Having said this, though, he went on to defend the most rigidly abstract–deductive version of its theoretical branch. His claim was that 'the theoretic branch of the science, that which treats of the nature, production and distribution of wealth, – is capable of all the certainty that can belong to any science, not founded on definitions' (Senior, 1966, p. 11). The reason for this claim to secure economic knowledge was to be found in the belief that it 'rests on very few general propositions, which are the result of observation, or consciousness' and all of which are of such common knowledge as not to require any further inquiry (ibid., p. 7). This was reinforced by the fact that 'the Science depends more on reasoning than on observation', the implicit suggestion being that the former is objective because it is common to all analysts (Senior, 1938, p. 5). From among the five main premises posited by Senior in the 'Lecture' (cf. the four specified in his *Outline,* 1938, pp. 26ff), two are of particular interest to us here. He deals with the human agents in their economic conduct by means of the assumption that 'every person is desirous to obtain, with as little sacrifice as possible, as much as possible of the articles of wealth'. And, in order to delimit the scope of the science, he supported this assumption with a definition of wealth as a further premiss. Wealth, he asserts, comprises 'things' which are scarce, produce pleasure or prevent pain and are able to be exchanged as values (1966, p. 35; cf. 1938, pp. 6ff). Senior was aware that these were two very different sorts of premises. The latter he claimed to be a 'matter of observation' along with the other three not cited here, but concerned with increasing labour productivity by means of machinery, the assumption of diminishing returns to agricultural land, and the Malthusian population theorem. In the case of his wealth assumption, at least, Senior's claim to an observed status for his *definition* was exaggerated because it most probably included an input from previous knowledge of political economy itself and from his own introspection and intuition. The idea that what constitutes wealth can be settled by the authority of observation was simply a misunderstanding on Senior's part.

His approach in the *Outline* was different, as the nature of wealth no longer appeared as one of the science's 'elementary propositions' (1938, p. 26). However, it was the other assumption about human agent motivation in matters economic that was of more significance, although Senior did not make much of it. He stated quite frankly that this premiss was 'a matter of consciousness' rather than of observation and that 'it can scarcely be said to require proof' (1966, p. 36). The matter was much more strongly stated in the *Outline* when he referred to the wealth motive as 'in Political Economy what gravitation is in Physics ... the ultimate fact beyond which reasoning cannot go, and of which almost every other proposition is merely an illustration' (1938, p. 28). By all of this he can only have meant that the security of the motive as a universal proposition about human nature derives from introspection by and general agreement amongst philosophers and political economists. On the basis of such criteria, its status can only be that of a useful a priori assumption which rather than not requiring proof is just not able to be proved one way or the other, as the assertion that it is a 'fact beyond which reasoning cannot go' tacitly recognized. The true significance of Senior's brush with this problem of what to do about the representation of human agency in political economy is that he realized that it could not be resolved by claims from observation. Later on, the same sort of realization would strike J.S. Mill, but with a much more profound intellectual impact.

From these premises are derived, by unspecified, but presumably deductive means, conclusions which have a status 'nearly as general' as the premises themselves. But Senior went on to make the distinction between those conclusions relating to the nature and production of wealth, which 'are universally true', and those relating to its distribution. The point of this separation was his recognition that the latter phenomenon is 'liable to be affected by peculiar institutions of particular countries'. However he wished to maintain the logically certain status of the science nonetheless, so he went on to say that, even in this respect, 'the natural state of things can be laid down as the general rule, and the anomalies produced by particular disturbing causes can be afterwards accounted for' (1966, pp. 7–8). Two things stand out here. One is that Senior is suggesting that the nature of the 'disturbing causes' will be comprehended sufficiently and can be represented formally enough to be added meaningfully to the general analysis. The second thing that is evident is the limited understanding of the nature of institutions which is reflected in Senior's implication that their complicating interventions can be handled as merely *mechanical* additions to the basic generalizations. The more appropriate, but more logically problematical, analogy would have been that of a *chemical* mix: the substance of the phenomenon could be qualitatively changed as a totality by adding in another cause. The latter would thus have recognized the complex of action, reaction and interaction between human agents and their institutional situations, which renders both in a continuous state of flux. Later we will see what J.S. Mill was able to make of this tricky, but very important, distinction between production and distribution as object phenomena in political economy.

Senior extended his defence of the essentially certain nature of the arguments of political economy into its practical branch as well. The branch was 'to ascertain what institutions are most favourable to wealth', but he recognized that its empirical nature would bring considerable difficulties for any attempt at formal analysis. In particular, in this context he referred to a more realistic conception of human agency as problematical. There was considerable perceptiveness in the following passage, the full implications of which were not pursued by Senior with the seriousness they warranted.

> The machinery of civilized society is worked by so many springs; the dislike of labour, the desire for immediate enjoyment, and the love of accumulation are so perpetually counteracting one another, and they produce such opposite conduct, not only in different individuals, but in whole masses of people, that we are liable to the greatest mistakes when we endeavour to assign motives to past conduct, or to predict the conduct which a new motive will produce. (1966, pp. 8–9)

In the face of these complex and fundamental impediments to any reliable understanding of human agency, it was still his intention to show that 'many conclusions, and those of the highest importance, in the practical branch, rest so immediately on the conclusions of the theoretic branch as to possess equal certainty and universality' (ibid., p. 11). It is surprising that the above compounding of complications affecting the representation of human agents was not perceived as already pertinent to the theoretical branch. Senior's intuition could have reasonably been expected to have noticed how immediately and intimately involved they were as, at least, 'disturbing causes' in relation to the theoretical premiss of the maximum–minimum motive in the pursuit of wealth. Once again, the required degree of perspicacity to recognize and confront these issues was to be displayed by J.S. Mill and it is to his contributions that we now turn our attention.

8   J.S. Mill and classical methodology

8.1   Introduction

In several crucial ways, John Stuart Mill's intellectual profile can be seen to be similar to that of Adam Smith. Hutchison's observations about Smith that follow could just as well apply to Mill and they set the stage for my analysis of the latter's contributions to economic methodology: he was 'in fact, and undoubtedly always considered himself to be, a philosopher, in a highly comprehensive sense'; he 'remained a philosopher from the beginning to the end of his life'; he 'would never have regarded his work as a whole as primarily economic'; and he 'thought of economics, or political economy, as only one chapter, and not the most important chapter, in a broad study of society and human progress, which involved psychology and ethics (in social and individual terms), law, politics, and the development of the arts and sciences' (1978, p. 5). One could quibble about the details of the statement as it applies to either Smith or Mill. However it conveys admirably the sweep of their respective concerns to deal with human or moral science in general as the means to any proper understanding of political economy, concerns that were ultimately the foundations for the very similar designs and objectives of their respective magna opera on the subject. Mill had an intense interest in the philosophy and the individual and social psychology of human nature. His consequent detailed comprehension of the human dimensions of the socioeconomic sciences led him to raise questions about the consistency and legitimacy of the received orthodoxy of methodology in political economy. It was the wide scope and depth of insight of his consequent inquiries which set him apart from the other classicals and their critics who may have touched on the issue.

Mill's methodological arguments were initially dominated by his intention to defend the abstract–deductive approach to the orthodox political economy that he had inherited. He soon came to see the limitations of the extant presentations of this approach and his intellectual challenge became the establishment of consistency between the demands of this scientific method-ology and the particular nature of economic phenomena, *especially with respect to the fact that the latter originate in the individual and/or collective conduct of situated human agents.* His understanding of the human origins of matters economic led him to realize that the epistemological claims for any axiomatic–deductive theory purporting to explain them had to be tempered relative to those which could be made in some of the physical sciences. He was convinced, though, that the moral sciences only lagged in their status among the sciences because of their failure fully to adopt the most rigorous methodological principles available for theory construction and testing. The thrust of his belief here was that the sciences had all gone through a progressive evolution towards the adoption of the definitive methodological model, and that this progression had taken place in the order of the complexity of their respective objects of knowledge. In his own words in the *System of Logic* (SOL), published in 1843, 'the backward state of the Moral Sciences can only be remedied by applying to them the methods of the Physical Sciences, *duly extended and generalized*' (p. 833, emphasis added). There are two things about this assertion that should be noticed. One is that Mill referred to *physical* sciences here as the distinctive methodological model because he considered it to be taken for granted that the moral sciences, like all sciences, were inherently natural sciences. The other is that the emphasized piece conveys a certain qualification to what he expected from the application of the physical science approach. It will be an integral part of my argument to follow that the source of this qualification to Mill's methodological monism was that he found there to exist a significant void between the status of axiomatic assumptions in human science, especially where these refer to human agency, and the empirical reality they were to represent. He was ultimately led to grant that this void was greater *and of a different nature* from that confronted in the physical sciences and, although he struggled to show that the void could, nevertheless be satisfactorily bridged, there came a point beyond which the human sciences just could not yet go in their emulation of the physical sciences because of the sheer complexity of object phenomena that originate in the inaccessible processes of the human psyche.

In particular, he came to realize that there remained a metaphysical dimension of all phenomena generated by human actions that was beyond the reach of empirical science. Mill maintained his sanguinity, however, that 'this blot on the face of science' could be removed, for he noted that, in relatively recent times, 'several other sciences have emerged from this [pre-scientific] state, and it was now the case that none ... remain in it except those which relate to man himself, the most complex and most difficult subject of study on which the human mind can be engaged'. So, while both methodologically and substantively the study of the 'physical nature of man, as an organized being' had established 'a considerable body of truths', it remained the case that 'the laws of Mind, and, in even greater degree, those of Society, are so far from having attained a similar state of even partial recognition, that it is still a controversy whether they are capable of becoming subjects of science in the strict sense of the term'. Thus, he continued, at the 'threshold' of any inquiry that is concerned to understand human phenomena, 'we are met by an objection, which, if not removed, would be fatal to the attempt to treat human conduct as a subject of science. Are the actions of human beings, like all other natural events, subject to invariable laws? Does that constancy of causation, which is the foundation of every scientific theory of successive phenomena, really obtain among them?' (SOL, pp. 833–4, 835). Mill was convinced that these absolutely crucial ontological questions about the origin of the object phenomena of the human sciences had potentially affirmative answers and he set out to establish that these applied to political economy in particular.

That Mill was no mere imitator and defender of the starkest versions of classical methodology has been noticed by others, most recently by Samuel Hollander in his massive study of Mill the political economist (1985, especially chapter 2; cf. his 1987, chapter 14). What has not been presented in its fullest detail is the source and precise nature of Mill's distinctive position amongst the late classicals. As indicated by his intellectual parallels with Smith suggested above, it was his philosophical and psychological interests which engendered his reflections on the epistemological claims made for the conclusions presented in economic theory. Mill was a methodological monist in the delimited sense that he believed that the logic of the physical sciences was the exclusive *source* of the logic for all sciences. He approached political economy with this preconception fixed firmly in his mind and it always remained so. But, unlike the majority of his antecedents and successors in economic science, many of whom held the same view, he was astute and forthright enough to realize that it would be necessary to leave its theories effectively incomplete and open-ended because of the intractable nature and complexity of the phenomena they were to explain. This did not turn him into a methodological dualist, in the strictest sense, who would consider the human sciences to require a distinctly different approach to theory creation and testing. It was Mill's ultimate driving notion that the human sciences had just not yet achieved the epistemological zenith that awaited them in the future. His challenge was to realize this methodological destiny by showing how human conduct, with all its impenetrable and complicating ontological character, could be represented and explained in a logically cogent manner on the basis of empirical criteria alone. In the end, though, after the most exhaustive of inquiries into the psychology of human agents and the logic of science, he concluded that there would always be hanging over the human sciences, including political economy, an epistemological remainder unable to be uniquely and definitively linked to the evidence of observation. That is, there was a sense in which any legitimately applicable methodology of human science could only approximate the strict demands of the axiomatic–deductive ideal. It was to Mill's lasting credit that he had the intellectual integrity and fortitude to confront this limitation and allow for a compensating methodological flexibility in his writings on political economy.

The way forward in the human sciences, then, as Mill saw it, was to inquire more deeply into the extent to which the logic of the physical sciences could be shown to be consistent with a proper recognition of the ontological essentials of humanly generated phenomena. Mill set out to clarify 'how far the unsatisfactory state' of inquiries directed at such phenomena by the human sciences 'is owing to a wrong choice of methods, how far to a want of skill in the application of the right ones; and what degree of ultimate success may be attained or hoped for by a better choice and more careful employment of logical processes appropriate to the case' (SOL, p. 835). In the case of political economy, the idea of making a 'better choice' as against a 'wrong choice', and of exposing any 'want of skill' in the application of the appropriate methodology demanded that Mill make very clear just what the nature of the objects under study in the science was. It was also these objects of study which were at issue in determining 'what ultimate degree of success', that is, scientifically defensible success, 'may be attained or hoped for' in the application of the physical scientific methodology to political economy.

Mill's first published piece of methodological significance in the present context was the 1828 article for the *Westminster Review* (CW, XI, pp. 2ff) in which he reviewed Richard Whately's *Elements of Logic* (2nd edn, 1827). It is to be recalled that this first literary endeavour that we mention here came when Mill was 21 years of age and had endured that arduous and rigorous education under the tutelage of his father about which the younger man informs us so fully in his AUT (cf. Bain, 1969). He was by this time familiar with his father's political economy and associationist psychology (J. Mill, 1966a and 1967) as well as with the Utilitarian philosophy espoused by the followers of Jeremy Bentham and his father (see Halévy, 1972, *passim*). Alexander Bain's assessment of the article was that it represented 'a landmark not merely in the history of his [Mill's] own mind, but in the history of Logic', even though he thought that Mill had overrated the significance of Whately's contribution per se (Bain, 1969, pp. 36–7). What Mill affirmed in his critique of Whately was, inter alia, that the adoption of syllogistic deduction as the fundamental methodology in political economy could be defended, provided the distinctive nature of its premises could be accurately formulated by inductive means. Mill would later express misgivings about the status of the deductive results generated by syllogistic arguments in particular and about the viability of formulating axiomatic premises by observation. Indeed it is appropriate to conclude that, more generally, and in regard to these methodological matters especially, the Whately piece provided him with a forum to express his thoughts about the logic of science, the impending problematics of which would only approach resolution after the next 15 years of often excruciating intellectual effort leading to the publication of the SOL (Kubitz, 1932, pp. 25ff; AUT, pp. 123f, 189, 231).

In the year following the Whately review, Mill was set another challenge which impinged upon the development of his thought on methodology. James Mill had written his 'Essay on Government' in 1820 for the Supplement to the *Encyclopaedia Britannica* and it was republished in 1825 in an essay collection. The piece was written in the abstract–deductive style, applying syllogistic reasoning to a priori premises about human agents that had become the trademark of the Utilitarians. It had been greeted by the young Benthamites, with whom Mill had formed a debating club called the 'Society of students of mental philosophy' (Robson, 1973, p. liii), as 'a masterpiece of political wisdom', although they did not accept all of its theses (AUT, p. 107). By contrast, the geometric approach to political theory therein elicited a critical response from Thomas Macaulay in an 1829 number of the *Edinburgh Review*. The elder Mill's response was disdainful and dismissive, but John Mill read the critique as warranting more serious consideration and he later reported on the incident as an important one in the AUT. He expressed his disappointment with his father's reply which 'treated Macaulay's argument as simply irrational' by citing Hobbes's aphorism 'that when reason is against a man, a man will be against reason' (AUT, pp. 165–6). What John Mill wanted to do was to apply some reason to the situation and to make clear thereby what was correct in the substance of the criticisms that had been levelled at his father. He thought that, overall, Macaulay's attack was generally ill-conceived because of its general dependence on the extreme notion that human sciences had to be wholly inductive in the experimental and demonstrative sense in order to be meaningful. However there were aspects of the critique which he felt had quite correctly drawn attention to his father's approach in this 'Essay' as overly dominated by the narrow and highly abstract conception of human agents from which he worked out his deductive conclusions. According to Macaulay, the axiomatic treatment of the motive of self-interest only allowed the truistic conclusion to be reached that agents will do as they choose and could indicate nothing about their actual conduct in particular situations (Mueller, 1956, p. 100).

Such suggestions made the young Mill ill at ease with his defence of a methodology which depended upon the concept of 'economic man' and his inclination was to believe that 'there was really something more fundamentally erroneous in my father's conception of philosophical method, as applicable to politics, than I had hitherto supposed there was' (AUT, p. 167). It was this challenge which gave a focus to what became the massive project of inquiry into logic and methodology that culminated in the SOL (AUT, p. 169; Kubitz, 1932, pp. 31ff; Anschutz, 1953, p. 81). In particular, Mill was of the opinion that both his father and Macaulay had misrepresented the methodologies which they defended. In Macaulay's case, he had failed to realize that the Baconian inductive process ultimately depended upon deductive argument to draw its conclusions. By contrast, James Mill had relied upon 'premises [that] were really too narrow, and included but a small number of the general truths, on which, in politics, the important consequences depend', and at the same time, while he was 'right in adopting a deductive method, he made a wrong selection of one, having taken as the type of deduction, not the appropriate process, that of the deductive branches of natural philosophy, but the inappropriate one of pure geometry, which not being a science of causation at all, does not require or admit any summing-up of effects' (AUT, pp. 165–9; cf. Robson, 1968, pp. 168–9). The key focus of these 'truths' was the nature of human agents and their representation. It was then this same focus that drew his attention to the need to question the form of the deductive process that had already concerned him in the Whately critique: 'I then asked myself, what is the ultimate analysis of this deductive process; the common theory of the syllogism evidently throwing no light upon it' (AUT, p. 167; cf. p. 189). He concluded that he should adopt the non-syllogistic mode of reasoning from mechanics and thus allow, by analogy with the 'Composition of Forces', for the 'adding in' of disturbing and countervailing dimensions to any too narrow perception of human conduct adopted for the purposes of establishing a core of logically sound theoretical argument. This was necessary in order adequately to cover the scope of human characteristics and motivations that may be pertinent in applying the theory to account for an observed phenomenon in human science or to justify recommending some social policy. These were methodological concerns which John Mill would confront again and again in the years to come.

By 1830, Mill was geared up for the writing of his own study of scientific logic (AUT, p. 167). He began the project somewhat in the reverse order relative to its ultimate presentation in the SOL because the first formalized step was to try to settle his ideas about the methodological demands of political economy in the light of the Whately review and the Macaulay incident. Not only was political economy the most advanced of the human sciences in terms of its concern with methodological issues, but Mill had also been inculcated into the subject from an early age by his father. In 1819, he was put through a rigorous study of Ricardo's *Principles* on a line-by-line basis, followed up by the preparation of written summaries of the topics covered. A few years later, Mill made marginal notes on the manuscript of his father's *Elements,* a work to some extent written from the father's lesson notes on Ricardo prepared for his son's instruction. Both works, along with others, were soon to be debated in great detail with his young Benthamite colleagues, sometimes under the leadership of Mill himself (AUT, pp. 31, 65, 123). All of this preparation must have left Mill with quite a build–up of manuscript notes and, around 1829–30, he decided to put together some essays on selected substantive aspects of the subject, along with one on its definition and methodology. He then spent some effort on their revision for publication up to the mid-1830s. While confusion surrounds the precise dating of these works, the important one for our purposes here, that on definition and methodology, was the only one actually published in the 1830s. It appeared in the *Westminster Review* in 1836. The other four had to await the success of Mill's SOL to be accepted for publication, along with a republication of the methodology piece, as the collection *Essays on Some Unsettled Questions of Political Economy* in 1844 (AUT, p. 189; Kubitz, 1932, p. 38 and n.; 'Editor's Note', CW, IV, p. 230). Mill originally gave the essay the title 'On the definition of political economy and on the method of philosophical investigation in that science', but he changed the latter part to 'on the method of investigation proper to it' for the 1844 version (DPE). What is most significant about this work is that Mill indicated by his approach that he was intuitively aware of an important methodological strategy. He apparently realized that the correct order of presentation of his argument was to define the nature of the phenomena with which the science is concerned and then to establish the methodological principles that could be shown to be logically consistent with the demands of that definition. Another fact worthy of attention in passing is that, despite the publication of the much more sophisticated treatment of the methodology of the human sciences in Book VI of the SOL, Mill still had sufficient confidence in the DPE to allow it to be presented to the public alongside the larger work with only minor changes from the original. This meant that the status of the DPE went beyond being merely a preparation for the SOL treatment. Indeed its crucial and central role in Mill's intellectual development was not less than that it comprised the foundations for the construction of both the SOL and the *Principles of Political Economy* (PPE) which were to follow.

8.2   Reflections on the methodological inheritance

Mill's DPE was effectively divided into three logically sequential sections. The first considered the issue of defining the nature and scope of political economy. Secondly, this definition was shown to involve a specific representational treatment of the human agents whose conduct forms the substance of economic activity. Then, finally, as a *consequence* of the definition having been established on the basis of the ontological nature of the phenomena with which the science is concerned, the methodology 'proper to it' could be considered in the light of the received orthodoxy. Especially were the epistemological expectations appropriately associated with its explanations thus shown to be sensitively dependent upon the fact that the object phenomena originate in situated human conduct. Understanding the phenomena of political economy required the explicit recognition that they are the results of the choices, decisions and self-conscious actions of human agents going about the most fundamental and dominant of their life-world tasks, the satisfaction of material needs manifested as wealth. Their conduct was to be perceived as chronically dependent upon their inherited situational context, including their social-functional relations with other agents and a host of institutional entities.

Mill began the DPE essay by distinguishing between the notions of a science and an art as they apply to political economy. Put most simply, 'Science takes cognizance of a *phenomenon,* and endeavours to discover its *law*; art proposes to itself an *end,* and looks out for *means* to effect it'; the rules of an art, which in political economy are directed at 'making a nation increase in wealth', depend upon those of the relevant science that is 'conversant with the laws of nature ... and teaches us how things take place of themselves' with respect to 'the laws which regulate the production, distribution, and consumption of wealth' (DPE, pp. 312–13, original emphasis). It was the *science* of political economy that was of concern to Mill and two matters pertinent to its definition were mentioned in this context. First, some delimitation and definition of what constitutes wealth was quite apparently a prerequisite for eliciting the laws relevant to the science. This term, Mill observed, 'is surrounded by a haze of floating and vapoury associations, which will let nothing that is seen through them be shewn distinctly'. His contribution to a clarification of the matter was to define wealth as 'all objects useful or agreeable to mankind, except such as can be obtained in indefinite quantity without labour' (DPE, p. 314). This left the scope of political economy rather open-ended, for, when the production of such objects was considered, the boundary between it and physical science (and engineering) faded by virtue of the essentially physical nature of this most fundamental of its processes.

So it was that, secondly, the science of political economy was required to be familiar with the 'laws of nature' from the particular perspective of its focus on production. As Mill pointed out, production is at its roots a problem of the effective application of physical scientific knowledge. This suggested that a close relationship had to be sustained between such knowledge and the understanding of economic phenomena, for both involved 'one and the same subject-matter; namely, the objects which conduce to man's convenience and enjoyment' (DPE, p. 316). At the same time, the science of political economy was to be kept distinct from the physical sciences and the distinguishing characteristic upon which Mill focused was that the phenomena of the former were the products of the active intervention of human agents in the physical world. Thus, as well as its common concern with the physical laws of nature, political economy had additionally to come to grips with the laws of human nature which ultimately direct economic conduct: 'Everything which can possibly happen in which man and external things, are jointly concerned, results from the joint operation of a law or laws of matter, and a law or laws of the human mind.' On this basis, political economy was classified as a '*moral* or psychological science' (DPE, p. 316, original emphasis).

More specifically, Mill was already inclined to distinguish the physical from the human sciences on the grounds that the ontological foundations of their objects of inquiry appeared to be different in nature. The former, he wrote, 'treat of the laws of matter, and of all complex phenomena in so far as dependent upon the laws of matter', as distinct from the former 'which treat of the laws of mind, and of all complex phenomena in so far as dependent upon the laws of mind'. Thus 'Laws of mind and laws of matter are so dissimilar in their nature, that it would be contrary to all the principles of rational arrangement to mix them up as part of the same study. In all scientific methods, therefore, they are placed apart'. However, for Mill, this separation was only apparent and could not be sustained in the practice of human science. He went on immediately to add that there could be no science which included mental phenomena among it objects which did not presuppose the existing knowledge of the physical sciences. For, as was self-evident as a matter of fact, 'even the phenomena of the mind itself ... [are] partially dependent upon the physiological laws of the body'. Moreover 'all the mental sciences, ... not excepting the pure science of mind, must take account of a great variety of physical truths; and, ... may be said to presuppose them, taking up the complex phenomena where physical science leaves them'. From this perspective, 'Political Economy ... presupposes all the physical sciences' in its focus on the production and distribution of the objects of real wealth, but 'It then inquires what are the phenomena of *mind* which are concerned in the production and distribution of those same objects; it borrows from the pure science of mind the laws of those phenomena, and inquires what effects follow from these mental laws, acting in concurrence with those physical ones' (DPE, pp. 317, 318, original emphasis).

At this point, then, Mill came up with the following interim definition of political economy which emphasized the above distinctions: '"the science which treats of the production and distribution of wealth, so far as they depend upon the laws of human nature." Or thus – "The science relating to the moral or psychological laws of the production and distribution of wealth"' (DPE, pp. 318–19). What made this definition, which 'still falls short of the complete accuracy required for the purposes of the philosopher' (DPE, p. 318), but an interim one was soon revealed to be the fact that it was not specific enough about the involvement of human agents in the science. Two additional qualifications had to be included: one was that, in their economic conduct, agents operate with the functional cooperation of others as part of a society; and the other was that, in their economic conduct, agents draw upon and manifest only some particular aspects of their total natures *qua* human beings and direct their attentions to very specific objectives. These additional conditions are apparent in what Mill posited as the 'complete' and 'correct definition of Political Economy as a portion of the field of science': "'The science which traces the laws of such of the phenomena of society as arise from the combined operations of mankind for the production of wealth, in so far as those phenomena are not modified by the pursuit of any other object"' (DPE, p. 323).

It is quite apparent that the above definitional endeavours give a distinct primacy to the involvement of human agents in the generation of the relevant object phenomena. For Mill, it was Man, 'considered as a being having a moral or mental nature, [who] is the subject-matter of all the moral sciences', including political economy. This nature may be specified on three different levels of general representation and understanding: Man as an isolated individual, 'as if no human being existed besides himself'; Man in immediate contact with other individual Men; and Man 'living in a state of *society*, that is, forming part of a body or aggregation of human beings, systematically co-operating for common purposes' (DPE, p. 319, original emphasis). Each of these levels depends in part upon those which precede it, with the ultimate empirical existence of human beings necessarily involving them in an inherited social situation.

The isolated individual is the object of 'pure mental philosophy' or 'the science of mind' which includes 'all the laws of the mere intellect, and those of the purely self-regarding desires'. These laws and desires are presupposed by the second level which compounds with them the 'laws of human nature which relate to the feelings called forth in a human being by other individual human or intelligent beings, as such'. At this level, the study of 'the science of mind' is extended to provide the formal foundations for the *art* of morals or ethics by inquiring into the aspects of human nature and conduct which relate to and depend upon 'the *affections,* the *conscience,* or feeling of duty, and the love of *approbation*' (DPE, p. 319, original emphasis). It is significant to notice here that Mill confined the *scientific* claims to the roots of moral conduct rather than to the conduct itself. In order to defend this claim, Mill invoked the notion of personal introspection as a source of certain knowledge of the laws of human nature and of the 'external circumstances capable of exciting the human will to action'. His argument was that 'the desires of man, and the nature of the conduct to which they prompt him, are within the reach of our observation. We can also observe what are the objects which excite those desires'. Such knowledge 'every one can principally collect within himself', on the condition that he is prepared to give due 'reasonable consideration of the differences, of which experience discloses to him the existence, between himself and other people'. This latter admission, of course, severely weakened Mill's prospects of ever identifying any universal and reliable laws of human nature, but he passed the point by and went on to claim that 'knowing ... accurately the properties of the [human] sub-stances concerned, we may reason with as much certainty as in the most demonstrative parts of physics from any assumed set of circumstances' (DPE, p. 329). Once again, though, the behavioural results obtained by reasoning from the laws would depend upon the assumed circumstances; that is, upon the particular situational conditions assumed to be confronted by individual agents.

As an extension of this level of argument to the ultimate level of Man in society, Mill was prepared to try for a *science of the conduct of individuals* on the basis that, when sufficiently specified, human objectives and their situational context would contain, constrain and direct such conduct in a regularized manner. He referred to 'certain principles of human nature which are peculiarly connected with the ideas and feelings generated in man by living in a state of *society*', principles which are reflected in the conduct of individuals acting within 'a union or aggregation of human beings' and directed at 'a common purpose or purposes' (DPE, p. 320, original empha-sis). These principles have their origins in the 'elementary laws of the human mind' identified at the previous two levels, but now explicitly contained by the conditions of society to 'give rise to results of a sufficiently universal character, and even (when compared with the still more complex phenomena of which they are the determining causes) sufficiently simple, to admit of being called, though in a somewhat looser sense, *laws* of society, or laws of human nature in the social state' (DPE, p. 320, original emphasis). A note of epistemological reserve crept in here with the concession that the relevant laws had a 'somewhat looser' status than may be expected in a physical science. Nonetheless this body of analysis of the active human agent, includ-ing 'every part of man's nature, in so far as influencing the conduct or condition of man in society', constituted the *science* which Mill chose to call *social economy*. It dealt with 'the whole of man's nature as modified by the social state, ... [and] the whole conduct of man in society' (DPE, p. 321, original emphasis).

Now it is quite apparent that this outline of the scientific approach to an understanding of the conduct of situated human agents was broader than the perspective taken by political economy itself in accordance with Mill's final definition. Precisely how the perspective of the human agent had to be nar-rowed for Mill's immediate purposes was reiterated by his emphasizing that economics 'is concerned with him solely as a being who desires to possess wealth, and who is capable of judging of the comparative efficacy of means for obtaining that end. It predicts only such of the phenomena of the social state as take place in consequence of the pursuit of wealth'. Mill felt that there was an empirical rationale for this emphasis because 'there is, perhaps, no action of a man's life in which he is neither under the immediate nor under the remote influence of any impulse but the mere desire of wealth' (DPE, pp. 321, 322). But, as a science, political economy had to make the concept of its ideal agents even narrower than thus implied. Their conduct under scrutiny had not only to be focused on the pursuit of wealth, but it also had to be exclusively so focused as to abstract from 'every other human passion or motive', with the exception of two perpetually countervailing 'antagonizing principles to the desire of wealth, namely, aversion to labour, and desire of the present enjoyment of costly indulgences'. The ultimate result was a concept of political economy in which human agents were considered 'to prefer a greater portion of wealth to a smaller in all cases' and 'as occupied solely in acquiring and consuming wealth; and [which] aims at showing what is the course of action into which mankind, living in a state of society, would be impelled, if that motive, except in the degree in which it is checked by the two perpetual counter-motives ..., were absolute ruler of all their actions' (DPE, pp. 321–2).

Having set up this ideal representation of the human agent as fundamental to political economy, Mill proceeded to give it a methodological imperative. It was self-evident, he suggested, that no economist would be 'so absurd as to suppose that mankind are really thus constituted' in this narrow way. The rationale for such a representation was rather that '*this is the mode in which science must necessarily proceed*' (DPE, p. 322, emphasis added; cf. p. 327). And, even more directly, he asserted that the definition of a science, which must include the ontological nature of its objects of study, 'is inseparably connected ... [with] the *philosophic method* of the science; the nature of the process by which its investigations are to be carried on, its truths to be arrived at' (DPE, p. 324, original emphasis).

At the most general level, Mill's argument was that such investigations proceed in all sciences by means of identifying progressively more complex causes for phenomena and by assuming that isolated causal contributions that are cited can be mechanistically 'added up', as it were. Analogous to the addition of centripetal and tangential forces in the explanation of planetary motion is the case of the conduct of the human agent: 'In order to judge how he will act under a variety of desires and aversions which are concurrently operating upon him, we must know how he would act under the exclusive influence of each one in particular' (DPE, p. 322). Mill's point here was that it is legitimate to isolate particular contributing causes of events because all such causes can be accumulated analytically to build up a complete explanation. This belief was important in political economy where formal analyses could only proceed by severely restricting the responses and conduct of situated human agents in order to prepare a core of abstract theory and then to be able to add in subsequently any 'disturbing causes' which would bring the deduced results closer to reality. It was a necessary consequence of the human bases of the science that, when a phenomenon is observed, 'no two individual cases are exactly alike, ... [and] no *general* maxims could ever be laid down unless *some* of the circumstances of the particular case were left out of consideration' (DPE, p. 327, original emphasis). The significance of the initially omitted factors must be assessed in terms of their importance as contributing causes so that the relevant theory, which is always only an abstract approximation to the complete causal origins, can be effectively expanded to allow for explanations of any real world phenomenon of the type (DPE, p. 323). What becomes apparent in these arguments by Mill is that he was, right from the beginning of his methodological work, highly sensitive to the epistemological limitations inherent in a human science such as political economy by virtue of its human essence. Where these limitations became most evident was in the practical endeavour to apply economic theory to comprehending and influencing the course of real world events. And, as he delved further into the criteria for establishing legitimate methodological principles for political economy in the face of the existing conflict between the abstract–deductive orthodoxy and its empirico-historicist rivals, the ramifications of the limitations only became more pronounced.

Mill's perception of the methodological controversy was that 'in whatever science there are systematic differences of opinion ... the cause will be found to be, a difference in their conceptions of the philosophic method of the science', especially in relation to their 'different views concerning the nature of the evidence appropriate to the subject'. He developed this thesis by ascribing the foundations of the issue to differences between observer–analysts with respect to their purposes of scientific inquiry. He distinguished between 'two kinds of reasoners' he called 'practical men' and 'theorists' by claiming that, respectively, they 'argue wholly *upwards* from particular facts to a general conclusion' or they 'aim at a wider field of experience, and, having argued upwards from particular facts to a general principle ..., then argue *downwards* from that general principle to a variety of specific conclusions'. Thus the 'first of these methods is a method of induction, ... the method *à posteriori*', while the latter is 'a mixed method of induction and ratiocination ..., the method *à priori*'. It mitigates the distinction, but cannot eliminate it, however, when it is recognized that 'both classes of inquirers do nothing but theorize, and both of them consult no other guide than experience' (DPE, pp. 324–5, original emphases). In this respect, Mill *hinted at* the distinction between two modes of induction. One had the sense applicable to the a posteriori approach, in which reasoning derives logically entailed, demonstrative conclusions 'not [from] experience merely, but [from] specific experience'. The other sense referred to requires only the non-demonstrative derivation from general experience, with no logical entailment, of the assumptions to be used as hypotheses in deductive analyses (DPE, p. 325; cf. Blaug, 1980, pp. 14ff).

At this stage it was Mill's categorical view about methodology in the human sciences that they have no option but to adopt what he called the a priori form: 'we go farther than to affirm that the method *à priori* is a legitimate mode of philosophical investigation in the moral sciences: *we contend that it is the only mode*'; moreover, he compounded this claim by asserting that it is '*the only method by which truth can be attained in any department of the social science*'. By contrast, in its strictly logical form, 'the method *à posteriori*, or that of specific experience, is altogether inefficacious in those sciences, as a means of arriving at any considerable body of valuable truth'. The crucial reason for this latter failure was, Mill noted, that observation in the human sciences had largely to proceed without the benefit of the controlled experiments often available to the natural sciences (DPE, pp. 326, 327–9, emphases added). In the case of political economy, then, the orthodox writers had little option but to make it into an abstract and a priori science. As such, 'it reasons, and, as we contend, must necessarily reason, from assumptions, not from facts', where this 'is not a practice confined to mathematics, but is of the essence of all science which admits of general reasoning at all'. But, while he drew an analogy between the *logical status* of such hypotheses and the definitional axioms of the mathematical sciences such as geometry, which need have no links to experience, he maintained that, in the human sciences, this link must be preserved. His specification of the a priori methodology as cited above suggested this (DPE, pp. 325–6).

It was, then, a consequence of the desire to be scientific, in the sense that its conclusions could be demonstrated to be at least logically 'true', which led political economy into a position of assuming 'an arbitrary definition of man, as a being who inevitably does that by which he may obtain the greatest amount of necessaries, conveniences, and luxuries, with the smallest quantity of labour and physical self-denial with which they can be obtained in the existing state of knowledge'. This dependence on the concept of 'classical economic man' espoused here called for a careful and explicit delimitation of the epistemological claims to be made for political economy *as a science,* as Mill well knew:

Political Economy ... reasons from *assumed* premises – from premises which might be totally without foundation in fact, and which are not pretended to be universally in accordance with it. The conclusions of Political Economy, consequently, like those of geometry, are only true ... *in the abstract;* that is, they are only true under certain suppositions, in which none but general causes – causes common to the *whole class* of cases under consideration – are taken into account. (DPE, p. 326, original emphasis).

To this he added the caveat, which has largely gone unheeded from his own day to ours, that this methodologically qualified status of the science, and the essentially logical status of its revealed truths, *'ought not to be denied by the political economist. If he deny it, then, and then only, he places himself in the wrong* (DPE, p. 326, emphasis added).

Now there was only one way in which a human science in this abstract–deductive sense could reach out towards a concept of truth which accorded with a representation of the reality of its object phenomena. This was the process of 'adding' back the consequences of disturbing causes which were exceptional to the strictly general circumstances to which a pure theory related. Such a process was assumed by Mill and the classicals generally to be the simple one of mechanically compounding the theoretical case without there being any *qualitative* feedback effects on its operations. Mill was concerned that, at least, this process inevitably added a measure of uncertainty into the reasoning of political economy and all human sciences: 'an uncertainty inherent in the nature of [their] complex phenomena, and arising from the impossibility of being quite sure that all the circumstances of the particular case are known to us sufficiently in detail, and that our attention is not unduly diverted from any of them'. Having said this, though, he went on to defend the deductive methodology in the face of these ontological complications by asserting that the disturbing causes were fully calculable, just as the addition of friction was in the case of physical mechanics:

> When the disturbing causes are known, the allowance necessary to be made for them detracts in no way from scientific provision, nor constitutes any deviation from the *à priori* method. ... The disturbing causes have their laws, as the causes which are disturbed have theirs; and from the laws of the disturbing causes, the nature and amount of the disturbance may be predicted *à priori,* like the operation of the more general laws which they are said to modify or disturb, but with which they might more properly be said to be concurrent. The effect of the special causes is then to be added to, or subtracted from, the effect of the general ones. (DPE, p. 330)

Later he added that 'in any tolerably advanced science' there will be no 'exceptions' which are beyond its scope, properly defined. The situation is rather that 'what is thought to be an exception to a principle is always some other and distinct principle cutting into the former'. Thus 'there are not a *law* and an *exception* to that law .... There are two laws ... bringing about a common effect by their conjunct operation' (DPE, p. 338, original emphasis).

The effect of the realistic additions, then, was only to *extend and complicate* the substantive reasoning in human science. There was no need to change, according to Mill, the abstract–deductive methodology of the analyses in order to approach closer to the nature of reality, for 'that which is true in the abstract, is always true in the concrete with proper *allowances*'; all that is involved is 'following out the method of the abstract science into minuter details; inserting among its hypotheses a fresh and still more complex combination of circumstances, and so adding *pro hâc vice* a supplementary chapter or appendix, or at least a supplementary theorem, to the abstract science' (DPE, pp. 327, 331, original emphasis). But, in order to maintain consistency with his emphasis on the human origins of the phenomena to be dealt with in this way, Mill was led immediately to try to trace these disturbing causes to the nature and conduct of human agents. To do so, the disturbances at issue in economics were said to work either through a modification to the tenets of the basic wealth motive or through 'some other law of human nature', although this latter case requires knowledge from some other science to be invoked. Just how far this methodological certainty could be carried into the formal representation of an extended complexity of human agency Mill did not say at this stage. However he did accept that the scope of reliable reason would have a limit by virtue of the fact that the premises from which it must work are ultimately dependent upon the fallible process of generalization from human observations. Once observer–analysts' knowledge of situated human agency must move beyond what may be logically extrapolated from personal introspection, then uncertainties about the veracity of a theory are inevitable. If it were the case that a knowledge of 'what are the particular causes operating in any given instance were revealed to us by infallible authority, then, if our abstract science were perfect, we should become prophets'. As was obvious to Mill, 'the causes are not so revealed: they are to be collected by observation; and observation in circumstances of complexity is apt to be imperfect'. The reason for this fallibility was mostly able to be attributed to the intellectual limitations of observers, but, in a further comment left without elaboration, Mill slipped in that '*some of the causes may lie beyond observation*' (DPE, p. 332, emphasis added). Perhaps here we have the first tacit admission that there would always be an untapped metaphysical dimension to any explanation in human science, even allowing for the insights made possible by introspection. Later on, as we are to see, this tacit concern became more explicit (section 9.4 below).

Whatever may turn out to be the extent to which the claims to realism in an abstract–deductive model of human science are defensible, it was Mill's further belief at this stage that the ultimate test of the theories involved was always the consistency of their predictions with observed events. This meant that 'the *à posteriori* method, or that of specific experience' became the complementary approach required,

> not as a means of discovering truth, but of verifying it, and reducing to the lowest point that uncertainty before alluded to as arising from the complexity of every

particular case, and from the difficulty (not to say impossibility) of our being assured *à priori* that we have taken into account all the material circumstances. (DPE, p. 331)

Just how analysts were to proceed in doing this testing of their theories, or what epistemological standards could be expected to flow from it, Mill did not stop to elaborate. He used the term 'verification' to refer to the objective of the exercise, but quite evidently it was only the more delimited notion of consistency between observation and theoretical implication that was at issue. It remains problematical, though, to interpret his intentions when it came to the response to be induced in the analyst by a failure to find such consistency. He noted that it could draw attention to the existence of an overlooked, but important, disturbing cause. But there also existed the possibility that the failure was signalling a more fundamental inadequacy of the theory itself, a *refutation* in more modern terms, in that 'it often discloses to us errors in thought, still more serious than the omission of what can with any propriety be termed a disturbing cause. It often reveals to us that the basis itself of our whole argument is insufficient' (DPE, p. 332). The challenge for the theorists confronted by such an inconsistency between their representation of a phenomenon and its empirical reality was to discriminate between an inadequacy in the causal scope of their arguments and one which stems from a lack of correct theoretical insight. This was an important implication of Mill's brief reference to the theory assessment puzzles of political economy, but it left a lot of unanswered questions in its wake about which controversy continues to this day.

In the early essay that we have just been considering, Mill posed for himself some acute methodological concerns about the appropriate mode of theory construction and testing in the human sciences. The example of political economy as one of the most formally developed and influential of those sciences at the time served him well as a means to establish the objectives of his more general inquiries into logic and methodology that he had been working on at the same time. As already indicated, these inquiries were to be brought to fruition in the SOL, with its wide-ranging coverage of methodological issues in science, including the human sciences. One of the most crucial influences upon the course of Mill's inquiries during this period was the positivist philosophy of Auguste Comte.

8.3   Comte's positivism and the human sciences
It was during the period of the final preparation of the SOL from 1837 onwards that Mill came under the strongest influence of the French philosopher Auguste Comte. He had been aware of Comte's work much earlier and had been impressed by parts of it (AUT, pp. 173, 217ff). Now the work with

which he was concerned was the *Cours de philosophie positive*. He read the first two volumes already extant (1830, 1835) and, subsequently, the remaining four volumes as they appeared (1838–42). There followed a period of correspondence between the two during the 1840s (CW, XIII, pp. 488ff), but ultimately, the influence which remained most apparent in Mill's SOL involved Book VI on the logic of the human sciences, crucial chapters of which he revised in response to Comte's sixth volume before the manuscript was sent to the publishers (Robson, 1973, pp. lxviii–lxix, lxxvi). Comte's influences were to be as much strategically as methodologically vital in Mill's overall approach to his project in the human sciences, including the design of the PPE. What was involved here was the shift from the narrow perspective on political economy as an independent science to a general acceptance of 'the Comtian idea of the consensus of social facts and the correlative idea that social phenomena could not be studied separately, since it was clear that each social phenomenon corresponded to the total condition of society' (Mueller, 1956, p. 105). The main sources of this sort of conclusion are the two long and critical essays on Comte that Mill published in the *Westminster Review* in 1865. These were reissued a year later in book form, under the title 'Auguste Comte and Positivism' (ACP) and they provide us with a retrospective assessment by Mill of the merits and demerits of the Frenchman's vast work.

The impact that Comte had on the development of Mill's works has been well established by his own recollections in the AUT (pp. 173, 217ff, 231, 255n, 271) and by a number of scholars, probably beginning with Alexander Bain in 1882 (1969, pp. 63ff). In 1909, W.J. Ashley considered at some length the Comte–Mill filiation and wrote of how 'Mill was immensely attracted, and for the time possessed, by Comte's general conception of the Social Science or Sociology; and [how] in the concluding chapters of his *Logic* he took this over bodily'. Beyond this, Ashley continued, in the working out of his revamped version of 'Ricardian' political economy, Mill felt 'bound to put this science into some sort of relation with that general Social Science ..., of which he had gained, or solidified, his notion from the reading of Comte. Accordingly, he gave his book the title: "Principles of Political Economy, *with some of their Applications to Social Philosophy*"' (1964, pp. xiv, xviii, original emphasis). Hayek's is probably the strongest claim of influence: 'Mill ..., in the sixth book of his *Logic*, which deals with the methods of the moral sciences, became little more than an expounder of Comtian doctrine' (1955, p. 186). Similarly, referring to the Mill–Comte correspondence, Iris Mueller suggests that 'Mill was so impressed by the method and control of Comte's intellect that his letters often give the impression of a neophyte resting on bended knees to learn wisdom from an acknowledged master'. And, she reports, during the 1840s Mill vigorously defended Comte against an attack by the philosopher of science John Herschel (Mueller, 1956, pp. 93, 95n; see CW, XIII, pp. 673ff). Her conclusion is that 'although Mill was later to denounce Comte's social program, he remained to the end an adherent and defender of the scientific part of Comte's endeavours' (1956, p. 96).

More recently scholars have treated Mill as a more careful and discriminating critic of Comte's methodological and substantive ideas (cf. Lewisohn, 1987, *passim*; Ekelund and Olsen, 1987, *passim*; and Hollander, 1985, pp. 168ff, 955ff). John Robson sums up the filiation most aptly when he refers to a significant common intellectual ground between the two writers from the outset:

> The exact extent of the debt [of Mill to Comte] is difficult to establish because of the shared beliefs and frequent agreement: both aimed at a scientific reorganization of society, and therefore directed their minds to problems of method; both believed in the limitation of inquiry to [empirical] phenomena, and recommended a recognition of this limitation to reformers; both held that moral progress was possible and probable, if not inevitable. Within this large area of agreement – for them it was large – their debts and differences are to be seen. (1968, p. 96)

It was Mill's assessment that Comte's 'essentially sound view of philosophy' comprised, most importantly, his 'clear, full, and comprehensive exposition, and in part creation, of what he terms the Positive Philosophy'. Here Mill's summary of positivism as the 'fundamental doctrine of a true philosophy' is important, for it set the stage for the anti-metaphysical essentials of Comte's contributions with which he was concerned to begin his critique.

> We have no knowledge of anything but Phaenomena; and our knowledge of phaenomena is relative, not absolute. We know not the essence, nor the real mode of production, of any fact, but only its relations to other facts in the way of succession and similitude. These relations are constant; that is, always the same in the same circumstances. The constant resemblances which link phaenomena together, and the constant sequences which unite them as antecedent and consequent, are termed their laws. The laws of phaenomena are all we know respecting them. Their essential nature, and their ultimate causes, either efficient or final, are unknown and inscrutable to us. (ACP, pp. 265–6)

Mill's acceptance of a phenomenalist epistemology could not have been more clearly stated. What was firmly reinforced here was his rejection, with Comte, of any concern to probe beyond the empirically observed nature of phenomena, including those generated by human agency (cf. Hayek, 1955, p. 170). One of his intentions in the SOL was to counteract the metaphysical intrusions into English philosophy, but not for intellectual reasons alone. While he supported per se Comte's rejection of 'the habit of conceiving ...

mental abstractions as real entities, which could exert power, produce phaeneomena, and the enunciation of which could be regarded as a theory or explanation of facts', he sustained a strong practical orientation in so doing (ACP, pp. 270–71). Already, in 1854, he wrote to Theodor Gomperz, the German translator and editor of many of his works, that he believed the 'intuitionist' school of philosophy to be 'the greatest speculative hindrance to the reformation, so urgently required, of man and society; which can never be effected under the influence of a philosophy which makes opinions their own proof, and feelings their own justification' (CW, XIV, p. 239; quoted by Mueller, 1956, p. 97). Later he expressed the similar concern that, 'whatever may be the practical value of a true philosophy ..., it is hardly possible to exaggerate the mischiefs of a false one'. In particular the 'notion that truths external to the mind may be known by intuition or consciousness, independently of observation and experience, is, I am persuaded, in these times, the great intellectual support of false doctrines and bad institutions' (AUT, p. 233). Thus it should be emphasized that Mill's rejection of the metaphysical conception of human nature was of the utmost practical significance for his work in the human sciences. His ideas for the design of policies which would bring about economic and social reforms depended primarily upon the belief that the human mind, and hence the character and conduct of human agents, could be moulded and directed by manipulation of the environmental situations that they were caused to confront by policy means. Acceptance of the alternative 'innatist' position, espoused especially by metaphysical theologians, encouraged conservative attitudes towards reform. I return to this theme in section 9.4 below.

My main focus for the rest of this section will be on Mill's critical concern regarding Comte's misleading assessment of the current state and desirable direction of the prospective future development of the human sciences generally, and of psychology and political economy in particular. What particularly disturbed Mill about Comte's endeavours was his assertion that all of the extant individual components of human science were in a state of metaphysical backwardness and divisive disarray. Mill did not accept these assertions or the proposed corrective measure of immediately and exclusively developing a fully inclusive and unified positive science of sociology into which all burgeoning human sciences were to be absorbed. As far as Mill was concerned, some of the human sciences were already well developed as bodies of knowledge which met the epistemological demands of positivism in Comte's sense. There had been, Mill argued, a significant number of prominent writers on human–social themes, amongst whom he included 'Turgot, Adam Smith, and the political economists universally', who had 'a full conviction that social phaenomena conform to invariable laws, the discovery and illustration of which was their great object as speculative thinkers'. What Mill was prepared to grant, though, was that these human scientists 'did not get as far as M. Comte in discovering the methods best adapted to bring these laws to light' (ACP, p. 290). To assist in bringing about a correction of this latter shortcoming was the crucial objective of Mill's SOL in particular. What Mill found in Comte's sociology was an holistic science based upon a particular methodology which gave primacy to the generalized collective outcomes of human–social conduct as its immediate objects of empirical study. Methodologically he granted that the approach was 'highly instructive', even though it appeared to contradict the relevance of the established direct deductive approach to human–social phenomena, especially as reflected in orthodox political economy. Mill reminded his readers in ACP that the human essence of economic phenomena comprised a recognition that their 'elementary facts are feelings and actions, and the laws of these are the laws of human nature, social facts being the results of human acts and situations'. While the laws of human nature must remain as data for sociology, it was the cumulative biographical experiences of generations which in a developed society dominated the character and conduct of its agents. Therefore the apt perception, with which Mill agreed, was that 'human beings themselves, on the laws of whose nature the facts of history depend, are not abstract or universal but historical human beings, already shaped, and made what they are, by human society' (ACP, p. 307; cf. pp. 315ff). To reach an explanation of social phenomena by direct deduction from the laws of human nature thus became unworkable because of the complexity and historical extent of the factors affecting contemporary events. There was, then, as Comte advocated, a need to reverse the usual approach to science so that 'in sociology it is specific experience which suggests the laws, and deduction which verifies them' rather than the other way round. In sum, 'if laws of social phaenomena, empirically generalized from history, can when once suggested be affiliated to the known laws of human nature [then] the empirical generalizations are raised into positive laws, and Sociology becomes a science' (ACP, pp. 307–8). Mill's adoption of this inverse deductive methodology will be discussed more fully in section 9.3 below.

Probing further into the rationale for Comte's negative judgement about the status of human science, Mill had discovered a serious flaw in the direction of Comte's inquiries about the essential foundations on which such science was to be constructed. Mill considered it to be a 'grave aberration in M. Comte's view of the method of positive science' as it involves human–social issues that he 'rejects totally, as an invalid process, psychological observation properly so called, or in other words, internal consciousness, at least as regards our intellectual operations' (ACP, p. 296). This matter was of profound concern to Mill. For him, it was self-evident that the human sciences could only be founded, in a logically prior sense, on the properly constituted laws of the structure and operation of the human mind. Such laws of mind were to be empirically derived, largely with the aid of extrapolation to other agents of the introspective insights of each individual: 'The wisdom acquired by the study of ourselves, and of the circumstances which surround us, can alone teach us to interpret the comparatively little which we know of other persons and other modes of existence' (Mill, quoted by Mueller, 1956, p. 107).

By contrast, Comte gave no self-sufficient status 'to the science of Psychology, and always speaks of it with contempt'. On this matter, Comte was interpreted by Mill to be an unacceptably extreme empiricist and behaviourist, having rejected 'as an invalid process, psychological observation properly so called, or in other words, internal consciousness' (ACP, p. 296). Comte claimed access to knowledge of the human mind by means of the physical observation of other people alone, for he was of the opinion that 'we can learn very little about the feelings, and nothing at all about the intellect, by self-observation'. Even more specifically, he was read by Mill as espousing the view that 'we cannot observe ourselves observing, or observe ourselves reasoning: and if we could, attention to this reflex operation would annihilate its object, by stopping the process observed' (ACP, p. 296). Mill rejected these ideas as fallacious, adding the penetrating query 'how we are to observe other people's mental operations, or how interpret the signs of them without having learnt what the signs mean by knowledge of ourselves, he does not state' (ACP, p. 296; cf. Priestley, 1969, p. li). Such self-reflection was well within the capabilities of human agents by means of the capacity to attend to more than one mental representation at a time, supplemented by the ability to call up memories or such representations. Comte's reasoning about the incapacity of agents to study their own mental processes and substance was simply wrong (ACP, pp. 296–7). Then, as the final absurdity, Comte resorted to an upgraded version of phrenology to give ultimate empirical, and hence positive methodological impetus, to his pseudo-psychology and proceeded to place it under the rubric of Biology in his list of the sciences (ACP, pp. 297, 360). In sum, while 'Comte admitted phrenology to full scientific status, and believed that the basis of sociology was in physiology', Mill remained 'unwilling to substitute the unproven physiology for the association psychology which he believed to be the proper basis for social science' (Lewisohn, 1987, p. 269, cf. p. 271).

Most generally, it was Mill's complaint against Comte that, being wedded to such an extreme behaviourism and to the claims of phrenology, he had chosen to ignore the established nomological tenets of associationist psychology. Moreover, at the fundamental level of the formation of the mental character of individual agents and the inclinations of their conduct, he had failed to give due regard to the profound influence of biographical experiences and current situational circumstances. As a consequence, he had 'done nothing for the constitution of the positive method of mental science' and neglected the 'psychological branch of the positive method, as well as psychology itself'. All in all, these errors of omission and commission, his 'great mistake' in Mill's words, were not indicative of 'a mere hiatus in M. Comte's system, but the parent of serious errors in his attempt to create a Social Science' (ACP, p. 298). In particular it meant that his point of departure in his inquiry into the formation and the practical application of the human sciences was the false one that they currently had no positive status because they had confined their premises to metaphysical assumptions flowing from an unfounded psychology. Mill's belief was, on the contrary, that human phenomena could be approached using the positive scientific methodology because of their origin in the empirical laws of mind and the laws of the formation of human character that could be formalized as the science of ethology.

Mill was especially disturbed by Comte's treatment of political economy, which for Mill comprised 'the only systematic attempt yet made by any body of thinkers, to constitute a science, not indeed of social phaenomena generally, but of one great class or division of them'. Beyond Adam Smith, whose speculations were considered to be 'valuable preparatory studies for science', Comte deemed the progress in the study of economic phenomena to have been minimal, for the political economists 'have added nothing really new to the original *aperçus* of Adam Smith' and had continued to debate its concepts in the most scholastic way. Political economy had, Comte asserted, remained 'unscientific, unpositive, and a mere branch of metaphysics' (ACP, p. 305; cf. Ashley, 1964, pp. xiii–xiv). Not unexpectedly, he rejected the notion that there had been no progress in the works of the political economy since Smith, for 'every one who has read them knows that they have added so much as to have changed the whole aspect of the science'. Moreover he correctly sensed just how little Comte really knew about the subject, anyway: 'Any one acquainted with the writings of political economists need only read his few pages of animadversions on them … to learn how extremely superficial M. Comte can sometimes be' (ACP, p. 305). In this respect, evidently, Comte stands condemned for having undertaken 'to denounce political economy at some length, [whereas] his severity stands in strange contrast to his exceedingly slender knowledge of the object of his abuse'. For, as Hayek has discovered, 'even one of his admirers, who has devoted a whole book to Comte's relation to economics, could not help emphasizing, his knowledge of economics was practically nonexistent' (1955, p. 181). The only apparently saving grace for Comte in this matter was his reference in correspondence with Mill in 1844 to an acceptance that political economy could be ascribed a 'provisional' status in its presently extant form (CW, XIII, pp. 624ff). It seems probable, though, that as Ashley explained soon after the publication of the relevant letters, Comte misunderstood the import of Mill's suggestion (1964, pp. xxii–xxiii). What Mill appears to have intended was that the conclusions of political economy were 'provisional' in the sense that, while they applied in the context of the institutional arrangements of the contemporary capitalist system, they would require revision along with any transformation of that system. It was Comte's idea, by contrast, that political economy should be treated as a 'provisional' step towards the writing of an holistic sociology, after the realization of which it would disappear. As far as Mill was concerned, there was never any intention on his part that political economy was to be absorbed into a sociology of any sort.

On one important, and ultimately quite influential point, though, he was essentially in agreement with Comte: 'namely, that the study of the conditions of national wealth as a detached subject is unphilosophical, because, [with] all the different aspects of social phaenomena acting and reacting on one another, they cannot be rightly understood apart'. Comte had taken this insight too far in his rejection of *any* separable science of economic phenomena. What was involved was rather the implication that the generalizations of the science were necessarily to be considered as strictly relative to their particular socio-historical context, a conclusion which 'no political economist would deny' (ACP, p. 305). In Mill's view, though, some basic economic principles would always be intertemporally transferable, being sufficiently essential and abstract to provide generalized knowledge relevant to any stage of historical development. From this perspective, it was the 'Ricardian' heritage which could be so designated. Hollander's summary argument is worthy of careful critical consideration, for 'Mill's criticism of Comte in 1865 is precisely that which he had in mind while preparing the *Principles*'. In particular:

> It seems fair to conclude that nothing in the Comte–Mill nexus of the 1840s implies a breakaway on Mill's part from the orthodox (Ricardian) approach to political economy – subject always to the insistence upon specification of the appropriate institutional framework and recognition of the consequentially restricted scope of its generalizations, which Mill intended to emphasize by the organization of his *Principles*. What comes to the fore in the 1865 review is disappointment in Comte's continued failure to appreciate the possibility of remaining within the orthodox camp, while yet recognizing the historico-institutional dimension of social investigation and the need to avoid 'narrow-mindedness'. (1985, p. 174)

What requires more emphasis than Hollander gives it is that a crucial manifestation of the revisionist dimensions of Mill's PPE project was his refusal to model the human agent as mere 'economic man' in the 'narrow–minded' orthodox sense. The required representation of human agents had to allow for the cumulative and current effects of the facts of their perceived situations, including the demands of contemporary institutions. It was Mill's conviction that an understanding of human agency could only follow from an appreciation that it is environmentally sensitive and responsive, so that economic analysis could only provide a cogent basis for policy reform if it paid due regard to this fact.

The immediate impact of this focus upon human agency as the means of generation of actual and planned economic phenomena was that the methodological strategy and epistemological expectations of the PPE had to be modified relative to those narrow, scientistic criteria accepted in much of the 'Ricardian' literature. On the basis of this reasoning, Mill concluded that 'a person is not likely to be a good political economist who is nothing else' (ACP, p. 306). He effectively called for a conscious endeavour to maintain a concept of the human agent in political economy that was considerably broader in scope than 'classical economic man'. On his own admission, extant economic analysis, much of it presumably 'good', had depended exclusively upon this restricted model of the agent in order to facilitate its presentation in formal deductive–logical terms. Now he was effectively recommending a shift to a political economy based upon a model of anthropological or sociological proportions, with a much lower degree of abstraction than could be expected if the concrete deductive methodology of physical science is to be sustainable in representing economic phenomena. The result could only have been a PPE whose mixed methodological style as well as whose coverage was similar to that of Adam Smith's WN. Mill had no hesitation in admitting that his PPE was designed as a book covering more than the abstract science, with much of it devoted to the applications of political economy. It treated the science as part of a larger totality of human sciences and so interlinked with all the other branches that its conclusions could only be considered to be true conditionally (AUT, p. 243; cf. p. 242).

One further dimension of Comte's methodology which Mill adopted was the distinction which he made between static and dynamic analyses, drawing the analogy from biology rather than mechanics (Hayek, 1955, p. 178). Mill's summary of the distinction conveys admirably the potential for its application in political economy that must have so impressed him:

> Social phaenomena, like all others, present two aspects, the statical, and the dynamical; the phaenomena of equilibrium, and those of motion. The statical aspect is that of the laws of social existence, considered abstractedly from progress, and confined to what is common to the progressive and the stationary state. The dynamical aspect is that of social progress ... [and] evolution. The first is the theory of the *consensus*, or interdependence of social phaenomena. The second is the theory of their filiation. (ACP, p. 309, original emphasis)

Quite clearly the basic idea of such a division already existed in political economy, but Mill gave it added definition through his theoretical and applied treatments in the SOL and the PPE.

It was Mill's opinion that Comte had made no original or meaningful contribution to substantive aspects of the static analysis of society from any perspective. His dynamic analyses were, though, of some significance and found the general support of Mill, at least as far as their theoretical contents were concerned (ACP, pp. 309, 315ff, 324–5). In particular it was their foundation on the principle that the crucial basis of human progress was intellectual development that attracted his imprimatur because of its immediate consistency with the notion that human character and conduct could be manipulated by environmental conditioning. It was Mill's ever-present intention to resist the 'innatist' conceptions of the direction of human agency, for 'the passions are, in the individual man, a more energetic power than a mere intellectual conviction; but the passions tend to divide, not to unite, mankind: it is only by a common belief that the passions are brought to work together'. The inculcation of common belief sets brings cooperation in the place of conflict: 'All human society, consequently, is grounded on a system of fundamental opinions, which only the speculative faculty can provide, and which, when provided, directs our other impulses in their mode of seeking their gratification' (ACP, pp. 315–16). Such beliefs must be accounted for by situational influences, and by this means alone can the passions and interests which are so vital in providing the drive of individuals to act be given a common socially desirable direction. Mill argued this point by analogy:

> To say that men's intellectual beliefs do not determine their conduct, is like saying that the ship is moved by the steam and not by the steersman. The steam indeed is the motive power; the steersman, left to himself, could not advance the vessel a single inch; yet it is the steersman's will and the steersman's knowledge which decide in what direction it shall move and whither it shall go. (ACP, p. 317)

Mill's crusade for reform in much of his work was devoted to ensuring that, while the individual motivational forces were sustained by sufficient liberty, the desired direction and destination of economy and society were controlled by means of properly designed intellectual development. Comte was credited with being 'free from the error of those who ascribe all to general causes, and imagine that neither casual circumstances, nor governments by their acts, nor individuals of genius by their thoughts, materially accelerate or retard human progress' (ACP, p. 322). Having granted this, though, Mill was unable to give much support to the Frenchman's own programmes of social redesign that were the subject of his *Système de politique positive* (1851–4). It was especially Comte's espousal of altruism in place of egoism as the chief motivator of human agents, together with his advocacy of extremes of institutional controls, his 'mania' and his 'frenzy' for regulation, in place of a priority for properly contained liberty, which Mill found to be wholly misguided, at best (ACP, pp. 335ff). It was evident in retrospect that much room had been left by Comte for Mill's own developments in social theory and for the consequent strategy of economic and social reform which he worked out in the PPE (ACP, p. 327). But, before this could be achieved, he considered it essential to reflect long and hard on the proper methodological foundations for such a practically oriented social science, the scope of which reached well beyond the established principles of political economy. It is to this endeavour within the SOL that we now turn.

9 Mill's extended methodological inquiry

9.1 Introduction

Parallel with his work on the DPE, Mill wrote the early draft of significant parts of the SOL dealing with the most basic topics of philosophy and logic and with the problem of deduction, later to constitute Books I and II and part of Book III of the work. At that time, he had also hoped to deal 'at once with the problem of Induction, postponing that of Reasoning, on the ground that it is necessary to obtain premises before we can reason from them' (AUT, p. 167). However, this was not to be. Mill recalled that he had been much troubled by the inductive dimension of methodology: 'I had come to the end of my tether; I could make nothing satisfactory of Induction, at this time. I continued to read any book which seemed to promise light on the subject, ... but for a long time I found nothing which seemed to open to me any very important vein of meditation' (AUT, p. 191). The 'long time', in fact, was to last five years during which time work on the SOL was brought to a halt. The breakthrough came in 1837 with the publication of William Whewell's book *History of the Inductive Sciences*. This work provided Mill with an accessible survey of the inductive process as it had been established and practised across the whole of the sciences and this, together with a rereading of John Herschel's *A Preliminary Discourse on the Study of Natural Philosophy* (1831), enabled him rapidly to complete that part of Book III which had brought him to a standstill (AUT, pp. 217–19). After that, the remainder of the book was written and then the whole of it rewritten completely between 1841 and 1843, with some significant revisions, before the manuscript was sent to the publishers. The book finally appeared in the spring of 1843 with the full title, *A System of Logic Ratiocinative and Inductive: Being a Connected View of the Principles of Evidence and the Methods of Scientific Investigation* (AUT, pp. 229ff; Robson, 1973, pp. lxviff).

The main general objective of the SOL, according to Mill's own recollections, was to provide an accessible exposition of that scientific logic which may be applied in obtaining an understanding of phenomena generated externally to the mind. These phenomena are claimed to be represented to the mind by the combined consequences of sensory experience and mental associations. Its purpose, that is, was to oppose the widely held notion that knowledge of such phenomena could be generated a priori by human intuition and consciousness acting independently of experience. Mill intended to do so by showing that there existed a sound logic of science applicable to empirically observable phenomena, independently of any claims made about their metaphysical origins (AUT, p. 233). He made this latter point quite explicit in a paragraph added to the Preface of the sixth edition of the SOL (1865): 'The main doctrines of this treatise are on the whole compatible with either of the conflicting theories respecting the ultimate structure of the human mind – the *à priori* or intuitional theory, and the experiential theory' (p. cxvi). Thus, emphasizing that 'Logic is not the science of Belief, but the science of Proof, or Evidence', he expressed his objective most generally as 'to attempt a correct analysis of the intellectual process called Reasoning or Inference, and of such other mental operations as are intended to facilitate this: as well as, on the foundation of this analysis, and *pari passu* with it, to bring together or frame a set of rules or canons for testing the sufficiency of any given evidence to prove any given proposition' (pp. 9, 12). In the Preface to the work, he posed the particular issue to be addressed with respect to the human sciences in the light of this general aim as

> whether moral and social phenomena are really exceptions to the general certainty and uniformity of the course of nature; and how far the methods, by which so many of the laws of the physical world have been numbered among [the inferential] truths irrevocably acquired and universally assented to, can be made instrumental to the formation of a similar body of received doctrine in moral and political science. (p. cxiii)

The implications of Mill's sanguine espousal of the logic of the physical sciences as pertinent to the human–social sciences, considered in relation to the general objective stated above, came in Book VI of the SOL, which carried the title 'On the Logic of the Moral Sciences' (pp. 831ff). According to Kubitz, 'in presenting Book VI ... we are presenting the form which Mill's method took after he had solved the problem of induction [in Book III] and had worked through Comte's account of the social sciences', what comprised, effectively, 'merely a complete development of the method which he had already formulated for political economy' (1932, p. 242). My inquiries, as reported in this chapter, suggest that the reference here to 'merely a complete development' is potentially misleading. To an extent, it could obscure the shift in Mill's position on methodology between the DPE and the SOL brought about by the extension of the scope of the relevant object phenomena of the human sciences allowed for in the latter. It is true, as I noted earlier, that the two works were contemporaneously published. But I will argue that their particular substantive, and thus methodological, perspectives made them different rather than inconsistent. The DPE could provide only partial bases for the expansive social economics of the PPE, and Book VI of the SOL provided the methodological bridge from one to the other. The most important consideration in the need for the bridge was the failure of the concept of 'economic man' to represent adequately the situated human agency that Mill was to build his analyses around in the later book. Once he permitted the object ontology to direct the choice of methodology, Mill could not sustain the orthodox classical position. Moreover the idea that logical operations could continue to claim epistemological results that are independent of beliefs about the generation of the phenomena themselves became difficult to defend when he probed the ultimately transcendental dimensions of the mind that are responsible for human action. The consequently inevitable epistemological remainder that would be left in any explanation or prediction in the human sciences was finally admitted when Mill explicitly confronted and gave his first sustained attention to the significance of the metaphysical school of thought (cf. SOL, p. cxvi). I consider the consequences of this extension of his inquiries in section 9.4 below.

In the DPE, considered in the previous chapter (section 8.2), Mill defended the abstract–deductive methodology as the only one appropriate for political economy in its orthodox scientific version. He did so on the grounds of the accepted belief that it was possible to provide an adequately realistic abstract representation of the conduct of human agents in objective terms. This objectivity stemmed from the containment of the relevant dimensions of human agency by the strictly defined motivational and situational conditions assumed to constitute the economic environment. The perspective in Book VI of the SOL shifted to a broader and more philosophically sophisticated treatment of the problem of representing human agents for analytical purposes. In this context, the issue of the potential for objectivity in representing human conduct was posed under the rubric of free-will versus determinism, with Mill expressing support for the latter in the very special sense that made the belief consistent with the essential freedom of agents to choose and act as they wish. The thrust of his argument was that agent predictability is the relevant form of determinism here, in that it allows for their conduct to be argued as a reliable, rather than an absolutely necessary, function of their situations. As it is my intention to show in this chapter, this was the most essential of the human ontological premises from which Mill worked in elaborating and defending the methodology of the human sciences in the SOL and beyond.

9.2 The essentials of situated human agency

Mill introduced the issue of understanding human agency by comparing two extreme positions on the subject of the law of causality versus the freedom of the will. One was the 'doctrine of Necessity' with its assertion that as 'human volitions and actions [are] necessary and inevitable', the 'law of causality' must apply in human affairs as much as it does in other circumstances. This was contrasted with the alternative position that 'the will is not determined, like other phenomena, by antecedents, but determines itself; that our volitions are not, properly speaking, the effect of causes, or at least have no causes which they uniformly and implicitly obey'. For Mill, it was unequivocally the case that the tenor of 'the former of these two opinions is that which I consider the true one' (SOL, p. 836).

It was only the *tenor* of the 'doctrine of Necessity' which Mill espoused because the literal meaning of the position had been so often misunderstood to imply a human condition contrary to freedom. What he intended was to steer the argument towards one in which the causal roots of human conduct were not separated from the free choices of agents themselves. In the determinism of human agency there existed, he claimed, a constancy of causation such that,

> given the motives which are present to an individual's mind, and given likewise the character and disposition of the individual, *the manner in which he will act might be unerringly inferred*; that if we knew the person thoroughly, and knew all the inducements which are acting upon him, *we could foretell his conduct with as much certainty as we can predict a physical event.* (SOL, pp. 836–7, emphasis added)

Mill claimed a commonsense rationale for this strong assertion of human situational determinism. It merely reflected a widely adopted and accepted procedure by one agent who observes another and assumes that his/her choices and actions will comprise a regularized response to what is known of his/her character, state of mind and the circumstances confronted. The significant point remained, though, that with this mutual predictability between agents well known to each other did not come any reduction in freedom to act by choice. Thus 'We may be free, and yet another may have reason to be perfectly certain what use we shall make of our freedom'; but, at the same time, 'we do not feel ourselves the less free because those to whom we are intimately known are well assured how we shall act in a particular case' (SOL, p. 837).

When the doctrine was put as baldly as this, Mill realized that there should be a degree of scepticism about its veracity because common sense also suggests that human agents *can and do* act other than in a constrained and determined way. In a strictly existential sense, agents are wholly free to respond as they wish without situational concerns, for 'we know that we are not compelled, as by a magic spell, to obey any particular motive [and] that if we wished to prove that we have the power of resisting the motive, we could do so'. It was Mill's argument that, in such circumstances, the break with necessity in his sense was only apparent because the totality of the causation now included a '*new antecedent*', namely, the volition to resist the usual motive (SOL, p. 838, original emphasis). Mill was not arguing for an irresistible or uncontrollable necessity that may apply in cases where it is other 'agencies of nature' that are the causal origins of an event. Rather, in words that recall the 'disturbing causes' qualifications applied in political economy, 'when we say that all human actions take place of necessity, we only mean that they will certainly happen if nothing prevents [them]', with the appropriately tempered claim being that 'the given cause will be followed by the effect, subject to all possibilities of counteraction by other causes'. More specifically, 'human actions ... are never (except in some cases of mania) ruled by any one motive with such absolute sway that there is no room for the influence of any other' (SOL, p. 839).

At a somewhat deeper level of inquiry, Mill no longer worked from an assumed given character of the human agent. Instead he chose specifically to link that character into the moulding forces of the agent's situation: 'our characters follow from our organisation, our education, and our circumstances' (SOL, p. 840). Thus 'the doctrine of Causation of human actions, improperly called the doctrine of Necessity' was not to be aligned with fatalism. Mill's position was clearly that this doctrine asserted 'only that men's actions are the joint result of general laws and circumstances of human nature, and of their own particular characters, those characters again being the consequence of the natural and artificial circumstances that constitute their education, among which circumstances must be reckoned their own conscious efforts' (SOL, p. 932; cf. p. 936). Here, as before, there was no claim by him that individual volition had no role to play in the process. Individual agents were free to direct the formation of their characters either in coordination with their situations over time or by resisting, to some degree, these situational forces. Here Mill concluded with respect to the human character that:

> Its being, in the ultimate resort, formed *for* him, is not inconsistent with its being, in part formed *by* him as one of the immediate agents. His character is formed by his circumstances, ... but his own desire to mould it in a particular way is one of those circumstances, and by no means one of the least influential. (SOL, p. 840, original emphasis)

So it was, then, that at both the immediately observable level of human conduct and the implicit level of human character, Mill's thesis was that the contemporary and cumulative situations of human agents acted to dominate their choices and actions. In order to probe more deeply into these claims, and more definitely to resolve the issue of the influence of volition in particular cases, he invoked the notion that all human phenomena were founded upon laws of the human mind. Such an invocation, of course, left Mill the arch-empiricist facing just the sort of metaphysical inquiry that his work in the SOL was dedicated to avoid, indeed, to defeat. Somehow he had to give such implications a wide berth in order to avoid endangering his empiricist bona fides. Unfortunately, whatever he may have believed about his own arguments along the way, the problem would not disappear. Ultimately there came a point where he recognized explicitly that he could not avoid leaving a metaphysical residue after any explanation involving human agency in a causal sequence.

Initially in Book VI of the SOL, in line with his general aims outlined in section 9.1 above, Mill attempted to avoid the metaphysical extensions of his inquiry. He did so by denying any concern with the ontological question of 'what the Mind is' as distinct from its 'sensible manifestations'. He resolved to 'keep clear of all speculations respecting the mind's own nature' and to 'understand by the laws of mind those of mental phenomena – of the various feelings or states of consciousness of sentient beings', comprising 'Thoughts, Emotions, Volitions, and Sensations'. Such laws would include the means by which 'those feelings generate one another', and, for Mill, true laws of mind are only those in which 'a state of mind is produced by a state of mind' rather than as a reaction to some somatic state (SOL, p. 849). He rejected any notion that conscious states of the mind were able fully to be accounted for as products of the physiological states of the body, including the brain and nervous system. It was evident, though, as he realized, that some such somatic–mental connections must exist, and he granted that, as a matter of ultimate principle, there can be no other explanation for mind states. But what Mill wanted was to found his inquiry into human conduct on an independent science of mind or psychology. In this science, 'original mental laws' were to be established by means other than what was at the time a process of dubious validity, the deductive derivation of mental phenomena from physiological laws. As far as Mill was concerned, while the fact 'that every mental state has a nervous state for its immediate antecedent and proximate cause, though extremely probable, cannot hitherto be said to be proved', it remained 'incontestable that there exist uniformities of succession among states of mind, and that these can be ascertained by observation and experiment' (SOL, p. 851). Such was the associationist psychology that he had carried forward from his father.

The effect of this sort of argument was to make psychology into a largely inductive science in the strict sense that demonstrative explanatory laws were to be derived from observation and experiment alone. Just what form these inductive inquiries were to take in practice, Mill did not indicate here. However it is not unreasonable to suggest that some resort to personal introspection and extrapolation must have been accepted as the modus operandi for the simple, even trite, reason that mental phenomena in others are not 'observable' directly in any sentient sense or indirectly by inference from behavioural manifestations. At one point in the SOL, in the context of confirming the ethological influences on character formation, Mill hinted at this approach as the means of getting at the mental dimension: 'Any one who is willing to take ... the trouble of thinking himself into the doctrine ... will find it ... not only a faithful interpretation of the universal experience of human conduct, but a correct representation of the mode in which he himself, in every particular case, spontaneously interprets his own experience of that conduct' (SOL, p. 932). It is to be presumed that the associationist psychological premises or 'simple or elementary Laws of Mind', which Mill adopted from his father's work, *Analysis of the Phenomena of the Human Mind* (1967) and elsewhere were originally so devised as well (SOL, pp. 852ff). For my present purposes, it is unnecessary to consider the details of the associationist arguments, for nothing that follows depends upon them specifically. The one observation that needs to be made, though, is that these elementary laws were presumed to provide the mental essence common to *all* individual agents. This was an important claim for Mill to defend, because he proceeded from here to expound the rudiments of his science of ethology by means of which specific human psychological characteristics were, to by far the greatest extent, to be explained. In this connection, he explicitly denied that human character had any *significant* innate origins, in spite of the existence of individual differences of 'congenital predisposition' and 'the natural differences of individual minds'. Such differences were, Mill considered, 'of secondary importance when we are considering mankind in the average, or *en masse*'. As a consequence, the conduct of agents could only be explained by cumulative biographical experiences and contemporary situational influences (SOL, pp. 856ff, 873).

The methodological position which he took on these essential laws of mind was summarized in the following passage:

> The laws of mind ... compose the universal or abstract portion of the philosophy of human nature; and all the truths of common experience, constituting a practical knowledge of mankind, must ... be the results or consequences of these. Such familiar maxims, when collected *à posteriori* from observation of life, occupy among the truths of the science the place of what, in our analysis of Induction, have so often been spoken of under the title of Empirical Laws. (SOL, p. 861)

What began to emerge here was Mill's dominant thesis that human character and conduct are, as far as concerns the human sciences such as political economy, determined by cumulative environmental and situational conditioning. At the level of observation, it was possible, he argued, to elicit empirical generalizations about human agency. Such generalizations were not, though, self-supporting explanations of phenomena. Rather,

> an empirical law is a generalization, of which, not content with finding it true, we are obliged to ask why is it true? knowing that its truth is not absolute, but dependent on some more general conditions, and that it can only be relied on in so far as there is ground of assurance that those conditions are realized. (SOL, p. 861)

Thus empirical laws of observed human conduct cannot reveal 'the ultimate laws of human action; they are not the principles of human nature, but *results of those principles under the circumstances in which mankind have happened to be placed*' (SOL, p. 861, emphasis added). From this it followed for Mill that empirical laws were phenomenal generalizations for which explanations had to be found and which could be used as evidence to confirm conclusions drawn from theory. The thrust of his subsequent reasoning was that it was the challenge for human science to discover the *universal* laws which mediate between the essential laws of human nature and observed phenomena generated by human agency. These, he resolved, could only be identified by a study of the agent's situation and biographical experiences. This study would constitute the basis of Mill's projected 'Ethology, or the Science of Character' (SOL, p. 869).

The central claims of ethology were built up from the idea that the 'laws of the formation of character [are] the principal object of scientific inquiry into human nature'. Most essentially a human science required that

> it is possible to determine ... how any given mode of feeling and conduct, compatible with the general laws (physical and mental) of human nature, has been, or may be, formed. In other words, mankind have not one universal character, but there exist universal laws of the Formation of Character. And since it is by theses laws, combined with the facts of each particular case, that the whole phenomena of human action and feeling are produced, it is on these that every rational attempt to construct the science of human nature in the concrete and for practical purposes must proceed. (SOL, pp. 864–5)

Another fundamental claim made by Mill with respect to the ethological bases of human science was that the formation of character 'cannot be ascertained by observation and experiment'. The reason for this was given as the extreme complexity of the object phenomenon, the character and conduct of situated human agents. Such objects demanded a particular methodological approach in order to be coped with analytically: 'the Deductive Method, setting out from general laws, and verifying their consequences by specific experience, is alone applicable'. This made ethology 'the Exact Science of Human Nature; for its truths are not, like the empirical laws which depend on them, approximate generalizations, but real laws. It is, however, (as in all cases of complex phenomena) necessary to the exactness of the propositions that they should be hypothetical only, and affirm tendencies, not facts' (SOL, pp. 865, 870).

The overall result of this approach to human science was that it had to be based on two foundations: psychology, as the 'science of the elementary laws of mind', and ethology, as the 'ulterior science which determines the kind of character produced in conformity to those general laws, by any set of circumstances, physical and moral'. Thus the 'principles of Ethology are properly the middle principles, the *axiomata media* ... of the science of mind: as distinguished, on the one hand from the empirical laws resulting from simple observation, and on the other from the highest generalizations' (SOL, pp. 869–70). And, moreover, the 'science of the formation of character is a science of causes', for its arguments are founded on elementary laws of mind discovered inductively in accordance with what Mill considered to be the orthodox scientific model exemplified by astronomy:

> The subject is one to which those among the canons of induction, by which laws of causation are obtained, can be rigorously applied. It is, therefore, both natural and advisable to ascertain the simplest, which are necessarily the most general, laws of causation first, and then to deduce the middle principles from them. In other words, Ethology, the deductive science, is a system of corollaries from Psychology, the experimental science. (SOL, p. 872, cf. p. 863)

Mill went on to make the further point that, as ethology was a science in which theory construction about the formation of character depended upon deductive procedures, it had to be accompanied by continuous theory testing against empirical reality. As in all such science, the 'conclusions of theory cannot be trusted, unless confirmed by observation; nor those of observation, unless they can be affiliated to theory, by deducing them from the laws of human nature, and from close analysis of the circumstances of the particular situation' (SOL, p. 874). Any disconfirmation of theory by observation would suggest that a revision of theory may be required.

Having set up all these ethological principles, however, it was ultimately Mill's duty to inform his readers that no such science yet existed in any substantive sense. He assured them that the observed empirical conclusions about human agents had been established, and the elementary laws of mind which comprise psychology had been properly formulated. Thus the potential was there ready for intellectual realization, but that remained for the future (SOL, pp. 872–4).

Whatever their ethological backgrounds, all individual human agents operated in their life-world in a *social* situation comprising a set of relations with others, more or less defined and more or less distant. There were two aspects to this step in Mill's analysis of human agency: one was to reconsider the individual agent as intersubjectively dependent and socially affected; the other was to consider the individually unintended collective manifestations of situated and interactive individual agent conduct. The former perspective he quite correctly referred to as the basis of a 'science of man *in* society', and the latter he summarized aptly as the 'science ... of the actions of collective masses of mankind and the various phenomena which constitute social life', or, 'the study of Politics, and of the phenomena of Society' (SOL, p. 875, emphasis added). My reading of Mill's treatment of the problem of representing human agents in formal analysis suggests that he never really came to grips with the former aspect and social agency became identified only with collective agency. Mill was methodological individualist enough to have argued that:

> All phenomena of society are phenomena of human nature, generated by the action of outward circumstances upon masses of human beings: and if, therefore, the phenomena of human thought, feeling, and action, are subject to fixed laws, the phenomena of society cannot but conform to fixed laws, the consequence of the preceding. (SOL, p. 877; cf. p. 933)

What remained missing in Mill's model of the agent, including that of economic man, was any recognition that 'human thought, feeling, and action' are all profoundly functions of intersubjective relations with others. In this respect, his understanding of the collective outcomes of actions by individual agents as comprising merely the adding up of the consequences of such actions was incomplete and understated the complexity of such social phenomena. Intersubjectivity implies an interdependence between agents which defies inclusion in the adding up procedure.

Mill's concern in confronting the phenomena of politics and society was to reflect upon their potential for scientific treatment. He read the extant opinion on the subject as concluding with the 'vulgar notion ... that all pretension to lay down general truths on politics and society is quackery; that no universality and no certainty are attainable in such matters' (SOL, p. 876). It was his intention, especially in the light of Comte's indicative guidance (section 8.3 above), to provide evidence and argument to the contrary by setting out to discover a scientific methodology which could be applied consistently with the demands of the complex origins of the phenomena at issue. Mill's endeavours to contend with the problem of representing analytically situated individual and social agency in an ontologically valid way is taken up in the next section.

What is to be noted as the central conclusion of my inquiries in this section is that enough was said by Mill on the theme of human nature to confirm his important insight that the character and conduct of human agents are profoundly influenced by the situations in which they must operate. The ethological theory applicable to individuals may have had a more long-run orientation than will concern us in what follows, but the principle remains the same. Indeed, as I shall proceed to assume below, the character of individual agents, ethologically formed by biographical experiences, is appropriately taken as given in the short-run, along with the inherited social organizations, structures and institutions which constitute the agent's situation. Agents do not operate as isolated individuals in their life-world functions. They are social beings for whom living means relating to others in an intersubjective interdependence which affects their character and conduct in conjunction with the other dictates of their situations. It was when Mill tried to probe behind this continuous short-run frontier of human action in political economy as a human and social science that the validity of the 'economic man' category and the viability of the abstract–deductive methodology came into doubt. He ultimately found that behind the contained and constrained perspective on human agency there lurked a transcendental dimension of human nature which included the elementary individual laws of mind and the effect on them of agents' intersubjective connections with others. It became apparent to him that these laws and the nature of human interdependence were not, and could not be, derived or confirmed by direct general observation. The only observable aspect of the operations of the mind and their influence on human relations was their behavioural manifestations, but probing backwards was prevented by there being no sentient entities to bridge the void between these manifestations and their origins in the mind. The laws and connections, then, as the underlying causes of situated human conduct, were always to remain conclusions drawn from personal introspection and extrapolated to, but always beyond confirmation by, others. Political economy, and the human sciences in general, had either to confront and accept or to ignore this epistemological delimitation imposed by the ontological nature of the generation of their object phenomena. The classicals had largely taken the latter course, but it was in this respect that Mill was an exception.

9.3 Methodology and the representation of human agency

It was Mill's guiding hypothesis that the world of human being in all its facets could be studied scientifically, just as could the rest of nature. In order to begin to establish that this was a defensible approach to the study of human nature and situated human agency at the individual and social levels, Book VI of the SOL included an endeavour to find methodological and epistemological analogies amongst the recognized natural sciences. As already indicated above, one of Mill's most fundamental and constant concerns was to ensure that the approach to science was from the direction of the ontology of its object phenomena. The human sciences were characterized by the complexity of the phenomena with which they had to deal, a fact which immediately meant that analogies with other natural sciences had to take this into consideration and that their epistemological expectations should be tempered accordingly.

Concerning individual human being, Mill quite candidly expressed his misgivings about it as an object of science. Most essentially a human science was to inquire into the determination of 'the thoughts, feelings, and actions of human beings' and its challenge was to be able to argue ex ante about the appearance of these manifestations of character in particular cases. Ideally, according to Mill, the outcome of its arguments should be a prediction about these things that has 'the same certainty with which astronomy enables us to predict the places and occultations of the heavenly bodies' (SOL, p. 846). The methodology of the human sciences had to take off from a recognition that this expectation could not be realized for ontological reasons. The realistic image of the human individual as a scientific object which Mill now portrayed is worth quoting at length and studying carefully for the caveats which it foreshadowed regarding the epistemological expectations appropriate to human inquiry.

> The actions of individuals could not be predicted with scientific accuracy, were it only because we cannot foresee the whole of the circumstances in which those individuals will be placed. But further, even in any given combination of (present) circumstances, no assertion, which is both precise and universally true, can be made respecting the manner in which human beings will think, feel, or act. (SOL, p. 846)

Now, as far as Mill was concerned, the doubts expressed here did not arise through any lack of knowledge of the essential laws of human nature itself or because of individual differences at that level. He went on in the same passage:

> This is not, however, because every person's modes of thinking, feeling, and acting do not depend on causes; nor can we doubt that if, in the ease of any individual, our data could be complete, we even now know enough of the ultimate laws by which mental phenomena are determined to enable us in many cases to predict, with tolerable certainty, what, in the greater number of supposable combinations of circumstances, his conduct or sentiments would be. But the impressions and actions of human beings are not solely the result of their present circumstances, but the joint result of those circumstances and of the characters of the individuals; and the agencies which determine human character are so numerous and diversified, ... that in the aggregate they are never in any two cases exactly similar. (SOL, pp. 846–7)

What we have here is an image of human beings recognized as always chronically situated in terms of their cumulative biographical experiences and current environment. Whatever psychological laws they may adhere to in common are thus potentially overwhelmed by the influence of their circumstances. These latter are so extensive and variable that situated human agents and their conduct constitute scientific objects of extreme complexity. Hence Mill concluded the above piece by arguing that even if our science of human nature were theoretically perfect, that is, if we could calculate any character as we can calculate the orbit of any planet, *from given data;* still, as the data are never all given, nor ever precisely alike in different cases, we could neither make positive predictions, nor lay down universal propositions. (SOL, p. 847, original emphasis)

So far, then, it is apparent that observed situated human agency was, for Mill, the product of three separable constituents. First, human beings as isolated, sentient individuals operate according to some essential and common laws of mind which are potentially manifestable as states of consciousness. These states include thoughts, emotions, volitions and actions. Secondly, the actual manifestations of these mental phenomena and any action responses are the compound consequences of the laws of mind and the cumulative influences of biographical experiences. While the former laws were argued to be of empirical origin, the form of which can only have been personal introspection and extrapolation to others, the latter manifestations were foreshadowed to become the subjects of a deductive science, called ethology by Mill. The need for an abstract science of ethology was indicated by Mill in the above passage when he referred to the diversity of influences on human character formation. In the face of such complexity, demonstrative generalizations drawn from induction alone were ruled out. Only by means of the formation of abstract premises and the application of deductive logic could the human individual's character be modelled scientifically at all. At least as a matter of principle, then, human agents confronting their life-world situations and choosing their responses thereto could be represented as definitive beings. But, once again, the third constituent of their existence, namely the inherited situational influences under which they operate on a day-to-day basis, emerge as highly intractable in their complexity. Mill faced up to this ultimate impediment to scientific methodology by resorting to a reduction in the stringency of epistemological standards which qualify a body of connate knowledge as a science.

As a general condition for phenomena to become the objects of scientific discourse, Mill posited that they should comprise 'facts ... which follow one another according to constant laws', where these laws may or may not be known, but, at least, they had to be *known to exist* and thus be *knowable in principle*. However he came close to a non sequitur here when he applied the qualification that 'those laws may not have been discovered, nor even be discoverable by our existing resources' (SOL, p. 844). The trite question to be posed in response is: how can laws be known to exist and yet be undiscovered? It seems that Mill's presumption was that, if a body of knowledge appears to *approximate* a set of laws in the above sense, then it must constitute a science that merely deviates by some degree from being exact *in its present form*. The rationale for such deviation was identified as the complex ontological nature of the object phenomena in focus. This approach to the problem was in accordance with Mill's general understanding that the methodology and epistemology appropriate to a science were primarily to be shown to be consistent with the nature of the phenomena with which it was expected to deal.

He illustrated his notion of an inexact science by reference to examples from the physical sciences. Meteorology, with its objective of predicting the weather, and tidology, with its objective of predicting the tides, were both posited as inexact sciences. They qualified as sciences as a consequence of their being based on a set of well-established physical laws which combine with and manifest themselves through certain existing physical structures and conditions to produce the relevant observed phenomena. In these examples, the basic laws are not the problem. It is the complexity of their mediations of action which lead to inexact predictions. In the case of meteorology, Mill noted that, from a knowledge of the pertinent physical laws, it cannot 'be doubted that if we were acquainted with all the antecedent circumstances, we could, even from those more general laws, predict (saving difficulties of calculation) the state of the weather at any future time'. He believed that this claim in principle, although unsubstantiated by any confirmations in practice, was sufficient to render meteorology a science. The tempering condition was that, 'from the difficulty of observing the facts on which [its] phenomena depend, (a difficulty inherent in the peculiar nature of those phenomena) the science is extremely imperfect; and were it perfect, [it] might probably be of little avail in practice, since the data requisite for applying its principles to particular instances would rarely be procurable' (SOL, p. 844).

In certain crucial respects, tidology was in contrast to meteorology because its degree of inexactness was lower. The reason for this was claimed to be that its *most significant* causal forces were well established and that the forces diverting predictions from perfect accuracy were of a relatively insignificant and specifically local nature. It is significant to note, though, that, in all such circumstances, the deviations were also dependent upon known causal laws. They were thus, in principle, calculable in the presence of sufficient information. Mill concluded that tidology was 'not yet an exact science; not from any inherent incapacity of being so, but from the difficulty of ascertaining with complete precision the real derivative uniformities'. In all cases, unexplained but minor errors will appear in tidal predictions. But the science could still pass the practical test of relevance in that 'general laws may be laid down respecting the tides; predictions may be founded on those laws, and the result will in the main, though often not with complete accuracy, correspond to the predictions'. However, 'with allowance for the degree of their probable inaccuracy, we may safely ground our expectations and conduct [on them]' (SOL, pp. 845–6).

The case of Mill's third example from the physical sciences was different again. Astronomy was a science which had passed through the phase of inexactitude during which complete calculation of all the forces acting to position the planets was not possible with contemporary knowledge. By his own time, Mill could claim that:

> It has become an exact science, because its phenomena have been brought under laws comprehending the whole of the causes by which the phenomena are influenced, whether in a great or only in a trifling degree, whether in all or only in some cases, and assigning to each of those causes the share of effect which really belongs to it. (SOL, pp. 845–6)

The ultimate inference here was that it was possible, as a matter of principle, for all three of these sciences to reach the epistemological standards set by astronomy. It remained doubtful, though, that this would ever be possible in practice for meteorology by virtue of the overwhelming number, complexity and inaccessibility of the forces acting to determine the weather. In predicting the tides, the problem of uncertain and irregular disturbances was also never likely to be overcome completely, but in this case, it did not matter so much as the predictions remained accurate enough to be usable for the purposes required.

Now, for Mill, the closest analogy to the science of human nature and agency from amongst these three examples was tidology. Human science 'falls far short of the standard of exactness now realized in Astronomy; but there is no reason that it should not be as much a science as Tidology is, or as Astronomy was when its calculations had only mastered the main phenomena, but not the perturbations' (SOL, p. 846). As Peter Winch summarizes Mill's position, 'Just as the irregularity of the tides as between different places on the globe does not mean that there are no regular laws governing them, so in the case of human behaviour' (1958, p. 69). In order to effect this analogy, Mill's immediate challenge was to show that an approach to human science could be found in which only the 'main phenomena' were to be the subject of claims about reliable causation and in which the disturbing causes were insignificant for the main conclusions reached, but ultimately calculable, nonetheless. To quote Winch again, it had to be established in both sciences that 'individual divergences are to be explained by the operation of laws on highly diversified individual situations' (1958, p. 69). An appropriate model of human agents had to be found such that it represented them and the tenets of their situated conduct in what we may refer to as a *typified* form, given the phenomenal context concerned. In forming this perspective on the human agent, Mill claimed that many of those effects which it is of most importance to render amenable to human foresight and control are determined, like the tides, in an incomparably greater degree by general causes, than by all partial causes taken together; depending in the main on those circumstances and qualities which are common to all mankind, or at least to large bodies of them, and only to a small degree on the idiosyncrasies of organization or the peculiar history of individuals. (SOL, p. 847)

For the phenomena of human science that can be shown to depend on such a typified image of the agents involved and the effects of their conduct, 'it is evidently possible ... to make predictions which will *almost* always be verified, and general propositions which are almost always true'. Mill defended this epistemology of inexactitude by suggesting, in effect, that this is the best that the human sciences can be expected to do. In such sciences, 'it is sufficient to know how the great majority of the human race, or of some nation or class of persons, will think, feel, and act', for 'an approximate generalization is, in social inquiries, for most practical purposes equivalent to an exact one; that which is only probable when asserted of individual human beings indiscriminately selected, being certain when affirmed of the character and collective conduct of masses' (SOL, p. 847, original emphasis; cf. p. 603).

A satisfactory methodological state of the human sciences required more than the revelation of 'approximate generalizations' about human agency. Mill added the qualification that these must be shown to be 'corollaries from the universal laws of human nature on which they rest' (SOL, p. 848). As we have seen, this demanded the assumption of universal laws of mind which were to be combined with an ethological theory of that typified human character most pertinent to the phenomenon to be accounted for. The situational context through which the typical conduct of such an agent is directed would then be sufficient to account for the appearance of the phenomenon. In the particular case of the phenomena of political economy, it was the 'economic man' concept which was assumed adequately to represent the origins of such phenomena in the exigencies of human agency *for the purposes of pure theory*. It is quite apparent that Mill was sensitive to the epistemological limitations which this assumption imposed on the outcomes of economic theory and hence on the immediate practical relevance of its arguments.

In the SOL, Mill's further investigations into the methodology of the human sciences were pursued from the social–collective and thus typified, or functionally average, conception of human agency. His objective, consistent with Comte's endeavours (section 8.3 above), was now to consolidate the scientific status of human–*social* inquiry, often referred to by what was, at the time, the generic term 'Sociology', by eliciting a defensible methodology for it. Its defensibility was to have the sense that its tenets and demands were consistent with the ontological nature of the object phenomena of concern in such inquiry. That nature was characterized most fundamentally by its complexity, but it was Mill's intention that a science of human society should be shown to be viable according to the requirements of the established natural sciences nonetheless. His presumption was that it would be possible to formulate the laws of society, as they were entailed by the laws of human nature and agency that must constitute their roots, in a form as certain as those of astronomy. The resulting science could not, of course, hope to emulate fully the achievements in any physical science because of the extremely complex and contingent influences which situations impose upon agents in their collective operations. Thus 'The circumstances ... which influence the condition and progress of society, are innumerable, and perpetually changing; and though they all change in obedience to causes, and therefore to laws, the multitude of the causes is so great as to defy our limited powers of calculation' (SOL, p. 878).

What methodology, then, could be shown to be consistent with a scientifically acceptable representation of phenomena apparently so analytically intractable? Mill posited four options which had been revealed by his general inquiries into the logic of science in the SOL: first, the chemical or experimental methodology; secondly, the geometric or abstract methodology; thirdly, the physical or concrete deductive methodology; and fourthly, the inverse deductive or historical methodology. His intention was to establish that the first two of these were not legitimately applicable to the analysis of social phenomena and thereby to initiate his investigation of the potential viability of the other two.

I noted in the previous section above that Mill conceived of the human composition of society in terms which neglected the intersubjective relations between constituent agents and their effects on observed individual and social conduct. This reflection of his strict methodological individualism led him to argue *petitio principii* that the 'laws of the phenomena of society are, and can be, nothing but the laws of the actions and passions of human beings united together in the social state' on the premiss that 'men are not, when brought together, converted into another kind of substance, with different properties'. Rather it was the case that 'human beings in society have no properties but those which are derived from, and may be resolved into, the laws of the nature of individual man' (SOL, p. 879; cf. p. 932). This latter idea was literally correct, but Mill's reference was not to individuals as they are *in society,* comprising the interdependent and interactive atoms of social composition. What he intended, it seems, was that individuals were to be conceived of as they would be *in isolation* and their conduct then simply, so to say, added up. It was really this belief which ruled out the chemical or experimental methodology in social science according to Mill for, by this approach, he meant a purely demonstrative induction in which observation, experience and experiment comprise the only and sufficient means of eliciting phenomenal knowledge (SOL, pp. 879ff). With experiment ruled out as a method of investigation in the social sciences, the only practical means of applying this methodology were observation and experience. Such a delimited form of the search for general laws would only be appropriate if penetrating beyond composite empirical appearances was held to be impossibly intricate and complex, as was often assumed about chemical reactions and changes. Mill did not accept this barrier to inquiry because of his belief that social phenomena had an atomistic explanation which could be nomologically formulated from elementary laws of mind and ethological principles.

The alternative of the geometrical or abstract approach to human science had the advantage that it probed observed phenomena for their deeper, atomistic causes. Its operational methodology was deductive and that too was seen by most social scientists as advantageous in its delivery of logical precision (SOL, pp. 887ff). The ultimate limitation of the approach which ruled it out for these sciences was, according to Mill, that it treated the abstract representations of its object phenomena in a way that distorted their real-world form too much. In particular the geometric method, with its dependence upon syllogistic argument, excluded the sequential and interactive and conflicting aspects of causal forces in social science. Geometry comprised 'a science of co-existent fact, altogether independent of the laws of the succession of phenomena'. For Mill, the apt analogy was closer to mechanics than to geometry for these reasons, but most especially because of 'what so constantly occurs in mechanics and its applications, the case of conflicting forces; of causes which counteract or modify one another'. He specifically criticized, therefore, the 'geometrical theory of society' for its implication that each social phenomenon can be explained by a single force stemming from 'one single property of human nature' (SOL, pp. 887–8).

There followed in the present context a specific critique of Benthamite social theory as including an especially crass example of 'the geometrical method in politics'. As was noted earlier on, among the culpable in this respect was Mill's father, especially in his 'Essay on Government' which caused the Macaulay incident of 1829 (section 8.1 above). The critique centred on the claim that the key weakness of the theory of government expounded by Bentham and his followers was that they 'founded their general theory … on one comprehensive premise, namely, that men's actions are always determined by their [self-]interests' (SOL, pp. 889–90). These writers were, Mill granted, well aware that this was an assumption that required qualification by means of making allowance for additional motivations for human conduct. Then, considering what he had defended by way of methodology in political economy in his DPE essay on the subject (section 8.2

above), the following argument contains some profoundly different standards
and expectations of human science:

> [The Benthamites] would have applied, and did apply, their principles with in-
> numerable allowances. *But it is not allowances that are wanted.* There is little
> chance of making due amends in the superstructure of a theory for the want of
> sufficient breadth in its foundations. It is unphilosophical to construct a science
> out of a few agencies by which the phenomena are determined .... *We either ought
> not to pretend to scientific forms, or we ought to study all the determining agents
> equally, and endeavour, so far as it can be done, to include all of them within the
> pale of the science;* else we shall infallibly bestow a disproportionate attention
> upon those which our theory takes into account, while we misestimate the rest,
> and probably underrate their importance. (SOL, p. 893, emphasis added)

The methodological image that was being defended here was quite apparently contradicted by that which provided the foundations for the scientific
version of classical economics according to Mill's own exposition. Such an
interpretation was then reinforced by the continuation of the above passage:

> *The phenomena of society do not depend, in essentials, on some one agency or
> law of human nature, with only inconsiderable modifications from others. The
> whole of the qualities of human nature influence those phenomena, and there is
> not one which influences them in a small degree. There is not one, the removal or
> any great alteration of which would not materially affect the whole aspect of
> society, and change more or less the sequences of social phenomena generally.*
> (SOL, p. 894, emphasis added)

We shall see in what follows that, in these pieces, Mill had for some unknown reason painted himself into a methodological corner from which he
would have to extricate himself subsequently. No human science, as the case
of political economy had already indicated, could sustain the methodological
inferences that he made so mandatory here in response to the claimed limitations of one example.

Mill began his defence of the physical or concrete deductive methodology
in social science by continuing his espousal of the sentiments just expressed.
What he called 'the true method' was one which 'proceeds (conformably to
the practice of the more complex physical sciences) deductively ..., but by
deduction from many, not from one or very few, original premises; considering each effect as ... an aggregate result of many causes, operating sometimes through the same, sometimes through different mental agencies, or
laws of human nature'. Most importantly, this methodology, 'of which astronomy furnishes the most perfect ... example', is one which enables us to
infer 'the law of each effect from the laws of causation on which that effect
depends; not, however, from the law merely of one cause ... but by consider-

ing all the causes which conjunctly influence the effect, and compounding their laws with one another' (SOL, pp. 894, 895).

A caveat emerged at this point and it will be in focus for much of the rest of this chapter. It will then colour the interpretation of his methodological and substantive endeavours in the PPE with which I conclude in the next. The rationale for applying the method of abstraction and deductive logic in the social sciences was always the need for simplification of the human–existential complexity of the phenomena with which they must deal. But, warned Mill, 'the same superior complexity which renders the instrument of deduction more necessary, renders it also more precarious; and we must be prepared to meet, by appropriate contrivances, this increase of difficulty'. The precise nature of the object phenomena from which the complexity stems was cited as the fact that the 'actions and feelings of human beings in the social state are, no doubt, entirely governed by psychological and ethological laws: whatever influence any cause exercises upon the social phenomena, it exercises through those laws' (SOL, p. 896). Where the actual problem emerged was in the multitude of such causes of social phenomena inferred by this summary assertion and which must be compounded in any complete explanation and/or prediction that results from the analysis. On this basis, Mill concluded that, 'when, by attempting to predict what will actually occur in a given case, we incur the obligation of estimating and compounding the influence of all the causes which happen to exist in that case; *we attempt a task to proceed far in which, surpasses the compass of the human faculties*' (SOL, p. 896, emphasis added). It will be readily apparent that this conclusion posited a delimitation which could not be consistent with the earlier demand to which I referred above. That demand was simply that *all* relevant 'determining agencies' of a phenomenon should be included in a complete account of its generation. Now it was recognized that this was beyond the capacities of the observer–analysts who were to construct the generalized theory through which the phenomenon could be explained and predicted in the future. What was confirmed here was the important Millian insight that it is the ontological complexity of the objects of human science which effectively determines the methodology which is viable in theory construction and the epistemological expectations which are appropriate regarding the analytical results.

Specifically what was called for in the case of the human sciences was that some 'softening' of the methodology be permitted relative to that which would be applicable in the perfectible calculations of, say, astronomy. A first step in this modification of the methodology comprised an acceptance of the assertion that it would not be possible fully to 'calculate the result of the conflicting tendencies which are acting in a thousand different directions and promoting a thousand different changes at a given instant in a given society'. The compromise suggested by Mill was that we might and ought to be able, from the laws of human nature, to distinguish correctly enough the [conflicting] tendencies themselves, so far as they depend on causes accessible to observation; and determine the direction which each of them, if acting alone, would impress upon society, as well as, in a general way at least, to pronounce that some of these tendencies are more powerful than others. (SOL, p. 896)

The effect of this compromise was consolidated by the next step in Mill's retreat from a strictly deductive methodology. This was to foreshadow a Friedmanite positivism by claiming that '*the ground of confidence in any concrete deductive science is not the a priori reasoning itself, but the accordance between its results and those of observation à posteriori*': that is, what saves the deductive methodology in the face of complexity is its 'third essential constituent part' which Mill called 'Verification', 'that of collating *the conclusion of the ratiocination* either with the concrete phenomena themselves, or, when such are obtainable, with their empirical laws' (SOL, pp. 896–7, emphasis added). The danger here was the burgeoning loss of the immediate relevance of sustaining the real and essential constitution of the phenomena and their generation in the theoretical representation. The subsequent evolution of the accepted methodology in economics, so starkly explicated by Milton Friedman (1953), has clearly demonstrated the reality of this danger. Mill, however, had himself discouraged this inclination by accepting that deductive social science 'cannot be a science of positive predictions, but only of tendencies'. His grounds for this weaker epistemological demand were pragmatic: that 'knowledge insufficient for prediction may be most valuable for guidance' and that it 'is not necessary for the wise conduct of the affairs of society, no more than of any one's private concerns, that we should be able to foresee infallibly the results of what we do' (SOL, p. 898).

The driving force evident in Mill's subsequent argument, though, was still that, in order to preserve the maximum degree of viability of the deductive method in the face of the complex nature of its objects, social science had to narrow and simplify the scope of its assumptions and logical reasoning. He quite frankly summarized the required methodological outcome by noting that:

All the general propositions which can be framed by the deductive science are ... in the strictest sense of the word, *hypothetical*. They are grounded on *some suppositious set of circumstances,* and declare how some given cause *would* operate in those circumstances, supposing that no others were combined with them. ... This mode of inquiry, considered as a means of obtaining general propositions, must, therefore, on pain of frivolity, be limited to those classes of social facts which, though influenced like the rest by all sociological agents, are under the *immediate* influence [original emphasis], principally at least, of a few only. (SOL, p. 900, some emphasis added)

There was in this summary the attempt to ensure that some ad hoc empirical justification would be given for the simplification process undertaken. The requirement was that social science in which direct deduction from assumed premisses is the principal method of reasoning should confine its attention to those phenomena for which narrowly defined origins could be specified. What Mill was about to do, of course, was to reintroduce political economy as such a branch of the science in which this requirement was, indeed, able to be shown to be met.

It was Mill's contention, *contra* Comte, that there could be established separately identifiable and self-contained, but not independent, branches of social science. The basis for these distinct sciences was to be their focus on a specific range of observed phenomena with sufficiently restricted causal underpinnings. Political economy was cited as a well-established example of such a science and he proceeded over the next several pages of the SOL to reiterate, indeed to quote directly at considerable length, the argument defending its status as it had appeared in the DPE essay considered in section 8.2 (SOL, pp. 901ff). What was made more precise in the present context was the substantive delimitations in the form of the abstractions that enabled economic events to be accounted for by purely deductive reasoning, given the proclaimed dominance of the wealth maximization–sacrifice minimization motive for human conduct in such affairs. As a result, the reiterated exposition reinforced the message of the DPE that political economy was a qualified but legitimate example of a science, albeit an inexact one, in the mould of all natural sciences *and* that it required no distinctive methodology to realize its, albeit circumscribed, objectives.

At the same time, Mill took the opportunity to re-emphasize the importance of empirical confirmation, 'Verification by Specific Experience', as a required assessment complement to the deductive construction of theories (SOL, pp. 907ff). Now, though, a rather more sophisticated version of what is at issue in this procedure was formulated. In particular Mill presented a definite statement of the implications of the discovery of instances of refutation within observed data. The essential premiss was that, 'before our theory of the influence of a particular cause, in a given state of circumstances, can be entirely trusted, we must be able *to explain and account for* the existing state of all that portion of the social phenomena which that cause has a tendency to influence' (SOL, p. 910, emphasis added). Where a theory fails fully 'to predict the present and the past' ex post and thus leaves 'a residual phenomenon', this residual requires 'further study for the purposes of explanation'. By this was meant a process whereby 'we must either search among the circumstances of the particular case until we find one which, on the principles of our existing theory, accounts for the unexplained phenomenon, or we must turn back, and seek the explanation by an extension and improvement of the theory itself' (ibid.). The methodological demands made of political economy in particular here were rather stronger than the heuristic sort of expectations we saw expressed above. Before, theory could only be expected to establish tendencies and provide guidance which was not dependent upon accurate predictions. Now, the preconditions for the application of 'our speculations in political economy' were, quite unrealistically and unreasonably on his own earlier expressed terms, that 'we must be able *to explain all the mercantile or industrial facts* of a general character appertaining to the present state of [a] country: to point out *causes sufficient to account for all of them,* and prove, or show good ground for supposing, that these causes have really existed' (ibid., emphasis added).

Mill was not content to let the concrete deductive methodology stand alone as the only one relevant to the social sciences. He maintained, very largely as a consequence of his exposure to the work of Comte on the same theme (section 8.3 above), that there exists a 'general science of society, which inquires into the laws of succession and co-existence of the great facts constituting the state of society and civilization at any time'. This constitutes 'a kind of sociological inquiries to which, from their prodigious complication, the method of direct deduction is altogether inapplicable' and for which empirical generalizations must be sought by direct observation: it can 'proceed in no other manner than by making such generalizations – afterwards to be confirmed by connecting them with the psychological and ethological laws on which they must really depend' (SOL, pp. 897, 908). The object phenomena which were to be in focus now comprised the observed historical states of particular societies. For these sorts of phenomena it was what he termed the *inverse deductive or historical* methodology which he elicited from his studies of Comte to complement the more abstract use of deductive reasoning. Thus, in the concrete–deductive methodology considered above, 'the question posed was, what effect will follow from a given cause, a certain general condition of social circumstances being presupposed'. The contrast was now with 'a second inquiry, namely, what are the laws which determine those general circumstances themselves'. Mill classified the endeavour to answer this latter question as 'the general Science of Society, by which the conclusion of the other and more special kind of [direct deductive] inquiry must be limited and controlled'. The twist in this approach which set it apart from the purely inductive alternative was that the 'Empirical Laws of Society' revealed by it were to be connected 'with the laws of human nature, by deductions showing that such were the derivative laws naturally to be expected as the consequences of those ultimate ones' (SOL, pp. 911, 916).

The phenomena with which Mill was concerned in regard to this complementary methodology were the successive historically evolving social and economic states of society considered both as static sets of consistent, or equilibrium, conditions and as dynamic successions of these conditions. He attributed the recognition of this distinction between statics and dynamics in the human sciences to Comte and supported its introduction here with a long quotation from the latter's work (SOL, pp. 917ff; cf. section 8.3 above). The complexity of these actually existent states and their cumulative historical origins, along with their continuous processes of change, simply defied the direct application of the concrete–deductive methodology. What was at issue here was a study which involved 'the extensive and constant reaction of the effects upon their causes'. More specifically Mill gave emphasis to the origin of this 'peculiarity' of the human sciences in the ontology of their object phenomena:

> The circumstances in which mankind are placed, operating according to their own laws and to the laws of human nature, form the characters of the human beings; but the human beings, in their turn, mould and shape the circumstances for themselves and for those who come after them. From this reciprocal action there must necessarily result either a cycle or a progress. (SOL, p. 913)

Any one of these states, then, resulted from 'so long a series of actions and reactions between Circumstances and Man, each successive term being composed of an ever greater number and variety of parts, [that it] could not possibly be computed by human faculties from the elementary laws which produce it' (SOL, p. 916). Primarily, though, the 'fundamental problem ... of the social science, is to find the laws according to which any state of society produces the state which succeeds it and takes its place' (SOL, p. 912). This sort of dynamic research strategy, with its long-term perspective and implied links to the Progress of Man thesis, smacked of an historicism which Mill did not accept. Moreover, he stressed, 'it cannot be the ultimate aim of science to discover an empirical law', for the laws of social change could not be legitimately posited as natural or immanent, and their purely empirical appearance had to be supported by complementary laws of a more essential nature. In his terms, the 'succession of states of the human mind and of human society cannot have an independent law of its own; it must depend on the psychological and ethological laws which govern the action of circumstances on men and of men on circumstances' (SOL, pp. 914–15).

At this stage Mill offered little by way of substantive demonstration as to how the static and dynamic analyses of society might proceed in practice. He elicited several examples of political factors which comprised 'the conception I have formed of the kind of theorems of which sociological statics would consist' and which could, in principle, be obtained by empirical means (SOL, pp. 921ff). Their confirmation by means of relating them back to the laws of human nature remained problematical and was left as an unsolved facet of sociology. The situation with social dynamics was similar in that crucial aspects of the required arguments were not available. Thus 'Little progress ... can be made in establishing the filiation [of successive social states], directly from laws of human nature, without having first ascertained the immediate or derivative laws according to which social states generate one another as society advances; the *axiomata media* of General Sociology'. However the 'empirical laws which are most readily obtained by generalization from history ... are not the "middle principles" themselves, but only evidence towards the establishment of such principles'. The problem remains that 'all such results are still at too great a distance from the elementary laws of human nature on which they depend, – too many links intervene, and the concurrence of causes at each link is far too complicated, – to enable these propositions to be presented as direct corollaries from those elementary principles' (SOL, pp. 924–5). The consequence, Mill concluded, was that social dynamics had been left as nothing more than a descriptive science dependent upon relativistic empirical observations. He remained optimistic, though, that the time would come when 'no important branch of human affairs will be any longer abandoned to empiricism and unscientific surmise [and] the circle of human knowledge will be complete' (SOL, p. 930).

The way forward, argued rather vaguely by Mill, was to provide more specific and formalized links between the static conditions of society and the processes of their dynamic transformation. In part, such an endeavour would be assisted by identifying a central mediating element of human progression comprising the 'one element in the complex existence of social man [that is] pre-eminent over all others as the prime agent of the social movement'. That element was the one which had been cited by Comte, namely 'the state of the speculative faculties of mankind, including the nature of the beliefs which by any means they have arrived at concerning themselves and the world by which they are surrounded'. Mill continued here to reinforce his central thesis that any human–social science had to keep its arguments in touch with the fact that its phenomena have their origins in the always mutable and manipulable exigencies of situated human agents and agency. In relation to 'the most obvious case first', that of phenomena generated by providing for human material needs in the face of relative scarcity, he wrote that

> the impelling force to most of the improvements effected in the arts of life is the desire of increased material comfort; but as we can only act upon external objects in proportion to our knowledge of them, the state of knowledge at any time is the limit of the industrial improvements possible at that time; and the progress of industry must follow, and depend on, the progress of knowledge. (SOL, pp. 925–6)

However, with respect to the future of a science of society in which this determinant of progress could take its appropriate place, there remained the issue of properly formulating 'the law of the successive transformations of human opinions [and] whether this law can be determined, at first from history as an empirical law, then converted into a scientific theorem by deducing it *à priori* from the principles of human nature' (SOL, p. 927).

This prospective theory of the dynamics of knowledge joined Mill's proposal for a science of the ethological development of human character as unfinished business on the slate of the human sciences. The two general theories remained the missing links between the elementary laws of mind, for which he claimed empirical validity and which he espoused with such confidence on the basis of the tenets of associationist psychology, and the complete comprehension of the empirical regularities of human–social phenomena, such as those that were the objects of political economy. In the form that this latter science had at the time, most of these more complex facets of its human dimensions were simply ignored in favour of ensuring the viability of the abstract–deductive methodology by means of the 'economic man' axiom. The alternative was for economic phenomena to be treated as only accessible by inductive means and argued to be so overwhelmingly historically relative in nature as to defy the discovery of meaningful generalizations. What Mill had attempted in his methodological inquiries was, at least, always to begin with the ontological nature of the relevant object phenomena in all sciences. He had a preconceived conviction that the deductive approach derived from the physical sciences must be shown to be viable, nonetheless, if political economy's scientific status was to be sustained, at least as far as its core of 'Ricardian' principles was concerned. But he did not allow this entirely to drive his choice of methodology without a defence geared to the origins of economic phenomena in human agency and without recognizing that some of these phenomena could only be properly comprehended by means of alternative methodologies. Just what Mill was able to make of the methodological conclusions which emerged from the SOL as the foundations for the design and execution of his 'New' political economy in both its static and dynamic dimensions forms the subject of Chapter 10.

9.4   Metaphysical intrusions

Before proceeding to examine Mill's 'New' political economy, there is one further aspect of the foundations of his work that impinged upon the writing of the SOL and the PPE and warrants some explicit attention. The issue concerned is the treatment by Mill of the metaphysical school of psychology and philosophy. As I noted above, Mill was decidedly opposed to all transcendentalist psychology which attributed the functions of the mind to its innate state and the formation of ideas to intuition and reason alone. He saw the SOL as a text devoted to defending the legitimacy of the logical foundations of the opposite experiential and associationist thesis. In that thesis, all mental structures and constituents were the result of current and cumulative human sensory experiences (AUT, p. 233). In mounting a more specific attack on the anti-experiential and rationalist metaphysical doctrines which he found enjoyed a continued currency and dominance in Britain, Mill chose as his opponent the Scottish philosopher Sir William Hamilton. He found Hamilton's *Lectures on Metaphysics and Logic,* published in four volumes during 1859 and 1860, in particular to be of such moment that he abandoned plans to review the work in favour of a 500-page critical monograph. This he published under the title *An Examination of Sir William Hamilton's Philosophy* (EHP) in 1865, the work going through several editions during the remainder of Mill's lifetime. For Mill, Hamilton was, in Britain, 'the great fortress of the intuitional philosophy' and 'the chief pillar' of that philosophy which seemed to him to be 'erroneous' (AUT, pp. 269–70). This made his work the obvious medium through which to launch an assault on what Mill believed to be an essentially conservative philosophy of human nature.

It was from the political perspective that Mill emphasized that a great deal was at stake in the conflict between the two opposing philosophical doctrines represented in his SOL and Hamilton's *Lectures*: 'Now, the difference between these two schools of philosophy, that of Intuition, and that of Experience and Association, is not a mere matter of abstract speculation; it is full of practical consequences, and lies at the foundation of all the greatest differences of practical opinion in an age of progress' (AUT, p. 269). R.P. Anschutz observes that 'Mill's references to these two schools are so constant and consistent throughout his life that they appear to be the fixed poles of his intellectual world' (1953, p. 65). At issue here, in particular, was the idea that, if social and political reform were to be possible, the character and conduct of human agents had to have a significant situationally determined content that was denied by the metaphysical school. The deeming of 'intuition to be the voice of Nature and of God, speaking with an authority higher than that of our reason' (AUT, p. 270), and the consequent ascription of much of the individual and social conditions of human agents to the dominance of that 'voice', entailed a resistance to any change in society that depended upon influencing the way its members act and the institutions they create. Mill observed:

> I have long felt that the prevailing tendency to regard all the marked distinctions of human character as innate, and in the main indelible, and to ignore the irresistible proofs that by far the greater part of those differences ... are such as not only might but naturally would be produced by differences in circumstances, is one of the chief hindrances to the rational treatment of great social questions and one of the greatest stumbling blocks to human improvement. (AUT, p. 270)

Mill's attack on Hamilton, then, had a more pragmatic objective than may be expected from such a fundamental piece of philosophical polemic. The principle that human agents and their agency are the combined product of associationist laws of mind common to them all, together with their bio-graphical experiences and their situational environment, remained to the fore in his thought. He considered this to be an entirely experiential principle, with the laws of mind being known empirically, and this rendered the charac-ter and conduct of human agents, including their generation of economic phenomena, an apt object for study by positive scientific methodology. When writing the SOL, Mill asserted that issues raised by the metaphysicians were beyond the scope of the work, or, more correctly, that their existence did not influence what he had to say about the logic of experiential human science. That work dealt with ideas which were compatible with both the intuitionist and experiential perceptions of the human mind and readers were, from the sixth edition on, referred to the EHP as the source of Mill's thought on matters raised by the two perceptions (SOL, p. cxvi). When actually con-fronting the existence of an established belief in the pertinence of transcen-dentalist premises, though, he could no longer avoid being more explicit about the rationale for his rejection of such foundations for an understanding of human agency. In the process, what became of concern to Mill was the idea that laws that claim to deal with the mental origin and control of human actions have an object which is beyond observational reach in its usually understood sense. Indeed, as I will have occasion to conclude below, Mill's explicit recognition that there must be an unavoidable transcendental dimen-sion in any claims to knowledge about the structures and processes of the mind was to have a profound effect upon the degree of epistemological security which he could claim for his economic theses. Whether he was conscious of this or not is a matter of speculation.

The EHP is a work which appeared well after the SOL and PPE, but its object of critique had always been present as part of the intellectual atmos-phere in which Mill created his ideas. It was the dominance of that atmos-phere by metaphysical and theological philosophical principles which led him to write the SOL as a means of establishing the logical bona fides of an alternative and progressive science of human agency. Mill attributed much of the development and maintenance of the existing economic and social condi-tions in Britain, which so disadvantaged the vast majority of people, to the tenets of the extant philosophy, especially in their theological guise. They gave an intellectual legitimacy to the existing economic class structure, with all its social and political trappings, and to the powerful resistance to any proposals for reform designed to mitigate their effects. In this respect, the EHP provides a further retrospective assessment by Mill of a crucial element that influenced the composition of his arguments, this time including those aimed at convincing his readers of the dire need and real potential for economic and social reform. It was in the PPE that much of his programme of reform was set out against the implicit backdrop of the existence of an intellectual movement dedicated to resisting it. That movement became the explicit target of his critique in the EHP and the work contains some important further development of the representation of the human agent that Mill devised to counter the innatist and intuitionist image argued by his conservative opponents. Mill's attack on Hamilton was designed to defend his representation from an alternative which isolated the essential structures and operations of the mind, and hence the character and conduct of human agents, from the influence of situational experience. The consequence of this alternative was a theory of human agency which left no room for environmental redirection in the interests of socially desirable and consciously introduced change (cf. Ryan, 1979, pp. xi–xiii).

For metaphysicians such as Hamilton, the human agent was perceived as a being driven by the innate characteristics of the human mind. In epistemological terms, this placed an irremovable mediating barrier between the reality of things-in-themselves and the human experience of them as phenomena. Knowledge of the noumena of the real world, represented as perceived phenomena, could only be conditioned and relative in the sense that it was ultimately a function of these characteristics (EHP, pp. 4ff). Hamilton began from 'the characteristic doctrine of the Kantian metaphysics, that the mind does not perceive, but itself creates, all the most general attributes which, by a natural illusion, we ascribe to outward things' (EHP, p. 355). Thus no secure grasp of any true knowledge of reality was possible. Knowledge was always relative, conditioned as it was by the innate mindset of the agent. There was an important sense, though, in which Mill accepted this aspect of the intuitionist doctrine. An interventionist concept of the mind had always been an integral part of the associationist psychology, in that the mind ordered the sensations received, with something more than a mere replication of them and their chronological sequence being the result. What was really at issue in the conflict with the intuitionists was the *nature* and *origins* of the pattern of the mental mediation which was claimed (EHP, pp. 8–9). For the intuitionists, the origins were essentially innate and therefore genetic and physiological. The mind was unilaterally active and interpretative ideas were purely a priori on this account. For some of them, too, the intervention was so dominant in its nature that phenomena of the mind were claimed to be completely divorced from the thing-in-itself which was its perceived object. Hamilton was not of this Kantian bent and rather allowed that sensations conveyed attributes of things directly as they are in themselves. Human consciousness was, he argued, an explicit consciousness of external objects and not just of itself as representing such objects (EHP, pp. 110–11, 114–15,

149ff). By contrast to all this, the associationists espoused the experiential or a posteriori origins of mental mediations. Mediation by the mind meant intervention in mental processes, but the intervention was no longer unilaterally determined and the mind was now perceived as, in a sense, passive in that it only or largely responded to environmental influences. The mind was perceived as still 'working' the input of sensations into shape, but now only in ways which reflected the experiences of the agent (EHP, pp. 177ff).

The above arguments which appeared in the EHP largely focused upon the problem of human knowledge of external matter, but Mill was aware that the same sorts of puzzles arose when the nature and existence of the human mind-in-itself was an object of study. In particular he was anxious to show how far his psychological theory could be applied to understanding the mind, or ego, as its object (EHP, pp. 188ff, 204ff). There could be no doubt, he began, that knowledge of our own mind is relative, just as in case of material objects that we perceive. The mind is experienced as a consciousness of sensations, but we have no means of forming a separate conception of the mind-in-itself. Moreover Mill had to accept that introspective self-examination of the mind could provide no insight into the distinction between mental characteristics which were innately present and the contemporary state of the mind consequent upon its biographical experiences (EHP, pp. 138ff). The situation was made more complex by the existence of further dimensions of the mind which cannot be classified as a mere consciousness of sensations. As Mill noted, 'the thread of consciousness which composes the mind's phaenomenal life, consists not only of present sensations, but likewise, in part, of memories and expectations'. These are 'attributes comprised in our notion of the Ego, and ... are at the very foundation of it'. It followed that, if 'we speak of the Mind as a series of feelings, we are obliged to complete the statement by calling it a series of feelings which is aware of itself as past and future'. However memory and expectation 'have no equivalent in Matter, and cannot be reduced to any elements similar to those into which Matter is resolved by the Psychological theory' (EHP, p. 205). Both must be mediated by the state of belief that sensations once occurred or can occur again. He was immediately sensitive to a potentially paradoxical implication of this argument. How could an externally generated series of sensations be 'aware of itself' and establish belief in sensations not actually present? The suggestion could only be made that 'the Mind, or Ego, *is something different from any series of feelings*' (EHP, pp. 193–4, emphasis added). At this point, Mill's associationism ran up against a barrier of metaphysical speculation about the true nature of the mind-in-itself.

The position which he decided to take on the matter was to concede that the potential of positivism was epistemologically exhausted. His resignation concerning this limitation of knowledge about human agents was clearly evident:

The truth is, that we are here face to face with that final inexplicability, at which … we inevitably arrive when we reach ultimate facts; and in general, one mode of stating it only appears more incomprehensible than another … . The real stumbling block is perhaps not in any theory of the fact, but in the fact itself. … I think, by far the wisest thing we can do, is to accept the inexplicable fact, without any theory of how it takes place; and when we are obliged to speak of it in terms which assume a theory, to use them with a reservation as to their meaning. (EHP, p. 194; cf.pp. 204–5)

Mill was, though, able to turn this admission of defeat into a point in favour of his associationism. This point concerned the identification of the self by the ego.

Since the fact which alone necessitates the belief in an Ego, the one fact which the Psychological theory cannot explain, is the fact of Memory (for Expectation I hold to be, both psychologically and logically, a consequence of Memory), I see no reason to think that there is any cognizance of an Ego until Memory commences. … Our very notion of a Self takes its commencement (there is every reason to suppose) from the representation of a sensation in memory, when awakened by the only thing there is to awaken it before any associations have been formed, namely, the occurrence of a subsequent sensation similar to the former one. (EHP, pp. 206–7)

This amounted to an associationist theory of the existence of self-consciousness, even though it stopped short by taking the actual processes of memory and expectation formation as given but unexplained.

Mill was also aware that this same relativity of knowledge applied to the crucially important existential claim that we can know of and comprehend other minds. At the same time, the metaphysical barrier just confronted applied with a vengeance once individual agents try to establish the identity and nature of other minds-in-themselves. The latter issue was mentioned in passing only, but Mill stated his belief confidently that, once agents have established the nature of their own egos, they can, 'by fair experiential inference from … one Ego, … ascribe the same reality to other Egoes, or Minds' (EHP, p. 208). This is, of course, a claim that demanded rather more philosophical defence than it received from Mill.

The most significant consequence of the metaphysical matters which I have just been addressing was that the two schools of philosophical and psychological argument were founded upon very different conceptions of human agents. It followed from the innatist and intuitionist position that agents should be represented as autonomous beings whose existential character and conduct are to be ascribed to physiology and genetics or to God, in combination with volition, rather than to the cumulative effects of experience alone. If it is allowed that experience plays an exclusive or even only a dominant role in forming the human mindset, the result is a plastic agent whose character and conduct are socially moulded through more or less passive responses to particular biographical and environmental influences. Quite clearly, in the SOL at least, Mill defended the latter ethological image of agents and thus required the appropriately experiential theory of mind and laws of human nature to underpin it. However it proved impossible for him to dispense entirely with the idea of an autonomy in his concept of the agent. This autonomous element was recognized by Mill as the product of the need for human agents to have a self-identity if a stream of contemporary experience is to be compatible with the existence of memory and expectation. The latter require the formation of beliefs about past and future events in relation to an existential self and imply a unilaterally active and creative mind. This left him with a permanent metaphysical residue in his representation of the agent and a lack of ultimate clarity about which aspects of agency were experientially determined and which were of innate origin (Ryan, 1979, pp. xxiv–xxv, xlii, xlvii–xlix; cf. Hollis, 1977, pp. 23ff and 1987a, *passim*).

Mill also had to confront the apparent conflict between the notion that agents are plastic, moulded creatures and his staunch defence of the individual freedom of autonomous agents. How can agents be determined in their character and conduct, as would be implied by the doctrine of necessity, or the doctrine of circumstances, but still be free in an existentially meaningful sense, as would be the implication of the doctrine of free will, or the doctrine of self-formation? How could there be a coherent positive human *science* if agents were, in fact, existentially free to exercise their individual volitions, given their innate characters, as the cause of conduct (EHP, pp. 437ff)? Anschutz reads Mill as leaving this problem unresolved in his work by maintaining contact with both concepts of the human agent. Mill simply emphasized the concept which suited his purposes more: where scientific inquiry was involved, the plastic agent would dominate; where it was of concern to focus upon the essential freedom of agents, the autonomous agent would dominate (1953, pp. 171ff). The key to providing answers to the above questions, and to shedding some additional light onto Anschutz's claims about Mill's duality, and possible inconsistency, on the human agent issue is the critical consideration of the concept of human volition and its relation to the concept of freedom itself which was contained in the EHP and elsewhere. In section 9.2 above, the treatment of the issue in the SOL was considered. These ideas were reiterated and reinforced by Mill in the EHP, where he was confronting the metaphysicians directly.

Hamilton had asserted that 'Free-will and Necessity are both inconceivable', the former because 'it supposes volitions to originate without cause' and thus effectively denies the relevance of human motives to the direction and comprehension of conduct. The doctrine of necessity was rejected by Hamilton because of the intractable infinite regress involved the 'chain of causation going back to all eternity', implied by ascribing necessity to a human action (EHP, pp. 441–2; cf. pp. 444–5). But it was Mill's intention to defend a modified form of necessitarianism and he asserted the idea that volitions have causes which can be accounted for in the same way and with the same regularity and reliability as physical causes in natural phenomena. This amounted to an empirical determinism in which 'human actions are not exempt from the causality in terms of which we explain all other phenomena' (Ryan, 1979, pp. lxi, lxiii; cf. Anschutz, 1953, pp. 170–71). In Mill's words:

> as a truth of experience, ... volitions do ... follow determinate moral antecedents with the same uniformity, and (when we have sufficient knowledge of the circumstances) with the same certainty, as physical effects follow their physical causes. These moral antecedents are desires, aversions, habits, and dispositions, combined with outward circumstances suited to call those internal incentives into action. All these again are effects of causes, those of them which are mental being consequences of education, and of other moral and physical influences. (EHP, p. 446)

For Mill, these claims followed from the introspection of an agent's own volitions and the indirect observation of the volitions of others implied in foreseeing their actions, with the accuracy of such foresight depending upon the former agent's degree of familiarity with the other. Moreover the claims were reinforced by collective observations which reveal volitional responses representing the statistical average in which minor disturbances have cancelled each other out, 'leaving the total result about the same as if the volitions of the whole mass had been affected by such only of the determining causes as were common to them all'. Failure by analysts accurately to predict in collective human situations could only be attributed to incomplete knowledge and/or incomplete inclusions of the relevant agents and their operational conditions. In this respect, such situations were no different from their physical counterparts. It was this sort of empirically calculable determinism, harking back to the tidology analogy (section 9.3 above), which Mill defended rather than any metaphysical causal necessity in a strict sense (EHP, pp. 446–7 and 447n). He also claimed that there can be no contribution made to human agency by 'spontaneousness' in the sense that the cause of conduct is left without potential empirical specification. The problem here is that the claim put him squarely back in the camp of those with a purely plastic perception of agents. He had already allowed for the influence of an independent dimension of the mind, as we saw above. It was not possible for him consistently then to argue that all human conduct is explicable by virtue of imposed circumstances, as he now appeared to do. He rescued the situation by granting that an unexplained transcendental element of *judgement and estimation* could enter the choice process, even though the objective circumstances remained otherwise the same (EHP, p. 448n; cf. Ryan, 1979, p. lxiii).

Agents were considered still to be free in the light of the above argument, even though it involved a form of determinism. This appears paradoxical at first and a resolution requires careful attention to Mill's concept of freedom. The usually expected sense of freedom is the right and power to choose when faced with alternatives, without any taint of predeterminism. Such freedom assumes a model of the agent who is autonomous and exercises a free will, but this was not the model which Mill espoused in his defence of liberty within a social framework (cf. Hollis, 1977, pp. 23ff; 1987a, *passim*). His agents were depicted rather as plastic in that their form had been moulded to fit their place in the socioeconomic order of the age. These agents have mental profiles and characters, and exhibit conduct, which are the accidental, but causal, consequences of their cumulative biography and current situational environment. These qualities are not, then, reducible to any innate essence of human nature. With his inherent love of liberty for humankind, Mill had to elicit how the existence of freedom could be made compatible with the image of agents that he had portrayed. The link was assured by his maintaining a particular orientation of the individualism pertinent to the interpretation of the conduct of situated agents. Freedom for individuals existing as social agents was then taken to mean that they could satisfy their needs and desires within the range of choices facilitated, and delimited, by their situations. Agents are free, then, when they can get what they want and free actions are so defined as to refer to actually satisfiable desires. But, as individuals confronted with continuous choice situations which they wish to optimize, agents must be ascribed a rationality if their responses are to be goal-directed and coherent.

For Mill, agents were always constrained maximizers in their choices, which suggests the acceptance of their exercise of subjective assessment and preferences and the required element of volition and autonomy (Hollis, 1987a, pp. 374, 377–8). What emerged were agents who, in all situations *could* have chosen to act otherwise than they did, and *would* have done so had antecedent conditions been different *and/or* had they made a different subjective assessment of the same conditions. Agents learn how to get the most out of their talents and perceived socioeconomic situations and, to this end, Mill saw education as a vital link in the establishment of a free society and the development of knowledge as the key to its progress. It is well put that individual freedom in society can be assured if, 'when we find a man who has not got what he wants, we do not give him more but make him want less', for, where agents are sufficiently plastic, 'then it simply does not matter who gets what, provided that education sees to it that all want what they get' (Hollis, 1987a, p. 383). This sort of freedom was totally compatible with the determinism required to make social cohesion sustainable, especially in the face of the material inequities so obvious under the distributional laws and institutions of capitalism. But, at the theoretical level, its defence left Mill with the remnants of pure volition and transcendentalism to which reference was made earlier on.

The important unattended metaphysics of human agency upon which his argument depended comprised the *processes* of rational choice and decision as they are effected in accordance with the laws of mind acting in and through the situations which agents inherit. These processes can reasonably be expected to rely on agents' interpretations of their physical, intersubjective and social environments and, as their outcomes are always in the future, they can only be based upon the working of the imagination and the formation of expectations. Necessarily these dimensions of the mind are creative and originating, and thereby autonomous (Shackle, 1979, *passim*). Any attempt, therefore, to discover what, if any, nomological content can be ascribed to such processes, and then formally to represent them in analyses, must reach beyond empiricism and behaviourism into phenomenological endeavours to comprehend the functioning of the mind. For Mill the anti-metaphysician, this was not a notion which he found congenial. The potential for constructing positive human sciences was always foremost in his objectives, although he well realized that they would long remain inexact in the sense that tidology and meteorology were. But he simply refused to pursue the peculiar reasons for such inexactitude in these sciences into what he saw as the realm of pure speculation, even though we have seen him run up against the problem in the EHP, only to turn aside from it. Thus, as Peter Winch has observed, he continued to regard 'all explanations as fundamentally of the same logical structure; and this view is the foundation of his belief that there can be no fundamental logical difference between the principles according to which we explain natural changes and those according to which we explain social changes' (1958, p. 71). But, really, Mill could not escape the import of his own recognition that humanly generated phenomena were not just very complex versions of other natural occurrences, but rather *of a different ontological nature*. Accounts of such phenomena could not be adequately expressed by the tenets of physical science methodology which has its roots in empiricism (cf. Winch, 1958, pp. 71–2, 75). Already, however, in the PPE, Mill had built his arguments around an implicit denial of the need for a model of the human agent which included the transcendental and originating dimensions of mental processes, although, as we are about to see, he was at least thoroughly conscious that the 'economic man' concept, along with the narrow deductive methodology that it made possible in political economy, would not do. Even at the empirico-behavioural level, the complexities of situated human agency as the source of economic phenomena and the target of policy directives defied the use of such a simplistic representation and methodological strategy. The impact that this had on the design and substance of the PPE is my subject in the next chapter.

10 Human agency and socioeconomic reform

10.1 The intentions and design of the PPE

When, in his AUT, Mill looked back on the success and influence of his *Principles of Political Economy with Some of Their Applications to Social Philosophy,* he attributed these outcomes to the intentions of the work so clearly expressed in its title. Its merit, he claimed, was that 'it was not a book merely of abstract science, but also of application'. The success was also, he continued, due to his consequent treatment of the subject as 'not a thing by itself, but as a fragment of a greater whole; a branch of Social Philosophy, so interlinked with all the other branches, that its conclusions, even in its own peculiar province, are only true conditionally, subject to interference and counteraction from causes not directly within its scope'. Most especially, political economy 'in truth, has never pretended to give advice to mankind with no lights but its own; though people who knew nothing *but* political economy (and therefore knew that ill) have taken it upon themselves to advise, and could only do so by such lights as they had' (AUT, p. 243, original emphasis). In particular Mill felt that he had extended the scope of the 'Ricardian' orthodoxy just sufficiently to keep his analyses in contact with the real contingencies of human agency and their role in generating the economic processes which were of concern to him.

A challenge which Mill faced up to in the PPE, then, was to provide an up-to-date and policy-relevant version of 'Ricardian' economics, with a clear orientation towards a better understanding of human problems in the real world and of the potential means for their correction. This reading of Mill as essentially 'Ricardian' in his main economic treatise has been cogently argued by both Pedro Schwartz and Samuel Hollander in more recent times. Schwartz's summary is especially apt:

> By refusing to take part in the criticism of Ricardian analysis, Mill remained a disciple of Ricardo .... His aim [nonetheless], and one in which he was largely successful, was to restore Adam Smith's concept of a broad political economy, which instead of confining itself within the limits of narrow professionalism would use economic knowledge to interpret and change society. (1972, p. 240; cf. Hollander, 1985, pp. 165ff)

He hoped thereby to enable this version of the science, in which he retained an essential faith, better to resist the onslaught of theoretical and practical, academic and humanitarian, dissenters. They had variously labelled it as methodologically unsound in its neglect of inductive foundations, as too abstract to be useful, as morally insensitive and inhumane in its defence of laissez-faire and the status quo of economic distribution, and as subversive in its representation of an immanent logic of class conflict (cf. de Marchi, 1974, pp. 121–2, 123ff). Mill endeavoured to steer a course between all this dissent: 'Economics had acquired a reputation of a cruel science, that showed the nations the road to the acquisition of wealth through hard work and selfishness; ... it was "the dismal science" [and he] wanted to change it into a doctrine of hope, one that was not merely reformist ..., but progressive in the widest sense of the word' (Schwartz, 1972, p. 4). He aimed to do so by sustaining and building on the substantive strengths of the orthodox doctrine, while at the same time giving due recognition to its limitations: 'he patched up the theory where it showed the passage of time, and changed the practical import of the theoretical model by making different assumptions ... and giving entrance in the economic argument to political and ethical considerations' (Schwartz, 1972, p. 236; cf. pp. 66, 70, 193). At the same time, he was intent upon not engaging other political economists in polemic: 'I confess,' he remarked in a letter of 1852, 'I do not see the good that is to be done by swelling the outcry against pol. economists – or why they should be blamed because people do unjust or selfish things for the sake of money' (CW, XIV, p. 93; quoted by Hollander, 1985, p. 181).

This effort to renew the respect for political economy involved Mill in broadening the methodological approach to, and downgrading the epistemological expectations then associated with, the science in its narrow 'Ricardian' form. As I will contend below, he did so as a direct consequence of his expanding on the importance of the human dimensions of the phenomena to be understood. Mill wanted to show how to extend the rigour of the 'science' to provide the positivist intellectual bases for the humane 'art' of economic reform, an intellectual need that was made apparent to him by the analytically loose and unsound discussions of economic and social concerns which he felt surrounded him. Hollander refers to 'Mill's hostility to philanthropic do-gooders who based themselves on thin air' and sums up the situation thus: 'What Mill intended by his *Principles* was the liberation of public opinion from the influence of second-rate economists who gave economic theory a bad name by their apologetic misapplications of theory, and from the false belief that Ricardian doctrine and method itself amounted to social apologetics' (1985, pp. 179, 185; cf. pp. 178ff).

Mill's correspondence in the 1840s and 1850s is replete with *obiter dicta* which attest to the project he envisaged embarking upon in writing the PPE and these are a valuable source of insight into the mood of the book (quoted by Hollander, 1985, pp. 166–7):

- 'I think my next book will be a systematic treatise on Political Economy, for none of the existing ones are [*sic*] at all up to the present state of speculation' (CW, XIII, p. 630);
- 'I believe if I have done any good a large share of it lies in the example of a professed logician & political economist who believes there are other things besides logic & political economy' (CW, XIII, p. 453);
- 'The whole science requires extremely to be recast, ... and such a book if one were able to do it well would at once supersede all the existing treatises, which are, one and all, effete and useless except as matter of history' (CW, XIII, p. 642);
- 'the study ... languishes for want of a book at once free from gross error and teaching the applications along with the principles, which ... is the beauty of Adam Smith's book' (CW, XIII, p. 642);
- 'to attempt to do for political economy what A[dam] S[mith] did at the time when he wrote, to make a book which, while embodying all the abstract science in the completest form yet attained, incorporating all important improvements, ... [is] at the same time ... essentially a book of applications exhibiting the principles of the science in the concrete' (CW, XIII, p. 708);
- 'I confess that I regard the purely abstract investigations of pol. economy ... as of very minor importance compared with the great practical questions which the progress of democracy & the spread of Socialist opinions are pressing on' (CW, XIV, p. 87).

One of the most significant signals of Mill's 'New' version of political economy was his explicit consciousness of the role of situated human agency in the comprehension of economic events and their redirection by policy means. It was also in his AUT, in the context of his tribute to Harriet Taylor for her alleged contributions to the writing of the PPE (cf. Robson, 1968, pp. 50ff), that Mill singled out for specific mention the distinction which gave the book 'that general tone by which it is distinguished from all previous expositions of Political Economy that had any pretensions to being scientific .... This tone consisted chiefly in making the proper distinction between the laws of Production of Wealth ... and the modes of its Distribution ...'. It was Mill's claim that, by contrast, the 'common run of political economists confuse these together, under the designation of economic laws, which they deem incapable of being defeated or modified by human effort' (AUT, p. 255). The correctness or otherwise of this undocumented assertion about other economists does not really matter here. What is important is that Mill recalled his beliefs that the laws of distribution, and their institutional manifestations, were strictly relative and mutable. Human endeavour, in the guise of properly designed policy interventions, could alter this vital determinant of human economic and social welfare. It will be part of my argument below that these beliefs, along with the distinction from which they flowed, when carefully interpreted, comprised a foundation upon which much of the policy analysis of the PPE was constructed.

The treatment of production and distribution were the themes of Books I and II of the PPE. In these parts of his treatise, Mill was not concerned to separate out the dynamic from the static, nor the institutional from the theoretical, facets of his analyses. The result was that formal argument was constantly blended with real-world evidence in a manner that demanded from the outset a pluralistic approach to methodology. Book III, with its focus on value, exchange and money, was placed by Mill in the same logical order as he had learnt from his father's *Elements* and from Say's *Traité*. This order of treatment reflected an important aspect of Mill's strategy in the work. It allowed him to follow out the idea that production was the most imperative and essential of the economic activities of all human agents, independently of their position in history. Production was a process in which, directly or indirectly, all agents had to participate. It comprised the mediation between the material provisioning needs of agents, however determined, and the state of natural resources, the object of which was the physical, chemical or biological transformation of the latter to suit the satisfaction of the former. Its form had a human design which eventually evolved to include specialization and the division of labour. These developments imposed an increasingly social and institutional character on the mode of production which, along with the techniques of the process itself, became the subject of historical change. A crucial element in the institutional dimension of production was the system of income distribution, and its consequences for the distribution of effective demand for commodities, which evolved as part of the society which the production serviced. The system of distribution, for a given organization and efficacy of production, determined the state of material welfare enjoyed by agents through their different modes of participation in the production process. Now all this could never be independent of or unaffected by the system of value and exchange which developed to facilitate it. However it was Mill's implied judgement that the themes of Book III were logically anterior to the fundaments of production and distribution which were their raison d'être. In interpreting him here, we should recall that he argued his analytical framework in sequential terms rather than depicting anything resembling a general equilibrium format. It is worth noticing, though, that at one point he at least hinted at an awareness of the idea of an interdependence between the above three operations (PPE, p. 705). This construction of the PPE was also influenced by the fact that production and distribution were the necessary focus of his reform strategy, while the institutional and operational dimensions of value and exchange were largely left aside because of their secondary role in the determination of the socioeconomic conditions experienced by the working majority.

Mill had adopted from Comte the distinction between static and dynamic analysis and the PPE gave him the opportunity to make effective use of these two perspectives. What eventuated, though, as indicated above, was that, in Books I to III, he treated several key issues of dynamics as immediate extensions of the otherwise static analyses. Dynamics proper, as he thought of it specifically in secular terms, was to be the topic of Book IV: 'Influence of the progress of society on production and distribution'. We notice once again the focus on the two most essential processes of the economy, but the analyses planned now needed the concepts of value and exchange in order fully to track the temporal developments affecting the future of capitalist economy and society (cf. Schwartz, 1972, pp. 208–9). It was, nonetheless, the dynamics of production from Book I, including the growth of labour productivity, the labour force, the capital stock and production from land, which comprised the bases of these later analyses. Ultimately Mill's concern in his dynamics was not with the economic motion of capitalism, as it involved the trends of prices and income distribution, for its own sake, but rather with the welfare consequences for workers of such trends. This was the theme which again dominated in Book V, where the role of government in the economy was analysed. There Mill gave a lot of attention to the economics of taxation, some of which was carried forward into the arguments about policy and reform. In this latter respect, though, he emphasized other, more general functions and interventions of government as they could affect social welfare, again with the future conditions of the working class as the central issue.

The *design* of the PPE, then, was not bound by 'Ricardian' doctrine, even though much of its more formal analysis was intended to carry the doctrine forward. It was a work which had a broader scope and intention than merely to reiterate the old political economy, even in the revised form that included his own subtle and often ingenious theoretical developments (cf. Stigler, 1965, *passim*). It did become, in spite of Mill's intention not to produce a work aimed at predominantly theoretical exposition, *the* textbook of its age. This can, no doubt, be attributed to its detailed but readily accessible treatment of established classical economic theory; although, it should be added, such accessibility was bought at the price of a lesser concern for logical rigour (cf. Viner, 1987, p. 161). The effect of this dominant reading of the PPE was that, most especially, its more radical methodological messages for economists were lost. Those who thought of themselves as Mill's disciples, especially John Cairnes (1965), were dedicated to preserving and promoting the strongly scientific dimensions of the work. It was only the enemies of orthodoxy, the Historical School members such as T.E. Cliffe Leslie, who managed to grasp the idea that, in order to deal properly with its phenomena, political economy could not sustain its purely scientific image, as this appellation was understood from the physical sciences (Hutchison, 1978, pp. 77ff). Its objects of study, phenomena with their origins in the thoughts and activities of historically situated human agents, could not be accounted for fully by such narrow methodological means. The strictly deductive approach, with its necessary dependence on the 'economic man' axiom, was simply inadequate as a means of comprehending such phenomena or for the defence of policies designed to bring about reforms to the system in which they were generated. At least, the complexities of a multitude of 'disturbing causes' made the logically formal representation of phenomena impossible. Then again, the Historical School lacked the subtlety of analysis to be able to make much of the more heterodox side of Mill's methodological legacy. So it was that, with the onset of the 'Jevonian' revolution, the fate of future neglect for this legacy was sealed. The need explicitly to represent the choices, decisions and actions of human agents as self-conscious and chronically influenced by their cumulative biographies and current situations, and to adjust methodological ambitions accordingly, simply did not become part of the lore of economics. Methodologically the 'Jevonian' revolution did much the same to the more intellectually innovative theses of Mill's PPE as the 'Ricardian' had done to those of Adam Smith's WN.

My objective in this chapter is confined to providing an outline of the way Mill adapted the methodological thrust of the PPE to ensure its consistency with the scope of the work's substantive subject matter and with the demands this substance made on the adequate representation of human agency. In particular this will include a consideration of some selected parts of the book in which he addressed those 'New' issues where he found it necessary to shed the 'Ricardian' straitjacket in order to convey his own ideas in accordance with his expositional aims (cf. Schwartz, 1972, *passim*). First and foremost, it will be my argument, in section 10.2, that this need emerged already in the treatment of production and distribution. There Mill made an important, but often misinterpreted, distinction between the analytical demands of comprehending the respective structures and operations of these processes. The outcome of this endeavour, I will argue, was to find his approach to reform short of its vital grounding in the ethology, an issue which he had chosen to lay aside in favour of the more readily tractable and accessible subject of political economy. In section 10.3, I consider Mill's reflections on the pragmatics of the economic and social welfare consequences of perfectly free factor and commodity markets. The key point to which he drew attention in these reflections was that, when human agents do not behave as 'economic men', the price and distribution results of markets vary from the theoretical optimum. The theme of the following section, 10.4, is the role of human agency in the generation of socioeconomic progress. When analysing the secular dynamics of capitalism, Mill confronted most obviously the limitations of the representation of the human agent as mere 'economic man'. As a consequence, we will find him eliciting features of human character and conduct, more or less ad hoc, in response to the demands of the various issues considered. The result was a mix of styles of analyses ranging from the abstract–deductive to the empirico-descriptive. Section 10.5 is then devoted to Mill's endeavours to argue out the terms and consequences of constructivist interventions in the design of institutional reorganizations and government interventions. He was particularly concerned with the potential of these actions to effect an improvement in the future well-being of the majority of people who comprise the working class. It will be observed in this section that, although Mill was sceptical about governments in both theory and practice, he made out a case for a considerable degree of intervention as the basis for reform. Section 10.6 sums up with some last words on the realities of Mill's treatment of human agency and methodology as compared with the presumptuous and narrow readings which underpinned mainstream claims about his legacy. Few contemporary interpreters recognized the true import of what Mill had done for economics. Most of his influential successors were set, rather, on ensuring the perpetuation of economics as an objectively formal pseudo-physical science. They simply chose to ignore those of his arguments which implied a conscious need for economic analyses to be designed explicitly to cope with the contingent nature of human agency. The fate of his revisionist ideas on methodology, along with those of similar status and content adumbrated by Adam Smith a century before, is now history.

10.2 Essentials of production and distribution

Mill introduced the readers of his PPE to the nature of the subject ahead in the following terms that were highly indicative of the orientation of his 'New' view of the science towards its essential foundations in human agency and its significance as a basis for the effecting of reforms to economy and society:

> In so far as the economical condition of nations turns upon the state of physical knowledge, it is a subject for the physical sciences, and the arts founded on them. *But in so far as the causes are moral or psychological, dependent on institutions and social relations, or on the principles of human nature,* their investigation belongs not to physical, but to moral and social science, and is the object of what is called Political Economy. (PPE, pp. 20–21, emphasis added)

For Mill, the essential foundations of political economy were identified as the laws which govern the production and distribution of wealth. He went so far as to assert with respect to the PPE that they, 'and some of the practical consequences deducible from them, are the subject of the following treatise' (PPE, p. 21). However it is pertinent to notice immediately that there is a distinction already drawn here between the physical and human dimensions of the object phenomena of the science, a distinction that had appeared in the DPE as well (pp. 316ff). What Mill probably intended in the above passage was to delimit the scope of his treatise by separating off the engineering structures and operational requirements of production as a purely physical matter from the institutions and processes of human agency which are involved, directly or indirectly, in their technical development and actual implementation. It will be more apparent in a moment just how important these distinctions are for any interpretation of Mill's treatment of the production process and its relation to distribution. Before considering these issues, something should be said concerning the mode of inclusion of the theory of value and exchange in the construction of the PPE. While they remained an integral part of the economic process in its totality, the laws of value and exchange were relegated by Mill to a very particular status for his purposes. It is evident, he explained first of all,

> that of the two great departments of Political Economy, the production of wealth and its distribution, the consideration of Value has to do with the latter alone; and with that, only so far as competition, and not usage or custom, is the distributing agency. The conditions and laws of Production would be the same as they are, if the arrangements of society did not depend on Exchange. (PPE, p. 455)

Leaving aside his vexed claim that all was settled regarding the theory of value (p. 456), the point of the above argument was further to emphasize that the purely engineering structures and operations of production were separable from the way the products were handled post-production. There is a limited sense in which this was correct for the single production period immediately ahead: given the same engineering set-up, *ceteris paribus*, the generation of physical output is independent of any subsequent operations. But the issue was far more complex than Mill made apparent, for, even within the above single-period delimitation, other things cannot be equal in different systems with respect to the qualitative delivery of human agency factors to the process. Moreover the intertemporal dynamics will involve a continuous interaction between the engineering aspects and the reflexive changes instituted, consciously and unconsciously, by human agents. More significantly, though, the piece implied that some immediate relation was relevant between distribution and the nature of the value–exchange processes. Mill was inclined to ascribe minimal importance to this relation:

Even in the present system of industrial life, in which employments are minutely subdivided, and all concerned in production depend for their remuneration on the price of a particular commodity, exchange is not the fundamental law of the distribution of the produce, no more than roads and carriages are the essential laws of motion, but merely a part of the machinery for effecting it. (PPE, p. 455)

Just what Mill understood by and about this nexus has been debated at length, in most recent times with Hollander's neoclassical revisionism as the centrepiece (1985, chapters 5 and 6). It is not necessary for the present purposes to add to these discussions. The only thing to note here is that Mill's reference to the crucial roles of competition and custom in the value and distribution argument is pertinent and it will be looked at again in section 10.3 below.

Mill treated the issue of the relative analytical priorities to be ascribed to the various separable operations of the economy quite seriously. He found in established political economy an inclination not to do so which disturbed him considerably:

To confound these ideas, seems to me, not only a logical, but a practical blunder. It is a case of the error too common in political economy, of not distinguishing between necessities arising from the nature of things, and those created by social arrangements: an error, which appears to me to be at all times producing two opposite mischiefs; on the one hand, causing political economists to class the merely temporary truths of their subject among its permanent and universal laws; and on the other, leading many persons to mistake the permanent laws of Production (such as those on which the necessity is grounded of restraining population) for temporary accidents arising from the existing constitution of society. (PPE, pp. 455–6)

Now production most essentially comprised 'the extraction of the instruments of human subsistence and enjoyment from materials of the globe' and depended upon certain 'necessary conditions' of the physical environment and upon human knowledge of them (PPE, p. 21). Although Mill's above reference to the 'permanent' laws of production suggested the contrary, very little of the current state of the physical and technical conditions of production could be considered as immutable. He was well aware that human agency was a vital determinant of the development of physical production techniques and of the actual use made of them. In sum:

Whatever mankind produce, must be produced in the modes, and under the conditions, imposed by the constitution of external things, and by the inherent properties of their own bodily and mental structure. Whether they like it or not, their productions will be limited by the amount of their previous accumulation, and, that being given, it will be proportional to their energy, their skill, the perfection of their machinery, and their judicious use of the advantages of combined labour. (PPE, p. 199)

Political economy takes any natural conditions as given and, by combining them with 'other truths relating to human nature, it attempts to trace the secondary or derivative laws, by which the production of wealth is determined' (PPE, p. 21).

The primacy of human agency in the design and implementation of production was emphasized here by the addition of the reference to the laws of production being 'secondary or derivative'. This is a highly significant observation which is often missed in interpreting Mill's intentions in the distinction between production and distribution to which he gave such retrospective prominence in the AUT. It has often been the view of his critics that the distinction was just an unsustainable confusion on Mill's part involving a failure to recognize the interdependence and interaction between all the operations of the aggregate economy, *à la* general equilibrium (for example, see Schumpeter, 1954, p. 543; Schwartz, 1972, p. 64). More careful readings have already suggested that, while Mill may have been unclear about his intentions, he was not confused (see, for example, V.R. Smith, 1985, *passim*; de Marchi, 1988, pp. 153f). The simple fact of the matter, as Mill's above argument indicates, is that he well knew that the processes of production, as they operated in the reality of an economic system, were not fully represented by their given physical and technical dimensions alone. To an extent, then, Mill's claim that 'the laws and conditions of the production of wealth partake of the character of physical truths' was inclined to mislead readers as to his meaning (PPE, p. 199). What was intended was that a purely engineering relationship could be shown to exist between inputs and outputs once the physical conditions of production were fully specified. Outputs could be logically accounted for in terms of inputs and the intervening transformations. There can be no doubt, though, that these conditions included the human design and implementation of means to facilitate the processes and that these had to be consistent with the demands of the given physical–technical cum engineering dimensions if maximum efficiency was to be achieved. Mill indicated some recognition of this condition: 'howsoever we may succeed in making for ourselves more space within the limits set by the constitution of things, those limits exist; there are ultimate laws, which we did not make, which we cannot alter, and to which we can only conform'. For some reason, probably to soften the tone of determinism, from the third edition of the PPE onwards, he changed the wording after 'the constitution of things' to read 'we know that there must be limits. We cannot alter the ultimate properties either of matter or mind, but can only employ those properties more or less successfully, to bring about the events in which we are interested' (PPE, p. 199 and ed. n.). All that can be said about this change is that the facts of the case explained in the earlier version could not be changed by altering the wording of his text. The demand for consistency between the physical technicalities of production and the form of their human operation simply could not be gainsaid, especially if agents cared about efficiency. No determinism was implied, though, for it was but one influence on the total design of production, albeit probably the most important. Further human inventions and interventions would decide the manifest form of the optimal consistency, and hence of the process itself, along with the degree of the optimality actually realized (cf. V.R. Smith, 1985, pp. 279–80, for a different version of the rationale for the change of wording).

All in all, it is apparent that Mill did not treat production as a purely physical process that can be fully understood independently of the involvement of situated human agency. These dimensions were separable only in principle. In the first place, the technology embodied in the whole engineering set-up was the product of human ingenuity; and, furthermore, it remained entirely inert until activated by human intervention, thus making even its physical operation dependent upon the exigencies of human agency.

In the case of the laws of distribution, these were perceived by Mill as even more immediately the product of human interventions operating through evolved social and economic institutions. He treated distribution as 'a matter of human institution solely. The things once there, mankind, individually or collectively, can do with them as they like. They can place them at the disposal of whomsoever they please, and on what terms'. Given this, it followed that the 'distribution of wealth ... depends on the laws and customs of society. The rules by which it is determined, are what the opinions and feelings of the ruling portion of the community make them' (PPE, pp. 199–200). The clear message here, leaving aside the apparent uncertainty engendered by the more qualified claim made earlier in the PPE that distribution was only '*partly* of human institution' (p. 21, emphasis added), was that, if the distribution phenomena of the economy are to be understood, they must be founded on a proper representation and analysis of the conduct of human agents as conditioned by a particular set of relevant institutions and associated rules.

At the beginning of the work, Mill had foreshadowed that the 'conditions on which the power [institutions] possess over the distribution of wealth is dependent, and the manner in which the distribution is effected by the various modes of conduct which society may think fit to adopt, are as much a subject for scientific enquiry as any of the physical laws of nature' (PPE, p. 21). What he intended to convey was that there was an aspect of distribution analysis able legitimately to be treated by formal, deductive logic. Such would be the case once the institutions by means of which distribution was to be directed had been 'chosen' by a society; although in reality, for any one era, the 'choice' would be dominated by inheritance from previous social evolution. In Mill's era, the institutions of private property and the market were dominant. Given their presence, 'we have here to consider, *not the causes, but the consequences*, of the rules according to which wealth may be distributed. Those, at least, are as little arbitrary, and have as much the character of physical laws, as the laws of production' (PPE, p. 200, emphasis added). So, as was the case with production, the analysis had two aspects to be considered: one had its causal source in the exigencies of human agency, in this case the largely inherited 'choice' of institutions, while the other could be argued as a matter of deductive logic, in this case the distribution actually realized in the absence of any 'disturbing causes' (cf. V.R. Smith, 1985, pp. 268, 281). However the extent to which this was really true depended upon the pattern of interaction between agents and the institutional constructs being one to which the strict rules of logic could be applied. Such a claim could be made for Mill's economy only in the abstract cum ideal case of pure 'economic men' operating in perfectly competitive markets. Once any 'disturbing causes' were allowed for in individual motivation and in the organization and operations of the market, the distribution *outcome,* too, would depend upon contingent agent conduct. This conduct, directed by custom rather than competition alone, could not be logically deduced without ambiguity. Mill was well aware of this problem, for, as we shall see in the next section, in his analysis of markets he confronted explicitly the 'disturbing' role of custom.

Mill's concerns about the outcome of the distribution process extended beyond its direct welfare and equity implications. The significance of these facets of distribution were to be balanced against their effects on the economic motivations of human agents (V.R. Smith, 1985, pp. 281ff). Not only was this consequence unable to be calculated by deductive logic, but it introduced a reflexive dynamic relation between distribution and the psychological and social determinants of production. The simple hypothesis which Mill considered pertinent to any reform to the distribution outcome was that pecuniary rewards to agents affected their incentives to participate in economic activities. Most directly, his concern was with the provision of labour services in production under communist and socialist alternatives to capitalism, where some degree of guaranteed income equity would apply. In spite of widely held beliefs to the contrary, Mill argued that placing properly educated workers in a situation comprising a properly constituted cooperative economic order would engender collective other-directed incentives to replace self-interest as the motivation to maximize labour effort. His view was that the common property and income equality of communism, exemplified in microcosm by the contemporary factory cooperatives developed and operated by Robert Owen, could be expected to encourage a greater commitment to work than the present system in which worker disincentives were rife (PPE, pp. 204–5, 203ff *passim*). The French socialist alternatives were not affected by this problem, as guaranteed equity was not one of their objectives. On the contrary, their design was to make the motive of self-interest more effective by securing unequal rewards for differential skill and effort (PPE, pp. 210ff).

With respect to both production and distribution as operational phenomena, Mill showed that political economy as formal analysis could concentrate on the aspects which avoided the need to get involved in the more intricate and subjective contingencies of human agency per se. For this purpose, the human origins of the *form* of the production process and the *design* of the institutions and rules of distribution were simply given for the purposes of strictly scientific analyses. These origins were buried deep in the psychological and social evolution of humankind and Mill asserted quite candidly that

> the opinions and feelings of mankind, doubtless, are not a matter of chance. They are the consequences of the fundamental laws of human nature, combined with the existing state of knowledge and experience, and the existing condition of social institutions and intellectual and moral culture. But the laws of the generation of human opinions are not within our present subject. They are part of the general theory of human progress, a far larger and more difficult subject of inquiry than political economy. (PPE, p. 200)

All this careful avoidance of any claim to be dealing directly with the processes of human agency as such is rather puzzling. It was a feature of Mill's approach that the immediate objective of policy design and defence, involving the *reform* of production and the *redesign* of distribution, was to influence the actual conduct of human agents through their education and through careful attention to their environmental conditions. What Mill did in the above argument was to sidestep the need to analyse formally the essential psychological foundations upon which his reform strategies were to be based.

This failure in the present context set the stage for all that was to follow. Readers of the PPE were asked to accept as a matter of faith that the economic welfare outcomes of capitalism could be manipulated by means of institutional change directed at modifying human agency: that is, to accept the idea without the back-up of the ethological theory which would have demonstrated formally the means by which the character and conduct of human agents were to be redirected to this end (cf. Hollander, 1985, pp. 957–8). Mill knew that this science of the formation of human character and agency, particularly in its applied guise of *political ethology,* was missing from his intellectual repertoire. Readers who took the opportunity to refer to the appropriate places in the juxtaposed magnum opus, the SOL, would have discovered the extreme seriousness of this omission. There Mill expressed his grave concern about the lack of such a theory as the foundation for policy action:

The causes of the national character are scarcely at all understood, *and the effect of institutions or social arrangements upon the character of the people* is generally that portion of their effects which is least attended to, and least comprehended. Nor is it wonderful, when we consider the infant state of the Science of Ethology itself, from whence the laws must be drawn, of which the truths of political ethology can be but results and exemplifications. (SOL, p. 905, emphasis added)

On the basis of these misgivings, he went on to conclude that

the most imperfect part of those branches of social inquiry which have been cultivated as separate sciences, is the theory of the manner in which their conclusions are affected by ethological considerations. *The omission is no defect in them as abstract or hypothetical sciences, but it vitiates them in their practical applications as branches of a comprehensive social science.* (SOL, pp. 905–6, emphasis added)

The implication evident here was that, as long as 'economic man' comprised the sole representation of human agents in economic analyses, then the *abstract* science of political economy could be epistemologically secure, but, once the tenets of ethology were allowed for, and human agents could be moulded so as to take on contingent forms of character and conduct, those credentials were lost to it. In the above passage quoted from the PPE, he made the frank admission, to reiterate, that 'the laws of the generation of human opinions ... are part of the general theory of human progress, a far larger and more difficult subject of inquiry than political economy' (PPE, p. 200). We can recognize, then, with the benefit of our literary hindsight, that this theory had been left on the agenda of unfinished business because of its obvious analytical difficulty. However the adverse ramifications of the startling revelations from the SOL for the claims of political economy to be a science of reform were not permitted any fuller consideration in the PPE.

10.3   Reflections on the free market
As is well established, Mill's outlook was dominated by a belief in the demonstrable benefits of, and a consequently determined preference for, free human agency as the economic and social norm. His fundamental premiss in this respect was categorically stated: '*Laisser-faire*, in short, should be the general practice: every departure from it, unless required by some great good, is a certain evil'. The rationale behind this assertion was simply the belief that, 'as a general rule, the business of life is better performed when those who have an immediate interest in it are left to take their own course [, for] the individual agents have so much stronger and more direct an interest in the result, that the means are far more likely to be improved and perfected if left to their uncontrolled choice' (PPE, pp. 945, 946–7; cf.p. 951). In matters

economic, this meant an espousal of free markets in which all agents were exposed to the full pressures of competition, including markets for the factors of production and the commodities they produced. Under a regime of capitalism, the operations of markets centred around a concurrent set of private property rights over the means of production in all their forms and over all that was produced with their aid. Property rights represented a vital mediation in the process of distributing the value of output in any period of time between the participants who contributed to its production.

For Mill, the institution of private property was the centrepiece of the contemporary economic system and he inquired in depth about the extent to which it, in particular, was responsible for the malevolent distribution conditions of that system. His extensive and controversial discussions of the potential for other types of systems, communist or socialist, to deliver a better welfare allocation result were conducted largely in terms of whether the alternatives sustained private rights or required a transfer to collective owner ship and control of property (PPE, pp. 200ff). But the most important facet of any system as far as Mill was concerned was not the ownership regime but whether or not it maximized individual freedom: 'If a conjecture may be hazarded,' as he put it regarding any choice of economic system, 'the decision will probably depend mainly on one great consideration, viz. which of the two systems is consistent with the greatest amount of human liberty and spontaneity' (PPE, p. 208). These existential qualities, assisted by an appropriate education system, provided the greatest opportunity for the full development of the human spirit. A further desirable quality cited by Mill was that the system should demand competition between agents, thus ensuring the maintenance of the maximum of human effort and efficiency in the processes of production (PPE, pp. 794ff; see section 10.4 below). Mill treated alternative economic systems with some careful attention to theoretical detail and endeavoured to bring out the best of their potentials. He found these potentials to be considerable, but a proper comparison with capitalism demanded that, if the alternatives were to be idealized, then it, too, should be so presented. When this was done, Mill found that the evils of the contemporary system were due to its historical distortions rather than to its principles, a conclusion consistent with what Adam Smith had argued (PPE, pp. 207–9). However it remained a moot point which of the systems, considered in their *pure* or *ideal* state, could most assuredly deliver the maximum of material welfare, equally distributed, and the maximum of sociopsychological well-being to each individual agent. Mill was led, therefore, to the pragmatic conclusion that any evolution towards these alternative systems was some way off in terms of human futurity and that, for the present, political economists should concentrate upon the conditions of existence and progress belonging to a society founded on private property and individual competition; and ... the object to be principally aimed at in the present stage of human improvement [should be] not the subversion of the system of individual property, but the improvement of it, and the full participation of every member of the community in its benefits. (PPE, p. 214)

Mill's immediate focus in the endeavour to construct an argument for the sort of reform foreshadowed in this passage was the system of distribution. He explained that the position of individual agents in the distribution process was dependent primarily upon whether their mode of participation in production included the ownership of means of production or not. Remuneration accrued to agents, and they were effectively assigned to economic classes, as a consequence of the extent to which their participation in production was dominated by such ownership and/or by the delivery of labour services. Mill's analytical strategy, which gave emphasis to the ideal of the capitalist distribution outcome, was neatly summarized:

We have to inquire, according to what laws the produce distributes itself among these classes, *by the spontaneous action of the interests of those concerned*: after which, a further question will be, what effects are or might be produced by laws, institutions, and measures of government, in superseding or modifying that spontaneous distribution. (PPE, p. 235, emphasis added)

Free competition in the pursuit of self-interest by agents was the essence of capitalist distribution and the associated regime of price determination, but it is worth remarking in passing that Mill left any concerns about the influence on distributional outcomes of relative property endowments implicit at this stage. Later he would express serious concerns about all aspects of intergenerational property transfers which contributed to the perpetuation of unequal endowments and consequent unequal economic opportunities (PPE, 800f, 810ff, 887ff).

Most immediately, though, he went on to reflect upon the actual role which competition played in the distribution process. He proceeded on the premiss that the effective activation of customs could distort the free and competitive outcome in practice and berated the orthodox political economists for their exaggeration of the latter result at the expense of 'the other and conflicting principle'. He rationalized this neglect methodologically by quite openly asserting that

only through the principle of competition has political economy any pretension to the character of a science. So far as rents, profits, wages, prices, are determined by competition, laws may be assigned for them. Assume competition to be their exclusive regulator, and principles of broad generality and scientific precision may be laid down, according to which they will be regulated. The political economist deems this his proper business: and *as an abstract or hypothetical science*, political economy cannot be required to do, and indeed cannot do, anything more. (PPE, p. 239, emphasis added)

Implicit in the combined argument of this passage and the previous one was a representation of the human agent as 'economic man', driven only by the motives of self-interest and pecuniary maximization, exercised without situational constraint or direction of any kind other than the conditions of the market. Under these conditions, the logic of the market outcome could be precisely calculated. Once the 'softer' and more variable influence of customs on agent responses had to be allowed for, this logic would be disturbed to a greater or lesser degree and the market outcome rendered ambiguous.

Now it is important to note that the impact of custom on the processes of human agency went much deeper than the mere 'disturbing causes' generated by market power. Mill emphasized that political economy had the potential readily to make allowance for such monopoly impact. What he was concerned with were situations where, although there were no impediments to competition, nonetheless it failed to operate. Such malfunction was attributed to the direction of agency being dominated by pre-existing customs or common usage effects that had historically evolved (PPE, pp. 239 ff). It was Mill's assessment that the structures and operations associated with some particular economic outcomes were to a greater or lesser extent determined independently of competitive effects: landed property and the generation of rent (pp. 240–42, 320), the organization and income patterns in many trades and the settlement of professional incomes (pp. 243, 398–9), some wage and profit incomes (pp. 396–9, 409) and certain categories of prices (pp. 242–3). Mill's treatment of these cases was not extensive, but one of them can be examined as a means of demonstrating the idea he wanted to convey.

Mill recognized, quite astutely for his era, that, while wholesale prices may be competitively determined, at the retail level it is the habits and traditions of buyer and seller relations, including, at times, even considerations of 'equity or justice', or of 'ease ... or vanity' (SOL, p. 906), which most influence the prices charged and paid. More fully: 'Purchases for private use, even by people in business, are not always made on business principles: the feelings which come into play in the operation of getting, and in that of spending their income, are often extremely different.' Distortion of realized market prices resulted from, among other things, 'indolence, or carelessness', 'ignorance and defect of judgement, want of time for searching and making inquiry, and not unfrequently from coercion, open or disguised' (PPE, p. 460). Hollander correctly finds these insights of Mill's to be indicative of his rejection of 'economic man' as an adequate representation of human agents in accounting for observed market conduct: 'The maximizing man in the *Principles* refers to the real man in the market place rather than [to] a psychological fiction' (1985, p. 959; cf. p. 266). The conclusion reached by Mill with respect to the operation of real-world markets, especially those operated by non-professional participants or in which participation was based on other than 'business principles', was that competition could not be relied upon to be the exclusive determinant of the material outcomes generated. Thus, 'to escape error, we ought, in applying the conclusions of political economy to the actual affairs of life, to consider not only what will happen supposing the maximum of competition, but how far the result will be affected if competition falls short of the maximum' (PPE, p. 244). And it was these 'actual affairs of life' which were of central concern to Mill the reformer.

10.4   Human agency and socioeconomic progress

In making the case for preferring a free-market system, whatever its limitations, Mill was also concerned to show the extent to which it could deliver gradually improving welfare results by virtue of its own immanent dynamics. Book IV of the PPE was devoted most directly to this theme and he revealed some guarded optimism about the existing system in spite of its distortions. It was an observed fact, Mill asserted, that in 'all the nations we are accustomed to call civilized' there existed 'at least one progressive movement which continues with little interruption from year to year and from generation to generation; a progress of wealth: an advancement of what is called material prosperity' (PPE, pp. 705–6). The improvement of material conditions delivered by the secular growth and development to which Mill referred was dependent upon a complex of *interactive* effects stemming from the combination of growth in real output and increase in population, together with the realities of distribution. And, as he proceeded to argue in some detail, the roots of progress were to be found in the relevant dimensions of situated human agency. Mill had already analysed the economic dynamics of growth and distribution in Books I and II and his intention in Book IV was to give the processes some additional meaning in terms of their welfare consequences over the longer run.

For a *given* rate of population increase, several main factors were identified by Mill as contributing to the aggregate growth of material production: the accumulation of capital as means of production, the increasing productivity of labour, reorganizations of the operations of labour and industry and a growth in agricultural productivity and production (PPE, pp. 100ff). In turn, he was able to attribute each of these factors to certain induced behavioural characteristics of human agents, given the natural resource base with which the economy was endowed. The rate of growth and development depended essentially upon the engendered qualities of the agents and their organizational direction, both of which were identified by Mill as functions of the institutional facilities available as a consequence of evolution and design. The success of production, as far as it depended upon labour, 'like most other kinds of success, depends more on the qualities of the human agents, than on the circumstances in which they work'. (PPE, p. 103). While these circumstances could not be ignored, he went on to suggest a range of specifically human factors which could contribute to the improved productivity of labour: greater regular and habitual energy of labour; superior intelligence, skill and knowledge, which included the talent for inventiveness and innovation; the moral qualities of workers, including their trustworthiness; and the security and protection enjoyed by members of the society, including 'protection *by* the government, and protection *against* the government' (PPE, p. 112, original emphasis).

Whatever the qualities of workers, their productivity could be further enhanced by proper attention to the organizational circumstances of the delivery of their services. Mill referred here to the modes of 'co-operation, or combination' of workers, and he gave full credit to Adam Smith for his seminal emphasis on the importance of specialization and division of labour as a source of increased output per labour hour attributable to worker reorganization (PPE, pp. 116ff). Mill considered all of Smith's insights, but he found it necessary to qualify particular aspects of, and to add some glosses of his own to, the original exposition. He went on to amplify the idea of this source of productivity increase by recognizing that there were additions to productivity to be gained by increasing the scale of production in a manufacturing operation, given the appropriate concomitant market size (PPE, pp. 131ff). Access to these gains could not be automatically assumed, for in some industries a smaller scale may be needed to ensure the attention to detail demanded by the nature of production or the product. Mill included in his considerations of scale the advantages and disadvantages of financial organization on the joint-stock principle. As he explained, the case for this mode of financing could be readily made as the sole basis upon which large-scale production could proceed in the absence of sufficiently large individual fortunes. The necessary condition remained that individual savers must have adequate knowledge of and confidence in the joint-stock system for it to function, a condition that could only come with the commercial maturation of human agents generally (PPE, pp. 140–41). There was, though, in addition, a negative consequence to consider, namely the separation of ownership from direct administration and control of actual production. Mill expressed his decided misgivings about depending upon hired labour in general, misgivings which only increased where those hired were expected to carry out high level organizational functions which cannot be circumscribed by fixed rules and require initiative (PPE, pp. 137–8). He concluded on the mitigating note that, whatever the disadvantage of hired managers, at least, by means of careful selection, those with the greatest industrial and commercial skills would rise to the top. Thereby the economy could avoid the risks of mediocrity associated with owners who claim the right to manage, independently of their actual talents (PPE, p. 139).

All of the above contributions to the potential for growth in material prosperity were carried along with a *given* rate of increase in the labour force, together with the rate of accumulation of capital and the rate of gaining access to increasing production from land. Each of these elements of the 'law of the increase of production' was analysed by Mill under the rubric of its own 'law of increase', an approach which potentially required a circumscribed representation of human agents if the term 'law' was to be taken in its literal methodological sense. More on this in a moment.

It should be observed briefly first that, as a matter of general principle, and across a wide range of his works, Mill was preoccupied with matters of population control as a necessary condition for ensuring the increase of per capita economic welfare and social well-being. The expansion of the availability of labour needed to realize growth was a function of the rising level of total population. Thus there had to be a balance struck between the rate of this rise and the desire to achieve an improvement in the equity of welfare access without any accompanying radical redistribution or socialization of property. Population growth was dictated essentially by Malthus's principles and Mill believed there were, even by his own time, impending, and ultimately immutable, limits to food and raw materials production from finite access to land and productivity improvements (PPE, pp. 154ff, 187ff). Indeed he was so concerned with the potential of these problems that he endeavoured to persuade his readers of the benefits, at least in principle, of reaching a stationary state of sorts, a theme taken up in the next section. More significantly for Mill's thought as a totality, he believed with absolute conviction, and campaigned long and hard to persuade others to believe likewise, that the rate of population increase need not be treated as a *given* socioeconomic parameter. In the absence of successful artificial birth control measures, Mill's acceptance of the Malthusian principle of population, and hence labour force, growth led him to refer to 'the unlimited extent of its natural powers of increase' and to the very limited potential for natural or environmentally generated human responses which act as impediments to the realization of those powers (PPE, p. 159). But he believed that human beings were, at least, a cut above other animals in their sexual mores: they were 'more or less influenced by foresight of consequences, and by impulses superior to mere animal instincts: and they do not, therefore propagate like swine, but are capable, though in unequal degrees, of being withheld by prudence, or by the social affections' (PPE, p. 157). This belief gave him hope that controlling the rate of population increase was a real possibility. Worker education and more acceptance of and access to positive birth-control practices would mitigate the problem. On this matter, Mill's optimism about the capacity of properly constructed social situations to redirect natural human conduct knew no bounds. It was a theme which he addressed at every opportunity in the PPE (pp. 348ff, 367ff, 719ff, 763ff).

Returning now to the theme of economic growth per se, as things turned out in the chapters which purported to address the above-mentioned 'laws', what Mill's analyses actually demonstrated was that the processes involved had little claim to any law-like status. His exposition was comprised very largely of logically coherent, but nonetheless descriptive argument. We can but conclude that he intended the concept of a law to be interpreted rather loosely and in a way which he knew to be consistent with the subject matter he was presenting, rather than with any preconceived methodological demands. My reading suggests that, as he wanted to emphasize the human dimensions of growth and its consequences, he had little option but to avoid the axiomatic–deductive form of argument. There was no need for 'economic men' in these chapters, where the analyses were conducted at a minimum level of abstraction and with a high level of empirical content.

Mill set out from the assertion that 'nothing in political economy can be of more importance than to ascertain the law of ... [the] increase of production; the conditions to which it is subject: whether it has practically any limits, and what these are'. And, to sheet home the imperatives of his own project, he added that 'there is also no subject in political economy which is popularly less understood, or on which the errors committed are of a character to produce, and do produce, greater mischief' (PPE, p. 153). With this law dependent upon the laws of increase of the three factors, labour, capital and land, Mill went on to treat each in turn in the light of the above concerns.

In discussing Mill's brief consideration of the determinants of capital accumulation, it is appropriate to be mindful that he conflated several concepts which we would now deal with as separable, especially in their relation to the decisions and actions of human agents. In Mill's analyses, saving was immediately capital accumulation, capital accumulation was immediately the intention to invest in means of production, and every intention to invest was immediately realized and physically realizable. That is, there was an assumed direct linkage from the propensity to save to the actual rate of real economic growth which Mill did not question. This may seem to be a trite observation to make, but in terms of the role of human agents in the growth process, it led him grossly to understate the complexity of the dynamics of agency involved. When addressing the diverse factors that affect the propensity to save, though, Mill did broaden his inquiry well away from the motivational scope of 'economic man'. However, at the same time, he revealed a minimal appreciation of the separate status of the propensity to invest in additional productive capacity. Moreover his approach involved him in an assumption of perfectly elastic supply in the means of production producing industries, an assumption which was probably beyond the capacity of his economics to have perceived explicitly at that time. Most basically expressed, Mill's thesis was that, 'since all capital is the product of saving, that is, of abstinence from present consumption for the sake of a future good, the increase of capital must depend on two things – the amount of the fund from which saving can be made, and the strength of the dispositions which prompt to it' (PPE, p. 160).

Mill had a broad conception of the periodic fund from which saving could be undertaken. It included that part of the workers' income share in excess of their consumption needs. Just how workers were able to negotiate this excess of wage income over contemporary 'subsistence', and thus appropriate a part of the surplus that would otherwise accrue to capital owners, Mill did not stop to explain. But, even if he accepted the 'wages fund' idea for much of his life, there was still the possibility of sectoral redistributions of the aggregate wage bill as a consequence of differential trade union-negotiated wage outcomes. However, by the late 1860s, Mill had definitely adopted a more flexible view of wage determination, which allowed for a wage bill not limited by the exigencies of capital advances (cf. Schwartz, 1972, pp. 70ff, 90ff; Hollander, 1985, pp. 387ff). From the outset, though, he did make explicit his appreciation of a dual relationship between profits and saving: that profits represented one of the sources included in the saving fund, while at the same time being a part of the incentive to save. Quite as would be expected, he did not grasp the complexities introduced by this insight and he went on further to compound the conflations cited above: 'But the disposition to save does not wholly depend on the external inducement to it; on the amount of profit to be made from savings' (PPE, p. 161). He wanted to convey here that a variety of factors could be elicited to explain the propensities to save *and* to invest, these two remaining more or less identical for his purposes and most often referred to as conjoined under the rubric of the desire to accumulate. It was in regard to the range of these factors that he revealed a quite subtle understanding of the accumulation decision by agents and, as just indicated, certainly one which went beyond the bald motive of profit maximization characteristic of 'economic man'.

In their accumulation decisions, the key concern that Mill ascribed to agents was the trade-off between present and future access to goods. Such preferences involved agents in a present sacrifice, the expediency of which 'varies very much in different states of circumstances; and the willingness to make it, varies still more'. The profound difficulty confronted by agents in this matter was that of uncertainty: 'In weighing the future against the present, the uncertainty of all things future is a leading element; and that uncertainty is of very different degrees' (PPE, pp. 162–3). Any condition which was conducive to feelings of a lack of security of person or property on the part of agents would disincline them towards the sacrifices of accumulation, with any reduction in the strength of their resistance requiring 'the inducement of a higher rate of profit on capital, to make them prefer a doubtful future to the temptation of present enjoyment' (PPE, p. 163). However Mill noted that there were factors which could override the calculations of expediency on the basis of reason such that 'the disposition to save is often far short of what reason would dictate: and at other times is liable to be in excess of it'. Beyond the consideration that agents' intelligence must be sufficient to give a proper role to reason in calculating future benefits, and beyond the possibility of accumulation for special purposes relating to the well-being of heirs, Mill left individual factors behind and concentrated on providing a descriptive exposition of various national political and social conditions which may affect the propensity to accumulate (PPE, pp. 164ff).

An important outcome of these inquiries was his recognition of the potential for the stationary state to emerge, in part, as a result of a decline in the incentive to accumulate. Specifically, 'when a country has carried production as far as in the existing state of knowledge it can be carried with an amount of return corresponding to the average strength of the effective desire to accumulate ..., it has reached what is called the stationary state' (PPE, p. 169). Under these circumstances, a return to positive accumulation would require some productivity-improving or cost-saving innovations that increase the yields expected from investment and/or some increase in the propensity to accumulate itself. Implicit in these assertions about the potential arrival at the stationary state, and the possibility of checking it, was a complex set of arguments posited by Mill about the expectation of secular declining rates of return on additional investments as output expanded and the existence of a minimum rate of profits (PPE, pp. 402f, 733ff). Mill's ultimate rationale for accepting these consequences was to be found in the law of increase of production from land, but a host of forces and counter-forces were identified as contributing to the trend in the interim.

For Mill, the decline in the rate of profit on individual capitals was due to the existence of assumed limits to investment opportunities except at ever-lower returns as the aggregate stock of means of production increased: 'It must always have been seen, more or less distinctly, by political economists, that the increase of wealth is not boundless: that at the end of what they term the progressive state lies the stationary state' (PPE, p. 752). This decline in returns was, then, directed towards an ultimate minimum acceptable rate, characteristic of each economy, at which the given propensity to accumulate of human agents is negated by the low yields expected. Now, although in 'opulent countries' the rate is 'habitually near to the minimum', there were short-run dynamic 'counteracting circumstances' operating in an irregular temporal pattern to mitigate the decline. Thus 'it would require but a short time to reduce profits to the minimum, if capital continued to increase at its present rate, and no circumstances having a tendency to raise the rate of profit occurred in the meantime'. There was a hint here, too, that the stationary state could be permanently delayed: 'The expansion of capital would soon reach its ultimate boundary, if the boundary itself did not continually open and leave more space' (PPE, pp. 738, 739). Hollander finds in this argument 'a splendid illustration of the sense of the notion "tendency" to refer not to a necessarily observable trend but rather to one force amongst other and possibly conflicting forces on a particular variable' (1985, p. 457). Mill cited four, possibly simultaneously operating, counteractions: the periodic wasting of a portion of the fixed means of production in recessions brought on by overproduction; cost-saving innovations in production; cost savings from imports of cheaper means of production and wage goods; and the export of finance capital (PPE, pp. 741ff). He remained convinced, however, that none of these corrections could reverse the tendency towards a stationary state in which accumulation would cease. This was a state to be encouraged, in Mill's view, as we shall see below, for the economic peace and well-being it would bring to all people.

The differential characteristic of land (and natural resources generally) cited by Mill as crucial to the arrival of stationary-state conditions was that it was finite in its quantity for any one nation, including its colonies. It also had a given profile of arability and fertility, and these considerations together delimited the natural capacity of a nation to produce raw materials and food. These natural limits could only be transcended by the application of capital and technology to lift the productivity per unit of existing land and to extend the arable boundaries. Now it was Mill's opinion that the ultimate limits to the capacity of nations to support contemporary rates of expanding populations at reasonable levels of material welfare, given the state of technology, were temporally closer at hand than was generally assumed (PPE, p. 173). His analysis of the issue included a due recognition of the potential for improvement in the productivity of land to counteract the diminishing returns to its extension, but the tenor of his argument was designed to convince his readers that the threat of overpopulation was a very real and a very near one (PPE, pp. 187ff). For Mill, it was ultimately the limits to production from land which would finally render capital accumulation untenable because of the negative influence on rates of return of the rising costs of food, and hence real wages, and of raw materials. He added to the impact of his message by denying at length the long-term potential for imports, even under free-trade conditions, or emigration to compensate for any nation's domestic production limits (PPE, pp. 190ff).

Inherent in the current prospects for socioeconomic progress were, at least, some optimistic trends. Mill identified these as an increasing command over the powers of nature, an increase in the security of persons and property, a general improvement in the 'business capacities' of the people and an increase in the capacity of human agents to cooperate in productive endeavours (PPE, pp. 706ff). Each of these tendencies, in its own way, could be expected to lift the productivity of human agents individually and/or collectively. But Mill ended his exposition of their operation with the caveat that they would be unlikely to achieve much beyond delaying the limits to growth and the onset of population pressures on welfare. There ensued in the PPE an extensive discussion of the various economic and social facets of secular dynamics which struck Mill as important: trends in values and prices, trends in income distribution between rents, profits and wages, the tendency for profits to fall towards some minimum, the prospects for the arrival of a stationary state and, finally, the 'probable futurity of the labouring classes'.

Mill endeavoured to convey a feeling of sanguinity, not to say Utopianism, about any tendency towards a stationary state which was for him, as indicated above, a very real possibility given the impending limits to the expansion of output at realistic rates of return on capital. This inclination of Mill's was quite contrary to the established unqualified defence of progress to be found in the works of the 'old school' of political economy (PPE, pp. 752–4). However he appeared to believe that rational, properly educated agents could be led to see the ultimate advantages of stationarity as a socioeconomic destiny. Mill expressed his convictions in this matter in quite emotive terms, attributing the dominance of desires to accumulate ever-increasing wealth as indicative of a situation in which 'minds are coarse' and where they, therefore, 'require coarse stimuli'. He believed that such a condition was only a transitory one along the way towards a more mature and sophisticated handling of material progress by human agents. In personal terms, he registered his objections to the contemporary stress on material drives:

> I confess I am not charmed with the ideal of life held out by those who think that the normal state of human beings is that of struggling to get on; that the trampling, crushing, elbowing, and treading on each other's heels, which form the existing type of social life, are the most desirable lot of human kind, or anything but the disagreeable symptoms of one of the phases of industrial progress. ... [And,] those who do not accept the present very early stage of human improvement as its ultimate type, may be excused for being comparatively indifferent to the kind of economical progress which excites the congratulations of ordinary politicians; the mere increase of production and accumulation. (PPE, pp. 754–5)

The alternative was to accept the onset and consequences of a stationary state, including the concurrent need for strict restraints on population growth, which Mill claimed would bring about 'the best state for human nature ... in which, while no one is poor, no one desires to be richer, nor has any reason to fear being thrust back, by the efforts of others to push themselves forward' (PPE, p. 754). In fact he went so far as to advocate a halt to population increases even before the sort of ultimate limits referred to above were reached. He did so in an endeavour to avoid the effects of what he saw as the prospect of overcrowding, even though all people may be enjoying acceptable levels of material welfare.

In short, it was time to think of the human condition in broader terms; to begin to value the possibility of 'solitude in the presence of natural beauty and grandeur, [that] is the cradle of thoughts and aspirations which are not only good for the individual, but which society could ill do without'. He continued with what today would be read as a piece of 'Green' environmentalist propaganda:

> Nor is there much satisfaction in contemplating the world with nothing left to the spontaneous activity of nature; with every rood of land brought into cultivation, which is capable of growing food ...; every flowery waste or natural pasture ploughed up, all quadrupeds or birds which are not domesticated for man's use exterminated as his rivals for food, every hedgerow or superfluous tree rooted out, and scarcely a place left where a wild shrub or flower could grow without being eradicated as a weed in the name of improved agriculture. (PPE, p. 756)

Thus it was that Mill foreshadowed the demise of 'economic man'. In the stationary state, homo oeconomicus would be replaced by homo bucolicus. There would be a continuation of human improvement, but it would be diverted into moral and cultural endeavours, and any technological advances would be dedicated to the reduction of necessary human labour (PPE, p. 756).

Whatever the ultimate economic state, there were certain potential characteristics of the future course of the development of agents *qua* human beings which Mill believed warranted attention. His ostensible focus was on the 'labouring classes' as the majority most in need of the benefits of reform. But this apparently innocuous class concept led him to imply what amounted to a quite radical element of reform, if the argument is to be taken at face value. It was the fact of the identification of *a separate class* of those agents who perform labour that so disturbed Mill. Such an appellation was 'descriptive of an existing, but by no means necessary or permanent, state of social relations' (PPE, p. 758). What made the point so radical in its implications was that, although it evidently derived from the communist principles of the era, which he had discussed earlier in the PPE (pp. 203ff), these principles were not at issue here. Mill's present focus was on the future under capitalism, but he still referred to 'the great social evil ... of a non-labouring class' as tolerable 'only provisionally'. His position was amplified in the following passage: 'I do not recognise as either just or salutary, a state of society in which there is any "class" which is not labouring; any human beings, exempt from bearing their share of the necessary labours of human life, except those unable to labour, or who have fairly earned rest by previous toil' (PPE, p. 758).

This radical perception of a reformed capitalism involved Mill in advocating at least the idea of the demise of the traditional relationship between capitalists and workers, what he called 'the relation of hiring and service' (PPE, pp. 766ff). The argument for this demise depended upon an optimistic future scenario in which the workers in their 'social and moral aspect' would be transformed from a state of 'dependence and protection', with its guiding principle that 'all things which affect them collectively, should be regulated *for* them, not *by* them', to the opposite one of 'self-dependence', in which 'they will require that their conduct and condition shall be essentially self-governed' (PPE, pp. 759, 764, original emphasis). What Mill claimed to have observed in and around him was a social dynamic in which workers were choosing collectively to move away from their former condition: 'The working class have taken their interests into their own hands, and are perpetually showing that they think the interests of their employers not identical with their own, but opposite to them' (PPE, p. 762). Such self-dependence implied an uplifting of the intellectual capacities of the workers, for it required that 'to their own qualities must now be commended the care of their destiny', and the 'prospect of the future depends on the degree in which they can be made rational beings'. Mill's attitude here was that 'there is no reason to believe that prospect other than hopeful', because he was able to point to 'a spontaneous education going on in the minds of the multitude, which may be greatly accelerated and improved by artificial aids' (PPE, p. 763). These aids to the improved intelligence of the workers would include 'newspapers and political tracts' and 'institutions for lectures and discussions'.

Now, under these changing perceptions of their own position in society, Mill reasoned that the workers could not 'be permanently contented with the condition of labouring for wages as their ultimate state', nor could it be 'expected that the division of the human race into two hereditary classes, employers and employed, can be permanently maintained' (PPE, pp. 766–7; cf. p. 793). He stressed that his reform ideals did not extend to any revision of the structures and operations of industry in themselves, and he reiterated the productivity benefits to be gained from large-scale production. His vision was rather of an association and cooperation between all participants in the production process on the basis of equality of opportunity, but organized to be consistent with the demands of large-scale operations. Thus it was Mill's conclusion that 'the civilizing and improving influences of association, and the efficiency and economy of production on a large scale, may be obtained without dividing the producers into two parties with hostile interests and feelings'. On the contrary, 'the relation of masters and workpeople will be gradually superseded by partnership, in one of two forms: in some cases, association of the labourers with the capitalist; in others, *and perhaps finally in all,* association of labourers among themselves' (PPE, p. 769, emphasis added).

He went on from here to develop the implications of these ideals of reform by means of a mix of empirical observations about existing experiments along such lines and theoretical assertions about possibilities for their generalized application (PPE, pp. 769ff). Organizational change would begin, Mill thought, with the spread of profit-sharing cooperatives involving existing capitalists and workers. But what he foreshadowed, in the end, was the evolutionary transition to a form of syndicalism. This would ultimately replace capitalism and be founded on a revision of the existing form and distribution of property rights over the means of production: 'The form of association, ... which if mankind continue to improve, must be expected in the end to predominate, is ... the association of the labourers themselves on terms of equality, collectively owning the capital with which they carry on their operations, and working under managers elected and removable by themselves' (PPE, p. 775). A little later, Mill gave some indication of the way in which such a peaceful, non-revolutionary transition to the worker control of industry might proceed, albeit in the necessarily vague terms usually associated with gradualism.

> As associations multiplied, they would tend more and more to absorb all work-people ... As this change proceeded, owners of capital would gradually find it to their advantage, instead of maintaining the struggle of the old system with work-people of only the worst description, to lend their capital to the associations ... and at last, perhaps even to exchange their capital for terminable annuities. In this or some such mode, the existing accumulations of capital might honestly, and by a kind of spontaneous process, become in the end the joint property of all who participate in their productive employment. (PPE, p. 793)

If all this were to be so, then Mill was already beyond the scope of his present objective of reforming the system only to the extent consistent with the maintenance of individual property rights. Evidently the worker cooperatives in their ultimate form were to remain an evolutionary ideal beyond the reach of immediate reforms. These reforms would have to be confined to the creation of a form of corporatism within existing enterprises under the regime of capital and the capitalists.

On top of this advocacy of cooperation, Mill imposed the rider that 'while I agree and sympathize with Socialists in ... [the] practical portion of their aims, I utterly dissent from the most conspicuous and vehement part of their teaching, their declamations against competition' (PPE, p. 790). As competition applied to the operations of markets, where it amounted to a rejection of the development of monopoly power, this defence was quite consistent with Mill's vision. It may well have brought a reduction in the cost of consumer commodities and could even have ensured that, in prosperous times, workers potentially shared in the benefits by bidding up nominal wages as a consequence of an excess demand for labour. The difficulty which arose in regard to this matter was that Mill persisted with the idea that only competition between agents as self-interested, maximizing individuals could ensure the efficient delivery of labour services and the general development and realization of human economic potentials: 'To be protected against competition is to be protected in idleness, in mental dulness; to be saved the necessity of being as active and as intelligent as other people' (PPE, p. 795). However he did not explain how this, together with his further observations about 'the natural indolence of mankind; their tendency to be passive, to be the slaves of habit, to persist indefinitely in a course once chosen', could be squared with the image of workers as self-dependent and collectively anxious to improve their intellectual, economic and social lot. Somehow, though, it was the key institution of worker cooperatives that Mill envisaged would internally combine the optimum of association and competition between educated human agents, while at the same time effectively competing externally as market participants. In Schwartz's view, 'the point of competition must be stressed', for what Mill wanted to ensure was inducement of 'competition within the co-operatives, so that reward should be commensurate to the contribution of each, and competition among co-operatives, so that the public be protected from inefficiency' (1972, p. 225; cf. p. 226).

Schwartz goes on quite properly to cast some doubt on the prospects for Mill's 'probable futurity of the labouring classes' ever to have been realized (1972, pp. 231ff). Mill may well have had the 'over-intellectualized view of human nature' to which Schwartz refers; in particular, to have believed too confidently in the rational redirection of agent character and conduct by means of environmental manipulation. He even more probably misread the innate dynamics of economic class power which constantly enables capitalism to defend itself as a system against the encroachment of change that threatens to destroy it. Mill thus overestimated the power of the rational merits of cooperatives to transcend the class conflict and defeat the entrenched forces of conservative self-interest. However, in mounting such criticism, it should be recalled that Mill was content in the immediate future to allow that economic and social change would have to proceed under the auspices of capital and adapt its expectations, form and extent to that fact.

10.5   Interventions and reform: pros and cons

The strategy adopted by Mill in formulating the rationale for and defence of interventionist reform measures was to lead his readers through the secular dynamics of the existing system, giving particular emphasis to the ramifications of the trends for human material and social welfare. These dynamics were the subject of the previous section above. What this analysis enabled Mill to do was to come to grips with the causes of the two great issues which concerned him, inequity and injustice in distribution and the consequent existence of mass poverty. Having provided himself with these insights, he examined the contemporary role of government in the operations of economy and society with a view to setting out its potential to effect change within politically acceptable terms of reference.

In sum, Mill's portrayal of the current state of and future prospects for the material welfare of the bulk of the population under the existing economic, social and political conditions in Britain was not an entirely optimistic one. Moreover he believed that any alteration to this outlook was made less likely by the contemporary acceptance of the necessity for inequity by the privileged classes and by those people with intellectual influence and/or political power. This situation was compounded by the threat of an excessive rate of growth of population in the face of fixed beliefs and attitudes which railed against the positive methods of birth control required to mitigate it. It was Mill's objective to change these attitudes, in part by demonstrating the potential for properly designed economic and social policy interventions to effect reforms that did not involve radical redistributions of property or power.

With respect to the outcome of the changes induced by interventionist reforms, Mill made reference to the need to accept a balance between strict equality in distribution and the consequences of human agents being afforded equal opportunity. With the proviso that 'they all start fair':

> Many [agents] ... fail with greater efforts than those with which others succeed, not from difference of merits, but difference of opportunities; but if all were done which it would be in the power of a good government to do, by instruction and by legislation, to diminish this inequality of opportunities, the differences of fortune arising from people's own earnings could not justly give umbrage. (PPE, p. 811)

Such equality of opportunity could not be sufficient to correct mass poverty and, to Mill, it was apparent that other interventions with a more direct effect on maldistribution would be required. The balance to be struck, then, was to ensure the preservation of self-reliance and incentives to work when agents were given the opportunity by their institutional situations to be dependent and indolent: 'Energy and self-dependence are ... liable to be impaired by the absence of help, as well as by its excess'. He was ever hopeful that, for human agents, 'assistance is a tonic, not a sedative' on the ground that 'it is even more fatal to exertion to have no hope of succeeding by it, than to be assured of succeeding without it' (PPE, p. 961). It was to this test of preserving these key agent qualities that all intervention proposals designed to assist workers should be subjected. Thus Mill's aims in the PPE were 'egalitarian', but they reflected the fact that at the same time, 'he was no leveller' (Schwartz, 1972, p. 194; cf. p. 213). Finally one further test of balance had to be applied: that the system should ensure the maximization of liberty for all people, within a framework of protection for the rights of others, in a manner consistent with an acceptable degree of welfare reform. Mill had faith in the merits of laissez-faire, but he was a 'mature liberal' who believed that 'liberty was not a panacea for all social ills ... It was, however, a social good that should be carefully protected, as there was no guarantee at all that it would grow with the progress of civilization' (Schwartz, 1972, pp. 105, 152).

Mill chose to establish the requirements for transition of the economic and social conditions of workers towards a more equitable state within the confines of only moderate alterations to the existing system, supported by marginal additional interventions by government. The problematic that he confronted in this matter was to design interventions which maintain a balance between freedom and self-determination for agents and adequate social control to ensure that the liberty was enjoyed with equity. He had no time for 'impatient reformers, [who,] thinking it easier and shorter to get possession of the government than the intellects and dispositions of the public, are under a constant temptation to stretch the province of government beyond due bounds' (PPE, p. 799). But, this point having been made, the challenge was to specify just what the 'proper limits of the functions and agency of governments' were against the widespread resistance to any interventions as a consequence of the long history of their selective benefits or wholesale disbenefits. Mill addressed the issue by containing some government functions within the category 'necessary' and then setting out to identify those that may be designated 'optional'. The key principle of the 'necessary' interventions was the maintenance of protection and security for persons and property against the unwarranted interference of others. Included were interventions designed to forbid and prevent violence, unjustified force, fraud and deception committed by agents against other agents or their legitimate property. In addition, there were a number of services which governments should provide that were conducive to general welfare but which, for one reason or another, would not be otherwise made available. In order to perform all of these loosely defined functions, three dimensions of government intervention were argued by Mill to be necessary. First, it must raise the revenues required to fund their operations; secondly, it must establish all the laws which provide the reference points and sanctions associated with the interventions, with Mill emphasizing the laws of property and contract as most pertinent to his purposes; and thirdly, it is required to set up the systems by means of which the laws are to be administered and the sanctions applied, in particular, the judicial system and the police (PPE, pp. 800ff, 804).

Any functions which the government may be performing or be expected to perform under a reform programme that could not reasonably be included under the rubric 'necessary' were bound to be classified as 'optional'. These, Mill thought, should be subjected to careful critical scrutiny with respect to their legitimacy according to the criterion that they deliver net welfare benefits otherwise not attainable. Here he began his inquiry with those cases where such interventions have been applied because of faulty reasoning about their warrant and/or about their effects. Thus 'there are some things with which governments ought not to meddle, and other things with which they ought; but whether right or wrong in itself, the interference must work for ill, if government, not understanding the subject which it meddles with, meddles to bring about a result which would be mischievous' (PPE, p. 913). Building on the logic of the political economy expounded in the earlier Books of the PPE, Mill identified several commonly found or advocated interventions which fitted into this category. He included domestic industry protection policy, usury laws, price control regulations, the granting of monopolies over trade, laws against the combination of workmen, and the censorship of free expression and publication of opinion. Whatever their original intention, each of these interventions was bound to fail to varying degrees and to deliver, directly or indirectly, net economic and/or social disbenefits.

Of these interventions, only the last two are of concern here, as they directly involve conditions of human agency. It was quite to be expected that Mill would seek to reinforce the case against the anti-combination laws. The arguments which he put in this context were the negative ones that the fears of excessive wage gains were unfounded as a matter of practicality. The potential power of combinations tended to be exaggerated and, in the limited cases where it was not, the gains were most often at the expense of the real wages of other workers because of induced price rises or of a reduction in employment. These latter matters were still of concern to Mill and he moralized that, 'when the elevation of the character and condition of the entire body [of workers] has at last become a thing not beyond the reach of rational effort, it is time that the better paid classes of skilled artisans should seek their own advantage in common with, and not by the exclusion of, their fellow-labourers' (PPE, p. 931). In spite of these misgivings about the sectional advantage that may be made possible by combinations, Mill defended the rights of all workers to attempt to maximize their gains. The two aspects of combinations against which he made explicit objections were first, the possibility of compulsory membership or compulsory participation in union activities being made a condition of employment; and, secondly, the establishment of union objectives which were illegal or unconscionable in their effects (PPE, p. 933). In the end, though, Mill made his belief very clear that 'the best interests of the human race imperatively require that all economical experiments, voluntarily undertaken, should have the fullest licence, and that force and fraud should be the only means of attempting to benefit themselves, which are interdicted to the less fortunate classes of the community' (PPE, p. 934).

On the matter of censorship of expression of opinions, Mill was satisfied that, de jure, this was no longer a problem for British people. What troubled him was its continuation as a de facto force:

> In this country, ... the effective restraints on mental freedom proceed much less from the law or the government, than from the intolerant temper of the national mind; arising no longer from even as respectable a source as bigotry or fanaticism, but rather from the general habit, both in opinion and conduct, of making adherence to custom the rule of life, and enforcing it, by social penalties, against all persons who, without a party to back them, assert their individual independence. (PPE, p. 935)

In this matter of intellectual freedom, and in the previous one of economic freedom, Mill expressed what appeared, at first sight, opinions which bordered on the espousal of anarchy. This was not his intention, as he proceeded to show in his extensive reflections on the legitimate grounds for interventions by government in the last chapter of the PPE. The impact of most of these was on the processes of human agency and thus they amounted to containments for the common good of otherwise anarchical tendencies.

While he granted that he was unable to provide any universally valid generalizations about the boundaries of legitimacy of 'optional' government interventions, Mill cited two kinds around which some argument may be organized. These were the classifications 'authoritative' and 'unauthoritative' (PPE, pp. 936ff). The origin of this distinction was to be found in Mill's ideas about ethology as the science of the determination of human character and conduct (section 9.2 above). 'Authoritative' interventions were those which meant the exercise of direct control over human agency, backed up by the threat of sanctions for non-compliance. Mill's concern was that these interventions should be minimized and only applied to a very delimited range of human conduct, for 'there is a circle around every individual human being, which no government ... ought to be permitted to overstep: ... some space in human existence ... sacred from authoritative intrusion' (PPE, p. 938). The basic principle for setting the limit of penetration here was that only agents' conduct that affected others adversely according to contemporary social standards should be at issue. And then, even in cases where such effects could be shown to exist, the authorization of any prohibition of conduct demanded cogent justification and the continuous scrutiny of its actual outcomes. To avoid these complications, and for reasons of strongly held belief, Mill favoured those interventions that do not 'restrain individual free agency' and need not be backed by authority.

> There is another kind of intervention which is not authoritative: when a government, instead of issuing a command and enforcing it by penalties, adopts the course so seldom resorted to ..., and of which such important use might be made, that of giving advice, and promulgating information; or when, leaving individuals free to use their own means of pursuing any object of general interest, the government, not meddling with them, but not trusting the object solely to their care, establishes, side by side with their arrangements, an agency of its own for a like purpose. (PPE, p. 937)

Clearly Mill depended in this sort of argument on the ethological belief that the conduct of human agents could be effectively directed by manipulation of particular facets of the situational environment in and through which they acted. He had no theoretical resources to draw upon in order to generalize about this idea, but he proceeded to apply it to some cases of relevance to his reformist intentions (PPE, pp. 947ff).

Now, even in considering these cases involving the absolute minimum degree and extent of interventions designed to influence and direct the conduct of human agents, Mill reiterated over and over his belief that private individuals and associations do things better for themselves. Thus, on this premiss, for each intervention it had to be convincingly argued that agents could not adequately cater for their own best interests. Such situations could arise because of a lack of sufficient or correct information on the basis of which decisions and choices were to be made; education was for Mill a case in point here. Some categories of persons might also be judged to be incapable of exercising proper discretion concerning their best interests and thus require the protection of the law; children and the insane were obvious cases, but Mill was explicit that, in this respect, the subjugation of women in any of their life roles was not justified. On similar grounds, he wanted to see the prevention of contracts in perpetuity which bind people to commitments which extend beyond their capacities rationally to decide. A further ground for positive intervention was to ensure the effectuation of the legitimate interests of groups which were beyond their own capacities to realize; the reduction of working hours and the defence of the Poor Laws were taken up by Mill under this head. The need for the provision of publicly used services was subjected to searching consideration. Mill continued to favour private enterprise in such provision, even though in many cases a monopoly would be created. The position that he took was that these 'practical monopolies' should expect to remain under some degree of government control and direction (PPE, pp. 927ff; cf. Hollander, 1985, pp. 758ff). However there would always remain some services, warranted by genuine need, which would not be provided at all if left to private interests. Mill accepted that, as a matter of default, these should be taken on by the government.

10.6 Human agents in political economy: some final observations

It is apparent from the above exposition of those aspects of Mill's PPE which he, himself, considered the most important that his conception of human agents went well beyond the scope of the objective character and conduct of 'economic man'. The immediate consequence of this was that the methodological nature of his argument could not be contained within the bounds of a rigorous abstract–deductive logic. Whatever he continued to believe about the status of 'pure' political economy as a science, in which objectivity and logical precision were able to be sustained, it is certain that, for Mill, its analyses could never be ends in themselves. He realized that the type of events and phenomena with which he was to deal as a socially concerned economist involved dimensions of human agency which could not be represented only as the isolated pursuit of maximum self-interest and pecuniary returns at minimum cost. All agents operate in and through particular situational environments which shape and direct their character and conduct in various ways. It followed that a fuller understanding of economic matters as the consequence of human agency would have required at least the integration of a properly developed ethological theory into political economy. Mill gave no explicit recognition to this need, and made no further endeavour to work up the appropriate theory, even though it turned out to be the very foundation required for his reformist arguments to be analysed fully. The consequent hole in his explication was enlarged further by the fact that he made no effort to probe beyond the empirico-behaviourist principles of associationist psychology, even after being led to grant in the EHP that there was a transcendental dimension to human nature in which the ultimate explanation of decisions and conduct was to be found (section 9.4 above).

In these issues Mill was not alone in having the full scope of his analytical potential left unrealized. As was argued earlier, Adam Smith had similarly hinted at complexities that are unique to the human sciences, and this side of his contribution, too, had been overlooked in what became the orthodoxy in political economy under the influence of James Mill and Ricardo. John Mill's insight was to suffer the same fate, as his successors rushed on to defend the rigour and precision made possible by assuming a population of 'economic men'.

But one final consideration which should be added to make the above interpretation of Mill more complete is the thesis cogently argued by Hutchison to the effect that, in his later years, Mill moved increasingly away from any explicit defence of the 'old' version of political economy associated with Ricardo and found much to support in the work of the historicist T.E. Cliffe Leslie (Hutchison, 1978, pp. 58ff). Hutchison suggests that the end of the 'Ricardian' dominance came in the late 1860s and early 1870s. During this period, Mill himself came 'to share the disillusion and impatience with the prevailing doctrines, or some of them, which had owed so much to his own prestige and earlier support' (ibid., p. 63). It is perhaps an irony which was not lost on Mill that the part of his treatise in which the 'old' political economy was reiterated, and the part that he thought of as comprising the least important of his contributions, became the part which made him most famous. In part, this disillusion was, for good reasons, methodological. He felt sorely that the 'Ricardian vice' was ever-present in the actual uses to which political economy was applied. In an article of 1870, dealing with Leslie on the land question, Mill took the opportunity to berate the 'routine school of political economists who have mostly had things their own way ... [and] who share the common infirmity of liking to get their thinking done once and for all, and be saved all the trouble except that of referring to a formula'. This group he found to wield 'a set of catch words, which they mistake for principles – free-trade, freedom of contract, competition, demand and supply, desire for wealth, &c. – which supersede analysis and are applicable to every variety of case without the trouble of thought' (CW, V, p. 671; quoted by Hutchison, 1978, pp. 63, 64). By contrast, Mill stressed the need to realize 'that general maxims should be helps to thought, not substitutes for it' (p. 672). In the work of Leslie's on the land issue with which he was immediately concerned (1870), Mill found and quoted the following piece in support of his views (CW, V, p. 671):

> A school of economists of no small pretensions, strongly represented in parliament, supposes itself to be furnished with a complete apparatus of formulas, within which all economic knowledge is comprised – which clearly and satisfactorily expounds all the phenomena of wealth, *and renders all further investigation of the causes and effects of the existing economy of society needless, and even mischievous, as tending to introduce doubt and heresy into a scientific world of certainty and truth,* and discontent and disturbance into a social world of order and prosperity. (p. 89; quoted, with emphasis added, by Hutchison, 1978, p. 64)

Of course, the fact that economic argument could be so readily reduced to set formulae was attributable to those characteristics of political economy which were the very basis of its claims to be a science; that is, to its dependence on the concept of 'economic man' in combination with the methodology of abstract deduction. This was a situation in applied economics for which Mill certainly could not have been held responsible with any justice. As we have seen, the methodology of the PPE was such as to ensure that the transition from the analyses of 'science' to those of the 'art' was not taken for granted. Indeed it is not too much to say that Mill's concern to make explicit the nature and limits of this analytical transition comprised the raison d'être of the work.

The thrust of the methodological point had been made more obvious in one of Mill's letters of 1867. He referred to his support for

> the emancipation of political economy – its liberation from the kind of doctrines of the old school (now taken up by well-to-do people) which treat what they call economical laws, demand and supply for instance, *as if they were laws of inanimate matter, not amenable to the will of the human beings from whose feelings, interests and principles of action they proceed. This is one of the queer mental confusions which will be wondered at by and by.* (CW, XIV, p. 1320; quoted by Hutchison, 1978, p. 63, my emphasis added)

After readers have traversed my arguments above, this methodological frustration should come as no real surprise. The focus of its wording was explicitly upon the problematics of representing human agency in any objective, nomological form. The 'old' political economy, and Mill himself in a much more self-conscious and tentative way, had avoided facing up to this matter by means of the device of 'economic man'. The unfortunate fact is that, from this point onwards, few economists actually did 'wonder at' this 'queer mental confusion'. Indeed, on the contrary, orthodox economics went on to erect its ever more sophisticated and mathematically rigorous analyses on the very basis of it.

To a significant extent, Mill himself contributed to the way his political economy was read. His only methodological exposition taken up readily by those concerned with matters economic was that in the DPE essay. This was a piece which could be read as merely defending the 'old' position. Mill had clearly not intended to convey such a view, as certain, perhaps more subtle, aspects of the DPE and Book VI of the SOL attested. Very early on, J.N. Keynes commented on the contrast between 'Mill's theory of method as contained in the *Essays* [DPE], and his practice as manifested in the *Principles*. In the former, the conception of "economic man" occupies a position of central and all-pervading importance; in the latter, it plays a much humbler part ... [and] [m]oral and social considerations, in the widest sense, receive accordingly their due share of attention' (1973, pp. 19–20; cf. 116ff). This assessment, with its emphasis on the human agency dimension, gives just the right flavour to the situation. Hollander, nonetheless, argues that, 'despite some anomalies, on the whole there is close accord between the pronouncements of the [DPE] essay and the *Principles* so far as concerns the linkages between factual investigation, economic theory and policy recommendation; indeed the *Principles* can only be fully appreciated in the light of the essay'

(1985, p. 164). The truth element here is that the PPE may well have set out from the methodology of the DPE, but the intervention of the SOL research drew Mill's attention to the need to qualify that approach more decisively when considering the application of 'pure' economic theory to real-world problems and policies. To the extent that it is generally agreed that there was a strong link between the DPE and the SOL, Blaug reaches a contrasting conclusion. He avers a lack of any apparent connection between the methodology of the SOL and what was applied in the PPE. The latter 'contains neither an explicit discussion of methodology nor an harking back to the *Logic* to show that the *Principles* exemplifies sound methodology'. The resulting two methodological Mills can be accounted for, he suggests, by realizing that 'neither the critics nor Mill himself saw any relationship between the *Logic* and the *Principles*; for all practical purposes, they might just as well have been written by two different authors' (1980, pp. 72–3). There are, indeed, good grounds for such an interpretation, albeit with two qualifications. First, in support of Hollander, it seems correct to me to maintain that Mill's methodological principles, within the bounds of their own limitations, were consistently applied. It is all-important, though, to recognize that Mill made allowances for the changing nature of the various object phenomena dealt with by shifting the methodological emphasis away from the premises that were given prominence in the DPE. As a second qualification, attention should be drawn to the irony that it was because Mill was actually so well aware of the ramifications of the relationship that he avoided making it explicit. The missing link of a theory of ethology threatened to bring any such attempted articulation between the two works undone. Without the means of *formalizing* the interaction between the character and conduct of human agents and the multiple dimensions of their situations, Mill had no way of extending the deductive arguments to an understanding of more and more complex economic phenomena or to setting down how they could be modified in the desirable direction by policy interventions.

The pity remains, though, that Mill felt unable explicitly to carry forward the full power and scope of his expansive and pluralistic methodological insights into the PPE. We can only speculate that he felt the need of the ethology most acutely in the transition from the abstract to the real world and decided to leave his readers to pursue his varied methodological intentions as best they could. Viner's observation is apt at this point: 'The *Principles* ... has no single methodological character. As is the case with the *Wealth of Nations* of Adam Smith, some portions are predominantly abstract and *a priori*; in others, there is a substantial measure of factual data and of inference from history'. He goes on to conclude that the PPE 'would have been an inferior book, much less rich in content – and much smaller in size – if Mill had thrown out all that was ambiguous and lacking in strict logical consistency' (1987, pp. 161–2). What Viner has hit on here is the simple fact that, having understood properly the source of economic phenomena in the contingencies of situated human agency, Mill was then not prepared to ignore real-world issues which concerned him just because, for this reason, they could not be readily moulded to fit scientistic criteria. Perhaps the text from the 1867 letter quoted above should just be left to form the basis for an apt intellectual epitaph for Mill:

> He struggled for the emancipation of political economy from the kind of doctrines of the old school which treat what they call economical laws as if they were laws of inanimate matter, not amenable to the will of the human beings from whose feelings, interests and principles of action they proceed. These are queer mental confusions which will only be wondered at by and by.

Bibliography

Anschutz, R.P. (1953), *The Philosophy of J.S. Mill*, Clarendon Press, Oxford.

Anspach, R. (1972), 'The implications of the *Theory of Moral Sentiments* for Adam Smith's economic thought', *History of Political Economy*, **4**,(1).

Ashley, W.J. (1964), 'Introduction' to J.S. Mill, *Principles of Political Economy* [1909], Augustus M. Kelley, New York.

Ayer, A.J. (1987), 'Introduction' to J.S. Mill, *The Logic of the Social Sciences*, Duckworth, London.

Bagehot, W. (1973), *Economic Studies* [1898], Augustus M. Kelley, Clifton, New Jersey.

Bain, A. (1967), *James Mill: A Biography* [1882], Augustus M. Kelley, New York.

Bain, A. (1969), *John Stuart Mill: A Criticism with Personal Recollections* [1882], Augustus M. Kelley, New York.

Becker, J.F. (1984), 'Adam Smith's theory of social science', *Southern Economic Journal*, **28**, 1961, reprinted in Wood (ed.) (1984), vol. I.

Billet, L. (1984), 'The Just Economy: the moral basis of the *Wealth of Nations*', *Review of Social Economy*, **34**,(3), 1976, reprinted in Wood (ed.) (1984), vol. II.

Bitterman, H. (1940), 'Adam Smith's empiricism and the law of nature', *Journal of Political Economy*, **48**.

Bladen, V.W. (1965), 'Introduction' to J.S. Mill (1965).

Blaug, M. (1980), *The Methodology of Economics: or How Economists Explain*, Cambridge University Press, Cambridge.

Bonar, J. (1932), *A Catalogue of the Library of Adam Smith*, 2nd edn, Macmillan, London.

Bowley, M. (1949), *Nassau Senior and Classical Economics* [1937], Augustus M. Kelley, New York.

Bowley, M. (1973), *Studies in the History of Economic Theory before 1870*, Macmillan, London.

Bryson, G. (1968), *Man and Society: The Scottish Inquiry of the Eighteenth Century* [1945], Augustus M. Kelley, New York.

Buchdahl, G. (1971), 'Inductivist *versus* deductivist approaches in the philosophy of science as illustrated by some controversies between Whewell and Mill', *The Monist*, **55**.

Cairnes, J.E. (1965), *The Character and Logical Method of Political Economy* [1875, 2nd edn 1888], Augustus M. Kelley, New York.

Campbell, R.H. and A.S. Skinner (1976), 'General Introduction' to Smith (1976b).

Campbell, T.D. (1975), 'Scientific explanation and ethical justification in the *Moral Sentiments*', in Skinner and Wilson (eds) (1975).

Cannan, E. (1904), 'Editor's Introduction' to Adam Smith (1961).

Coase, R.W. (1984), 'Adam Smith's view of man', *Journal of Law and Economics*, **19**,(3), 1976, reprinted in Wood (ed.) (1984), vol. I.

Coats, A.W. (1984), 'Adam Smith's conception of self-interest in economic and political affairs?', *History of Political Economy*, **7**,(1), 1975, reprinted in Wood (ed.) (1984), vol. II

Cropsey, J. (1977), *Polity and Economy: An Interpretation of the Principles of Adam Smith* [1957], Greenwood Press, Westport, Connecticut.

de Marchi, N.B. (1974), 'The success of Mill's *Principles*', *History of Political Economy*, **6**,(2).

de Marchi, N.B. (1983), 'The case for James Mill', in A.W. Coats (ed.), *Methodological Controversy in Economics: Historical Essays in Honor of T.W. Hutchison*, JAI Press, Greenwich, Connecticut.

de Marchi, N.B. (1987), 'The empirical content and longevity of Ricardian economics', *Economica*, **37**, 1970, reprinted in Wood (ed.) (1987), vol. III.

de Marchi, N.B. (1988), 'John Stuart Mill interpretation since Schumpeter', in W.O. Thweatt (ed.), *Classical Political Economy: A Survey of Recent Literature*, Kluwer Academic, Boston.

de Marchi, N.B. and R.P. Sturges (1973), 'Malthus and Ricardo's inductivist critics: four letters to William Whewell', *Economica*, **40**.

Dobb, M. (1973), *Theories of Value and Distribution since Adam Smith: Ideology and Economic Theory*, Cambridge University Press, Cambridge.

Ekelund, R.B. and E.S. Olsen (1987), 'Comte, Mill and Cairnes: the positivist–empiricist interlude in late classical economics', *Journal of Economic Issues*, **7**,(3), 1973, reprinted in Wood (ed.) (1987), vol. I.

Endres, A.M. (1991), 'Adam Smith's rhetoric of economics: an illustration using "Smithian" composition rules', *Scottish Journal of Political Economy*, **38**,(1).

Evensky, J. (1987), 'The two voices of Adam Smith: moral philosopher and social critic', *History of Political Economy*, **19**,(3).

Evensky, J. (1989), 'The evolution of Adam Smith's views on political economy', *History of Political Economy*, **21**,(1).

Fletcher, R. (ed.) (1973), *John Stuart Mill: A Logical Critique of Sociology*, Thomas Nelson & Sons, London.

Friedman, M. (1953), *Essays in Positive Economics*, University of Chicago Press, Chicago.

Grampp, W.D. (1984), 'Adam Smith and the economic man', *Journal of Political Economy*, **56**,(4), 1948, reprinted in Wood (ed.) (1984), vol. I.

Halévy, E. (1972), *The Growth of Philosophical Radicalism* [1928], Faber & Faber, London.

Hausman, D.M. (1981), 'John Stuart Mill's philosophy of economics', *Philosophy of Science*, **48**.

Hayek, F. von (1955), *The Counter-Revolution of Science: Studies in the Abuse of Reason*, Free Press, New York.

Hayek, F. von (1978), *New Studies in Philosophy, Politics, Economics and the History of Ideas*, University of Chicago Press, Chicago.

Heilbroner, R.L. (1982), 'The socialization of the individual in Adam Smith', *History of Political Economy*, **14**,(3).

Hollander, S.H. (1973), *The Economics of Adam Smith*, Heinemann, London.

Hollander, S.H. (1979), 'The historical dimension of *The Wealth of Nations*', in O'Driscoll (ed.) (1979).

Hollander, S.H. (1983), 'William Whewell and John Stuart Mill on the methodology of political economy', *Studies in History and Philosophy of Science*, **14**,(2).

Hollander, S.H. (1984), 'Adam Smith and the self-interest axiom', *Journal of Law and Economics*, **20**,(1), 1977, reprinted in Wood (ed.) (1984), vol. I.

Hollander, S.H. (1985), *The Economics of John Stuart Mill*, two volumes, Basil Blackwell, Oxford.

Hollander, S.H. (1987), *Classical Economics*, Basil Blackwell, Oxford.

Hollis, M. (1977) *Models of Man: Philosophical Thoughts on Social Action*, Cambridge University Press, Cambridge.

Hollis, M. (1987a), 'J.S.Mill's political philosophy of mind', *Philosophy*, **47**, 1972, reprinted in Wood (ed.) (1987), vol. I.

Hollis, M. (1987b), *The Cunning of Reason*, Cambridge University Press, Cambridge.

Hume, D. (1962), *A Treatise of Human Nature* [1739–40], two volumes, edited with Introductions by D.G. Macnabb and by P.S. Ardal, Fontana/Collins, Glasgow.

Hume, D. (1975), *Enquiries Concerning Human Understanding and Concerning the Principles of Morals* [1777], edited by L.A. Selby-Bigge, 3rd edn, Clarendon Press, Oxford.

Hutchison, T.W. (1976), 'The Bicentenary of Adam Smith', *Economic Journal*, **86**,(343).

Hutchison, T.W. (1978), *On Revolutions and Progress in Economic Knowledge*, Cambridge University Press, Cambridge.

Jensen, H.E. (1984), 'Sources and contours of Adam Smith's conceptualized reality in the *Wealth of Nations*', *Review of Social Economy*, **34**,(3), 1976, reprinted in Wood (ed.) (1984), vol.I.

Jevons, W.S. (1957), *The Theory of Political Economy* [1871], Kelley and Millman, New York.

Jones, R. (1956), *An Essay on the Distribution of Wealth and on the Sources of Taxation* [1831], Kelley and Millman, New York.

Jones, R. (1964), *Literary Remains consisting of Lectures and Tracts on Political Economy* [1859], Augustus M. Kelley, New York.

Keynes, J.N. (1973), *The Scope and Method of Political Economy* [1890, 4th edn 1917], Augustus M. Kelley, Clifton, New Jersey.

Kubitz, O.A. (1932), 'Development of John Stuart Mill's *System of Logic*', *Illinois Studies in the Social Sciences*, **18**,(1–2).

La Nauze, J.A. (1937), 'The substance of Adam Smith's attack on Mercantilism', *Economic Record*, **13**.

Laudan, L. (1971), 'William Whewell on the consilience of inductions', *The Monist*, **55**.

Leslie, T.E.C. (1870), *Land Systems and Industrial Economy of Ireland, England, and Continental Countries*, Longmans Green, London.

Lewisohn, D. (1987), 'Mill and Comte on the methods of social science', *Journal of the History of Ideas*, **33**, 1972, reprinted in Wood (ed.) (1987), vol. IV.

Lindgren, J.R. (1973), *The Social Philosophy of Adam Smith*, Martinus Nijhoff, The Hague.

Lindgren, J.R. (1984), 'Adam Smith's theory of inquiry', *Journal of Political Economy*, **77**, 1969, reprinted in Wood (ed.) (1984), vol.I.

Losee, J. (1972), *A Historical Introduction to the Philosophy of Science*, Oxford University Press, London.

McCulloch, J.R. (1965), *The Principles of Political Economy with a Sketch of the Rise and Progress of the Science* [1825, 5th edn 1864], Augustus M. Kelley, New York.

Macfie, A.L. (1959), 'Adam Smith's *Moral Sentiments* as foundation for his *Wealth of Nations*', *Oxford Economic Papers*, **11**.

Macfie, A.L. (1967), *The Individual in Society: Papers on Adam Smith*, George Allen & Unwin, London.

Machlup, F. (1978), *Methodology of Economics and other Social Sciences*, Academic Press, New York.

Macnabb, D.G. (1962), 'Introduction' to Hume (1962), volume 1.

McNulty, P.J. (1967), 'A note on the history of perfect competition', *Journal of Political Economy*, **75**.

McRae, R.F. (1973), 'Introduction' to J.S.Mill (1973).

Malthus, T.R. (1936), *The Principles of Political Economy considered with a View to Their Practical Application* [1820, 2nd edn 1836], International Economic Circle, Tokyo.

Meek, R.L. (1967), *Economics and Ideology and other Essays: Studies in the Development of Economic Thought*, Chapman & Hall, London.

Meek, R.L. (1973), *Studies in the Labour Theory of Value* [1956], 2nd edn, Lawrence & Wishart, London.

Meek, R.L. (1977), *Smith, Marx, and After: Ten Essays in the Development of Economic Thought*, Chapman & Hall, London.

Mill, J. (1966a), *Elements of Political Economy* [1826], in Winch (1966a).

Mill, J. (1966b), 'Whether political economy is useful' [1836], in Winch (1966a).

Mill, J. (1967), *Analysis of the Phenomena of the Human Mind* [1829, 2nd edn 1869], Augustus M. Kelley, New York.

Mill, J.S. (1963), *The Earlier Letters of John Stuart Mill 1812–1848*; volume XIII of the Collected Works of John Stuart Mill, University of Toronto Press, Toronto.

Mill, J.S. (1965), *Principles of Political Economy with Some of Their Applications to Social Philosophy* [1848, 7th edn 1871]; volumes II and III of the Collected Works of John Stuart Mill, University of Toronto Press, Toronto.

Mill, J.S. (1967), *Essays on Economics and Society*; volumes IV and V of the Collected Works of John Stuart Mill, University of Toronto Press, Toronto.

Mill, J.S. (1969), *Essays on Ethics, Religion and Society;* volume X of the Collected Works of John Stuart Mill, University of Toronto Press, Toronto.

Mill, J.S. (1972), *The Later Letters of John Stuart Mill 1849–1873*; volume XIV of the Collected Works of John Stuart Mill, University of Toronto Press, Toronto.

Mill, J.S. (1973), *A System of Logic Ratiocinative and Inductive: Being a Connected View of the Principles of Evidence and the Methods of Scientific Investigation*; [1843, 8th edn 1872]; volumes VII and VIII of the Collected Works of John Stuart Mill, University of Toronto Press, Toronto.

Mill, J.S. (1978), *Essays on Philosophy and the Classics*; volume XI of the Collected Works of John Stuart Mill, University of Toronto Press, Toronto.

Mill, J.S. (1979), *An Examination of Sir William Hamilton's Philosophy and of The Principal Philosophical Questions Discussed in his Writings*; [1865, 4th edn 1872]; volume IX of the Collected Works of John Stuart Mill, University of Toronto Press, Toronto.

Mill, J.S. (1981), *Autobiography and Literary Essays*; volume I of the Collected Works of John Stuart Mill, University of Toronto Press, Toronto.

Morrow, G.R. (1969), *The Ethical and Economic Theories of Adam Smith* [1923], Augustus M. Kelley, New York.

Mueller, I.W. (1956), *John Stuart Mill and French Thought*, University of Illinois Press, Urbana.

Myers, M.L. (1983), *The Soul of Modern Economic Man: Ideas of Self-Interest – Thomas Hobbes to Adam Smith*, University of Chicago Press, Chicago.

O'Brien, D.P. (1975), *The Classical Economists*, Clarendon Press, Oxford.

O'Donnell, R. (1990), *Adam Smith's Theory of Value and Distribution: A Reappraisal*, Macmillan, London.

O'Driscoll, G.P. (ed.) (1979), *Adam Smith and Modern Political Economy*, Iowa State University Press, Ames, Iowa.

Popper, K.R. (1972), *Conjectures and Refutations: The Growth of Scientific Knowledge*, Routledge & Kegan Paul, London.

Priestley, F.E.L. (1969), 'Introduction' to J.S.Mill (1969).

Raphael, D.D. (1975), 'The impartial spectator', in Skinner and Wilson (eds) (1975).

Raphael, D.D. and A.L. Macfie (1976), 'Introduction' to A. Smith (1976a).

Raphael, D.D. and A.S. Skinner (1980), 'General Introduction' to A. Smith (1980).

Reisman, D. (1976), *Adam Smith's Sociological Economics*, Croom Helm, London.

Ricardo, D. (1951), *The Works and Correspondence of David Ricardo*, volumes VI–VIII, edited by P. Sraffa with the collaboration of M.H. Dobb, Cambridge University Press, Cambridge.

Richardson, G.B. (1975), 'Adam Smith on competition and increasing returns', in Skinner and Wilson (eds) (1975).

Robbins, L. (1952), *An Essay on the Nature and Significance of Economic Science* [1932, 2nd edn 1935], Macmillan, London.

Robson, J.M. (1968), *The Improvement of Mankind: The Social and Political Thought of John Stuart Mill*, University of Toronto Press, Toronto.

Robson, J.M. (1973), 'Textual Introduction' to Mill (1973).

Rosenberg, N. (1979), 'Adam Smith and laissez-faire revisited', in O'Driscoll (ed) (1979).

Rosenberg, N. (1984), 'Some institutional aspects of the *Wealth of Nations'*, *Journal of Political Economy*, **18**,(6), 1960, reprinted in Wood (ed.) (1984), vol.I.

Ryan, A. (1979), 'Introduction' to J.S.Mill (1979).

Ryan, A. (1987), *The Philosophy of John Stuart Mill*, 2nd edn, Macmillan, London.

Say, J.-B. (1964), *A Treatise on Political Economy: or the Production, Distribution and Consumption of Wealth* [1803, new American edn 1880], Augustus M. Kelley, New York.

Schumpeter, J.A. (1954), *History of Economic Analysis*, George Allen & Unwin, London.

Schwartz, P. (1972), *The New Political Economy of J.S. Mill*, Weidenfeld & Nicolson, London.

Senior, N.W. (1938), *An Outline of the Science of Political Economy* [1836], George Allen & Unwin, London.

Senior, N.W. (1966), *Selected Writings on Economics: A Volume of Pamphlets 1827–1852*, Augustus M. Kelley, New York.

Shackle, G.L.S. (1979), *Imagination and the Nature of Choice*, Edinburgh University Press, Edinburgh.

Skinner, A.S. (1979), *A System of Social Science: Papers Relating to Adam Smith*, Clarendon Press, Oxford.

Skinner, A.S. and T. Wilson (eds) (1975), *Essays on Adam Smith*, Clarendon Press, Oxford.

Smith, A. (1961), *An Inquiry into the Nature and Causes of the Wealth of Nations*, two volumes, edited by E. Cannan, Methuen, London.

Smith, A. (1976a), *The Theory of Moral Sentiments* [1759, 6th edn 1790], edited by D.D. Raphael and A.L. Macfie, volume I of the Glasgow Edition of the Works and Correspondence of Adam Smith, Clarendon Press, Oxford.

Smith, A. (1976b), *An Inquiry into the Nature and Causes of the Wealth of Nations* [1776], edited by R.H. Campbell and A.S. Skinner, volume II (in two volumes) of the Glasgow Edition of the Works and Correspondence of Adam Smith, Clarendon Press, Oxford.

Smith, A. (1978), *Lectures on Jurisprudence*, edited by R.L. Meek, D.D. Raphael and P.G. Stein, volume V of the Glasgow Edition of the Works and Correspondence of Adam Smith, Clarendon Press, Oxford.

Smith, A. (1980), *Essays on Philosophical Subjects*, edited by W.P. Wightman and J.C. Bryce; with Dugald Stewart's Account of Adam Smith, edited by I.S. Ross; volume III of the Glasgow Edition of the Works and Correspondence of Adam Smith, Clarendon Press, Oxford.

Smith, A. (1983), *Lectures on Rhetoric and Belles Lettres*, edited by J.C. Bryce, volume IV of the Glasgow Edition of the Works and Correspondence of Adam Smith, Clarendon Press, Oxford.

Smith, V.R. (1985), 'John Stuart Mill's famous distinction between production and distribution', *Economics and Philosophy*, **1**.

Sowell, T. (1974), *Classical Economics Reconsidered*, Princeton University Press, Princeton.

Spengler, J. (1975), 'Adam Smith and society's decision-makers', in Skinner and Wilson (eds) (1975).

Spiegel, H.W. (1979), 'Adam Smith's heavenly city', in O'Driscoll (ed.) (1979).

Stewart, D. (1980), 'Account of the Life and Writings of Adam Smith, LL.D.', in A. Smith (1980).

Stigler, G.J. (1965), 'The nature and role of originality in scientific progress', in *Essays in the History of Economics*, University of Chicago Press, Chicago.

Stigler, G.J. (1975), 'Smith's travels on the ship of state', in Skinner and Wilson (eds) (1975).

Strong, E.W. (1987), 'William Whewell and John Stuart Mill: their controversy about scientific knowledge', *Journal of the History of Ideas*, **16**, 1955, reprinted in Wood (ed.) (1987), vol. I.

Taylor, O.H. (1960), *A History of Economic Thought*, McGraw-Hill, New York.

Thomson, H.F. (1984), 'Adam Smith's philosophy of science', *Quarterly Journal of Economics*, **79**, 1965, reprinted in Wood (ed.) (1984), vol.I.

Torrens, R. (1965), *An Essay on the Production of Wealth* [1821], Augustus M. Kelley, New York.

Viner, J. (1962), 'Some problems of logical method in political economy', *Journal of Political Economy*, **25**, 1917, reprinted in E.J. Hamilton *et al.* (eds), *Landmarks in Political Economy*, Phoenix Books, Chicago.

Viner, J. (1972), *The Role of Providence in the Social Order*, American Philosophical Society, Philadelphia.

Viner, J. (1984a), 'Adam Smith', in *International Encyclopaedia of the Social Sciences*, Macmillan, New York, 1968, reprinted in Wood (ed.) (1984), vol.I.

Viner, J. (1984b), 'Adam Smith and laissez faire', *Journal of Political Economy*, **35**,(2), 1927, reprinted in Wood (ed.) (1984), vol.I.

Viner, J. (1987), 'Bentham and J.S. Mill: the Utilitarian background', *American Economic Review*, **39**, 1949, reprinted in Wood (ed.) (1987), vol. I.

Walras, L. (1954), *Elements of Pure Economics or the Theory of Social Wealth* [1874], translated by W. Jaffé, George Allen & Unwin, London.

Whewell, W. (1964), 'Prefatory Notice' to Jones (1964).

Whitaker, J.K. (1975), 'John Stuart Mill's methodology', *Journal of Political Economy*, **83**,(5).

Wightman, W.P. (1975), 'Adam Smith and the history of ideas', in Skinner and Wilson (eds) (1975).

Wightman, W.P. (1980), 'Introduction' to A. Smith (1980).

Winch, D. (ed.) (1966a), *James Mill: Selected Economic Writings*, Oliver & Boyd, Edinburgh.

Winch, D. (1966b), 'Biographical sketch', in Winch (ed.) (1966a).

Winch, D. (1966c), 'James Mill on scope and method', in Winch (ed.) (1966a).

Winch, D. (1978), *Adam Smith's Politics: An Essay in Historiographic Revision*, Cambridge University Press, Cambridge.

Winch, P. (1958), *The Idea of a Social Science and its Relation to Philosophy*, Routledge & Kegan Paul, London.

Wood, J.C. (ed.) (1984), *Adam Smith: Critical Assessments*, four volumes, Croom Helm, London.

Wood, J.C. (ed.) (1987), *John Stuart Mill: Critical Assessments*, four volumes, Croom Helm, London.
Young, J.T. (1985), 'Natural price and the impartial spectator: a new perspective on Adam Smith as a social economist', *International Journal Of Social Economics*, **12**.

Index

Anschutz, R.P. 146, 195, 200, 201
Anspach, R. 56
Ashley, W.J. 159, 164
associationist laws of mind 196
associationist psychology 19, 21, 24, 145, 163, 174–5, 194, 197, 199, 239
astronomy 177, 180, 183, 185

Bacon, F. 124
Baconian inductivism 146
Bagehot, W. 130, 131
Bain, A. 127, 128, 145, 159
behaviourism 163, 203
Bentham, J. 145, 186
Benthamite social theory 186
Benthamites 146, 187
biology 17, 163, 166
birth control 224–5, 234
Bitterman, H. 25
Blaug, M. 130, 132, 155, 242
Bonar, J. 32
Bowley, M. 87, 124, 138
business principles 222

Cairnes, J.E. 209
Cambridge Inductivists 135
Campbell, R.H. 32, 33, 34, 38, 112
Campbell, T.D. 35, 43, 46
Cannan, E. 13
capital 88–9, 92–3, 97, 99, 107, 222, 225, 228, 232
    rate of profit on 227
capitalism 30, 69, 97, 103, 105, 115–16, 165, 216–17, 230
capitalist economy 115, 209
capitalists 232
causal laws 182
class conflict 233
classical economics 1, 187, 209
    methodology of 123–4, 131, 142, 144
classicals 1, 4, 134, 142, 144, 156, 179
co-operative economic order 216
Coats, A.W. 111

Colbert, J.-B. 85
combinations 223, 236
commodity prices 116
commodity value
    forms of 87
communism and socialism 216, 219
communist principles 230
competition 52, 94, 100, 104, 109–10, 112, 116, 213, 219, 220, 222, 233, 240
competitive markets 216
composition of forces 147
Comte, A. 158, 160, 161, 162, 163, 164, 165, 166, 167, 168, 170, 178, 184, 190, 191, 192, 193, 209
    Cours de philosophie positive 159
    positivism of 158
    Système de politique positive 167
Cooper, A.A.
    Earl of Shaftesbury 11,13
corporatism 232
cost saving innovations 228
Cropsey, J. 47

das Adam Smith Problem 31–2, 63
de Marchi, N.B. 128, 137, 206, 214
deductive logic 123, 188, 215–16
deductive methodology 131, 137, 156
deductive science
    ethology as 177
Descartes, R. 26
determinism 171, 172, 215
disturbing causes 123, 125–6, 138, 140, 153, 156, 158, 210, 216, 221
Dobb, M. 87
Draconian laws 61, 103, 105
dynamics of capitalism 211
dynamics of production 209

economic classes 196, 220, 233
economic dynamics 222
economic growth 95, 116
    rate of 222
economic harmony 53, 65

economic institutions 215
economic laws 207, 243
economic man 1–3, 49, 62, 76, 117–18,
    123–4, 127, 133, 146, 155, 165,
    166, 171, 178–9, 184, 194, 203,
    210, 216, 221, 225–6, 239, 240–41
economic phenomena 164, 166, 194,
    203
  science of 165
economic system 83–4, 87, 90, 94, 100,
    108, 214, 219
economics
  as science 4, 19
economy
  free-market 84
Edinburgh Review 146
education system 107, 219
eighteenth century
  intellectual context of 7
  scholars of 14
Ekelund, R.B. 160
empathy 40–41, 43
empirical determinism 201
empirical laws of society 191
empiricism 143, 163, 173–4, 193, 203
Enlightenment 22
epistemological expectations 179, 180,
    188, 206
ethological laws 188, 191, 192
ethological theory 239
ethology 164, 175–9, 181, 184, 186,
    194, 210, 217–18, 237, 242
Evensky, J. 84
exchange 3, 107, 208
experimental science
  psychology as 177

free markets 218–19
free trade 228, 240
free-will
  and necessity 200
  versus determinism 171
freedom of contract 240
French socialism 216
Friedman, M. 189
Friedmanite positivism 189

genetics 199
geometry 186
Gomperz, T. 161

Halévy, E. 7, 8, 10, 17, 126, 128, 145
Hamilton, Sir William 196, 197, 200
  Lectures on Metaphysics and Logic
    195
Hayek, F. von 13, 159, 160, 164, 166
Heilbroner, R.L. 28, 31, 34, 35, 41, 52,
    62, 63, 70, 75, 76
Herschel, J. 160
  A Preliminary Discourse on the Study
    of Natural Philosophy 169
Historical School 209, 210
historicism 192
Hobbes, T. 8, 9, 10, 11, 12, 13, 36, 48,
    113, 114, 146
holistic sociology 165
Hollander, S.H. 87, 126, 127, 129, 131,
    132, 133, 134, 137, 138, 144, 160,
    165, 205, 206, 213, 217, 226, 228,
    239, 241, 242
Hollis, M. 7, 200, 202
homo bucolicus 230
homo oeconomicus 230
human agency 1
  contingency of 205, 211, 216–18
  in economies 34, 65
  essentials of 211
  invention and innovation in 82
  justice and 9, 15, 33–4, 38, 48–9, 53,
    56–7, 59–60, 63, 65, 67, 70
  laws of 185
  metaphysics of 203
  psychological dimensions of 2
  realities of 129
  representation of 179, 210
  self-interest in 4, 7–14, 29, 31, 34,
    36–9, 42, 48, 50–53, 57–8, 62–6,
    69, 85, 93–4, 97, 100, 106, 111,
    114–15, 146, 186, 217, 220, 233,
    239
  situational determinism in 172
  theory of 24, 34
human agents 1, 3
  bettering condition motive of 51, 76,
    77, 80, 95, 115
  categories of 91, 97
  collusive practices of 94, 98, 100,
    103, 104
  compared to animals 72, 73, 74, 78,
    79, 224
  conscience of 44

creativity of 4
in economic analyses 218, 239
economic dimension of 2
as entrepreneurs 96
free 3, 4, 10, 84, 86, 110, 171, 173,
  200, 235
genetic makeup of 1
innate abilities of 75
institutional constructs and 216
interests of 10, 13, 29, 31, 36–9, 42
and justice 15, 64
manual dexterity of 80–81
mental phenomena of 19
mental processes of 163
model of 183
as objects of science 24
passions of 11, 14–15, 35, 38, 40–41,
  43, 47–8, 75, 94, 100, 167, 185
as philosophers 8
productivity of 229
prudence and 49, 63, 66
psychology of 144
reasoning capacity of 14, 20, 35, 46–
  7, 74
relations between 13, 29, 35–9, 42,
  47, 53–8, 63–4, 76, 90–91, 114,
  149, 177–9
representation of 148, 197, 221, 224
self-consciousness of 4, 61, 210
sentiments of 11, 15, 21, 26, 29, 35–
  42, 44–7, 62, 114
situated 3–4, 12, 31, 34, 36–9, 45–6,
  62, 65, 85, 105–7, 115, 137, 142,
  148, 152, 157, 161, 165–7, 171,
  173, 175–7, 179–80, 193, 197,
  201, 203, 210, 217, 223, 242,
  243
socialization of 34–5, 62, 80, 90, 107
trucking disposition of 77, 79, 80
virtues of 10, 12, 13, 15, 36, 40, 45–
  50, 53, 55, 59, 63
human consciousness 197
human inventions 215
human mind 22, 28, 34, 143, 161, 192,
  196, 199
innate characteristics of 197
laws of 143, 150, 163–4, 173–5, 177,
  179, 181, 186
science of 150–51, 177
theory of 128

transcendental dimensions of 171
human mind-in-itself 198
human nature 1, 63
altruism of 167
benevolence of 13, 15, 48–9, 52–3,
  55–7, 63–4, 79
competition and 34
egoism of 8–10, 36, 38–9, 111, 115,
  117, 167
emulation and 51, 69, 74, 76
essence of 40
laws of 128, 185
and memory 16
metaphysical conception of 161
philosophy and psychology of 1
primal 34, 75
principles of 33, 36
psychological contingencies of
  85,128
psychology of 11, 142
science of 176, 181
sentimental constitution of 46
theory of 18, 33, 39
transcendental dimensions of 179,
  239
human phenomena 143, 164
ontology of 135, 138
human sciences 2–3, 7, 17, 143–4, 145,
  146, 147, 150, 155–8, 161–2, 164,
  166, 170–71, 175, 179–80, 187,
  192, 194, 203, 239
epistemological limitations of 154
Hume, D. 14, 15, 16, 17, 18, 19, 20, 23,
  24, 25, 55, 113, 114
Hutcheson, F. 12, 13, 14, 15, 29, 114
Hutchison, T.W. 126, 128, 129, 132,
  142, 210, 239, 240, 241

ideas
association of 22, 27–8
systems of 27–8
income
distribution of 3, 87, 89, 92, 95–7,
  105, 116, 208–9, 221–2, 229
equity of 216
forms of 89–90
individualism 202
inductive foundations 206
industry protection policy 236
inexact sciences 182, 203

interest 89
intuitionist philosophy 161, 170, 195
intuitionists 197
investment 227
invisible hand 52, 93, 101, 116

Jensen, H.E. 84, 109
Jevonian revolution 210
Jevons, W.S 1
joint stock company 112
joint-stock principle 223
Jones, R. 135, 137
    *An Essay on the Distribution of
        Wealth* 137
    inductivism of 137
    on rent 138
justice 112, 115, 221
    administration of 67
    as security from injury 67–9

Kantian metaphysics 197
Keynes, J.N. 130, 241
Kubitz, O.A. 145, 146, 148, 170

La Nauze, J.A. 99
labour
    combinations of 102–3
    division of 3, 64, 75–8, 80–82, 89, 92,
        223
    productive and unproductive 95
    specialization of 2, 64, 75–81, 92, 223
labouring classes 229, 230
laissez-faire 129, 206, 218, 235
landed property 221
landlords 89, 91, 95, 97
large-scale production 231
law of causality 171
laws
    and customs of society 215
    of distribution 207, 213, 215, 217
    of economics 138
    of human action 176
    of human nature 150–52, 157, 162,
        176, 180, 184–5, 187, 189, 191–
        3, 217
    of matter 150
    of motion 213
    of nature 149, 215
    of production 207, 212–13, 216
    of psychology 180, 188, 192

of social change 192
of social existence 166
of social phenomena 162
of society 12, 128, 143, 152
of value and exchange 212
Leslie, T.E. Cliffe 209, 240
Lewisohn, D. 160, 163
liberty 202, 235
Lindgren, J.R. 32, 60
Locke, J. 7, 20, 113
    empiricism of 7, 16
logic
    of class conflict 206
    of human science 196
    of the market 221
    of moral sciences 170
    of political economy 236
    of science 144–5, 147, 185
Losee, J. 24

Macaulay, T. 146, 147, 186
Macfie, A.L. 14, 15, 32, 47, 49, 50
Macnabb, D.G. 15, 18
Malthus, T.R. 132, 133, 134, 135, 136,
    137
    Principles of Political Economy 135
Malthusian principle of population 140,
    224
Mandeville, B. de 12, 13, 25, 113
markets 92, 93, 94
    competitive 85, 86, 109
market prices 92, 101, 103, 109, 221
Marx, K.H. 31
McCulloch, J.R. 130, 135, 138
    Principles of Political Economy 138
McNulty, P.J. 109
mechanics 156, 166, 186
Meek, R.L. 32, 68, 80, 87
mental phenomena 174, 180, 181
mental philosophy 146
mercantile
    agents 100, 102–5, 109, 115
    capitalism 30, 38, 69, 71, 73, 84–5
    distortions 71, 118
    economy 98, 104, 116
    era 106
    groups 96–7, 104–7
    privileges 85, 111, 118
    regulations 111
    states 59

system 52, 85, 93–4, 98, 100–101, 104, 106, 115, 117
Metaphysical School 171, 194, 195
metaphysics 164, 173–4, 194
meteorology 182, 183, 203
method
  à posteriori 154, 155, 157
  à priori 154, 155, 156
  of deduction 117, 174, 176–7, 181, 186–7, 189, 194, 203, 210, 225
  of induction 154, 169, 174–5, 177
methodological individualism 185
methodological monism 143, 144
methodology 27, 113, 117–18, 147
  abstract-deductive 137, 142, 156, 171, 179, 194, 211, 239–40
  axiomatic 116, 117, 123, 142, 144
  chemical or experimental 185
  concrete deductive 166, 191, 192
  in economics 1, 3, 119, 124, 128, 142, 186, 189
  empirical 17
  empirico-descriptive 211
  geometric or abstract 185
  historical 118
  of the human sciences 148
  inverse deductive or historical 185, 191
  Newtonian 1, 14, 23
  physical or concrete deductive 185, 187
  pluralistic 242
  scientific 17, 113, 129,162, 164, 203
Mill, James 130, 132, 145, 147, 239
  abstract-deductive method of 125, 127, 129
  Analysis of the Phenomena of the Human Mind 127, 175
  Elements of Political Economy 125, 126, 129, 147, 208
  in *Encyclopaedia Britannica* 128, 146
  'Essay on Government' 146, 186
  History of British India 128
  intellectual origins 126
Mill, John Stuart
  on the association of ideas 15
  on associationist psychology 174–5, 194, 196–9
  on capital accumulation 225–8
  on certainty of economic conclusions 130

and classical methodology 142, 144
on competition and custom 213, 216, 220–22
on the definition of political economy 150–52
final methodological position of 240–43
on free markets 218
influence of Auguste Comte on 158, 168, 178, 184, 190, 209
influence of James Mill on 126, 128–9, 145–7, 174–5, 208
and the Metaphysical School 194
methodological inheritance of 148
methodological legacy of 118–19, 210
as methodological monist 144
as philosopher 142
on political economy as science and art 149–50
on production and distribution 141, 207–8, 210–11
reform strategy of 167, 205, 217, 234–6
representation of human agency 137, 139, 140, 179
on socio-economic class reforms 230–33
on socio-economic progress 222–5, 229
on static and dynamic analysis 209
mode of production 208
money 89, 98–9, 208
monopolies 105, 236
monopolists 101, 106
monopolizing spirit 71, 105
monopoly 106, 112, 238
  natural 101
  power 96, 100–101, 104, 107–8, 110–12, 115, 221, 233
  price 101–2
moral
  balance 90
  gravity 12
  philosophers 113
  philosophy 7, 25, 27, 31–2, 71, 114–15
  rules 46, 59, 62–3, 66, 71, 100
  sciences 2, 41, 114, 136, 142–3, 150, 155, 211
  theory 44

Morrow, G.R. 34, 35, 40, 41, 43, 45, 48
Mueller, I.W. 146, 159, 161, 163
Myers, M.L. 9, 11, 13, 16

natural liberty
   system of 85
natural phenomena
   physical causes in 201
natural prices 92–4, 101, 109
natural sciences 179, 185
Newton, Sir Isaac 12, 16, 20, 23, 26, 29,
   113
   and gravitation 7, 11, 13, 24, 26, 28–9
   methodology of 1, 14, 17, 23
Newtonian science 7, 8, 15–16, 23–4, 126
Newtonian system 28
noumena of the real world 197

O'Brien, D.P. 94, 131, 132
object phenomena
   dimensions of 212
   ontology of 3, 148, 153, 179, 182,
      184, 188, 192
O'Donnell, R. 87
Olsen, E.S. 160
ontology 2
overproduction 228
Owenite scheme 216

phenomena
   of human nature 178
   of human science 184
   of mind 150
   of political economy 184
   of society 151, 178, 187
phenomenology 203
philosophical method 146, 153–4
philosophy
   of human nature 175, 195
   of science 113
phrenology 163
physical sciences 1, 27, 143, 150, 182–
   3, 185, 187, 194, 211
Physiocrats 85–6, 95
physiology 163, 174, 199
   laws of 150, 174
Poor Laws 238
Popper, K.R. 24
population growth 229–30
   rate of 222, 224–5

price control regulations 236
price determination 220
Priestley, F.E.L. 163
production
   physical technicalities of 215
   psychological determinants of 216
   social determinants of 216
production and distribution
   essentials of 211
profits 89, 92, 97, 101, 102, 220, 227,
   228
progress of Man thesis 192
progressive state 166, 227
propensity
   to accumulate 227
   to invest 226
property
   endowments of 220
   labour origins of 68
   private 87, 89, 215, 220, 235
   rights 68, 114, 219, 232
   security of 227, 235

Raphael, D.D. 14, 15, 20, 24, 32, 44, 45,
   50
   rent 89, 96–7, 101, 220
Ricardian
   doctrine 209
   dominance 240
   economics 159, 205–6
   heritage 165
   literature 166
   principles 194
   revolution 210
   vice 240
Ricardians 130–31, 139
Ricardo, D. 126, 129, 130, 131, 132,
   134, 138, 239, 240
   abstract-deductive method of 125,
      129–30, 133–4
   links with James Mill 129
   methodological consciousness of 134
   methodological position of 132, 133,
      134
   Notes on Malthus 134
   Principles of Political Economy 125,
      129, 130, 134, 135, 147
   reactions to 134
   strong cases of 133, 135
Richardson, G.B. 109

Robson, J.M. 146, 147, 159, 160, 169, 207
Rosenberg, N. 84, 85, 104, 106, 112
Royal Society of Edinburgh 33
Ryan, A. 197, 200, 201

saving 226
Say, J.-B. 124, 125, 127
   Traite d'Economie Politique 124, 208
Schumpeter, J.A. 214
Schwartz, P. 205, 206, 209, 210, 214, 226, 233, 235
science of society 191, 193
Senior, N.W. 135, 139–41
   An Outline of the Science of Political Economy 139
   Four Introductory Lectures on Political Economy 139
   Introductory Lecture on Political Economy 139
sentimentalist tradition 19
sentimentalists 37, 113
sexual mores 224
Shackle, G.L.S. 203
Skinner, A.S. 14, 20, 32, 33, 34, 38, 80, 112
Smith, Adam
   on active role for the human mind 21
   on the allocative role for income distribution 92
   antecedents of 8
   approach to science of 19
   as an ascetic 50
   on Bernard de Mandeville 25
   on capital accumulation 94–6
   character of his work 31
   on the 'commercial' economy 70–71, 83–4, 86–7, 91, 96–8
   on contemporary philosophical issues 20
   and David Hume 14, 24, 55
   on the development of law and government 32
   early philosophical works of 9
   ethical theory of 41
   and Francis Hutcheson 12–13
   on the history and theory of jurisprudence 67
   and the Hobbesian image of human nature 36
   on human nature and competition 34
   on the imagination 14
   on immanent social harmony 63
   on the inadequacy of reason 47
   on the innate limitations of human agents 47, 54
   intellectual heritage of 7, 13
   on invention and innovation processes 82
   on justice and police 67
   on justice and political economy 65
   literary remains of 20
   on mercantile agents 104–5
   methodological ideas of 22
   methodological legacy of 113, 117–18, 123–4, 126–7, 131, 142, 144, 161–2, 166, 205–6, 210–11, 242
   moral philosophy of 31
   as a natural law theorist 35
   on the natural state of economy and society 66
   on the nature of philosophical inquiry 27–8
   on Newton's work 23–4, 26, 28–9
   normative analysis of 29
   on the notion of system 22
   on origin and nature of the moral rules 46
   on the origins of property 68–70
   and the philosophy of science 19
   and the Physiocrats 86
   pin manufacturing example of 89
   primary methodology of 23
   on productive labour 89
   on progress in scientific knowledge 20
   on social rationalism 45
   on the Stoical ideal of self-command 37
   on subjectivist philosophical inquiry 23
   reform strategy of 107–11, 118
   on the representation of human agents 62, 113, 129, 138–9
   sceptical view of knowledge of 24
   scientific bent of 24
   sociological system of 32
   on the specialization and division of labour 78–82, 223
   system of liberty of 84, 112, 118

theory of economy and society 38
on the transcendental role of reason 45
typified vision of human nature of 35
unified project in moral philosophy of 8, 31
unity in his work 33, 62
on wealth 98–9
Smith, V.R. 214, 215, 216
social
 apologetics 206
 dynamics 192, 193
 harmony 38, 42, 46–7, 49, 52, 53, 57–8, 61, 63, 65–6, 114
 phenomena 166, 187, 188
 philosophy 205
 sciences 32, 142, 170, 186, 191
 system 38, 60, 108
socialists 232
socialization of property 224
society
 early and rude state of 88
 geometrical theory of 186
socio-economic progress 211, 222, 229
sociological statics 192
Sowell, T. 129, 130, 131
spectator 15, 37, 42–7, 58
Spengler, J. 28
stationary state 166, 224, 227–9
Stewart, D. 33, 34
Stigler, G.J. 111, 209
Sturges, R.P. 137
subjectivism 123
surplus 89, 94
sympathy 29, 37–44, 47, 49, 52, 54, 58, 62–5, 114
syndicalism 232
system
 of government 69
 of justice 66

of laws 60, 66
of liberty 108, 112, 118

Taylor, Harriet 207
Taylor, O.H. 7, 9, 11, 12, 18, 19, 40, 75
theory of government 186
theory of human progress 217–18
Thomson, H.F. 14
tidology 182–3, 203
Torrens, R. 138
 Budget 132
 Essay on the Production of Wealth 132
transcendentalist psychology 194
Turgot, A.R.J. 161

usury laws 236
Utilitarians 126, 145–6
Utopia 110
Utopianism 229

value in exchange 88
value-exchange processes 212
verification 189–90
Viner, J. 31, 38, 43, 44, 46, 47, 55, 56, 84, 92, 112, 209, 242, 243

wage-labour 87, 91
wages 51, 73, 88–9, 92, 94, 96–7, 102–3, 220, 226, 228, 233
wages fund 226
Westminster Review 148, 159
Whately, R. 146, 147
 Elements of Logic 145
Whewell, W. 135, 137
 History of the Inductive Sciences 169
Winch, D. 126, 127, 128
Winch, P. 183, 203
worker control of industry 232
worker cooperatives 232